SPECIAL DAMAGE

The Cultural Lives of Law
Edited by Austin Sarat

SPECIAL DAMAGE

THE SLANDER OF WOMEN AND THE GENDERED HISTORY OF DEFAMATION LAW

Jessica Lake

STANFORD UNIVERSITY PRESS
Stanford, California

Stanford University Press
Stanford, California

© 2026 by Jessica Lake. All rights reserved.

This book has been partially underwritten by the Susan Groag Bell Publication Fund in Women's History. For more information on the fund, please see www.sup.org/bellfund.

No part of this book may be reproduced or transmitted in any form or by any means, electronic or mechanical, including photocopying and recording, or in any information storage or retrieval system, without the prior written permission of Stanford University Press.

Library of Congress Cataloging-in-Publication Data

Names: Lake, Jessica, author.
Title: Special damage : the slander of women and the gendered history of defamation law / Jessica Lake.
Other titles: Cultural lives of law.
Description: Stanford, California : Stanford University Press, 2026. | Series: The cultural lives of law | Includes bibliographical references and index.
Identifiers: LCCN 2025011940 (print) | LCCN 2025011941 (ebook) | ISBN 9781503635258 (cloth) | ISBN 9781503644694 (paperback) | ISBN 9781503644700 (ebook)
Subjects: LCSH: Libel and slander—United States—History—19th century. | Libel and slander—Australia—History—19th century. | Libel and slander—England—History—19th century. | Women—Legal status, laws, etc.—United States—History—19th century. | Women—Legal status, laws, etc.—Australia—History—19th century. | Women—Legal status, laws, etc.—England—History—19th century.
Classification: LCC K930 .L35 2025 (print) | LCC K930 (ebook) | DDC 346.7303/409034—dc23/eng/20250319
LC record available at https://lccn.loc.gov/2025011940
LC ebook record available at https://lccn.loc.gov/2025011941

Cover design: Lindy Kasler
Cover art: Josephine E. Butler, *Slain by Slander*, 1861. Engraving.

The authorized representative in the EU for product safety and compliance is: Mare Nostrum Group B.V. | Mauritskade 21D | 1091 GC Amsterdam | The Netherlands | Email address: gpsr@mare-nostrum.co.uk | KVK chamber of commerce number: 96249943

FOR MUM AND DAD, WITH LOVE

CONTENTS

	Acknowledgments	ix
	Introduction	1
ONE	The Slander of Subjects and Citizens *New Jersey*	18
TWO	Savage Speech Against Civilized Females *New South Wales*	38
THREE	Unsullied Purity and the First Slander of Women Act *North Carolina*	57
FOUR	Free White Females and Social Intercourse with Blacks *Georgia*	79
FIVE	"Deprived of Her Natural Guardian" *South Australia*	99
SIX	Stained Whiteness and the Cult of True Womanhood *New York*	121

SEVEN   "There Is a Total Disregard for the Rights of Women"   138
Victoria

EIGHT   Barbarous Common Law and   152
Double Standards of Morality
England

Conclusion   173

Notes   187
Index   221

ACKNOWLEDGMENTS

A monograph is both the result of quiet, solitary concentration and—if one is lucky—collaborative, cooperative work with a range of helpful people. This book would not have been possible without the assistance, support, and expertise of many friends, family, and colleagues and a number of organizations.

The idea for this book began in 2020, as I returned to work after two years as carer for our very sick child. So, my first thank-you is to the staff at the Children's Cancer Centre of the Royal Children's Hospital in Melbourne, particularly Dr. David Hughes. Without your dedication and expertise in treating and curing our son, it is possible I may never have returned to academic scholarship.

In early 2021, I was delighted to join the newly established Institute for Humanities and Social Sciences at the Australian Catholic University, an enterprise that bucked the trend within Australian universities by investing money, time, and esteem into humanities research. My position as research fellow in the Gender and Women's History Research Centre allowed me to pursue the beginnings of this project and draft grant applications for funding. I am indebted to the warm and witty company and astute advice offered by colleagues and mentors there, particularly Joy Damousi, Sue Broomhall, Kate Fullagar, Amanda Nettelbeck, Sarah Bendall, Kristie Flannery, Clare Davidson, Ellen Warne, and Ben Mountford.

In late 2022, I was fortunate to be given a Discovery Early Career Researcher Award (DECRA) by the Australian Research Council, which enabled me to travel and conduct original archival research for this project across different locations in the common law world—in the United States, the United Kingdom, and Australia. It also, crucially, ensured I had the necessary time to read, reflect, plan, and execute a project of this size and scope. Similarly, I thank the Francis Forbes Society for Australian Legal History for their funding and support of parts of this project, and for the opportunity to present some of my findings to their members at the Supreme Court of New South Wales in November 2023.

Research for this book involved traveling overseas and interstate on multiple occasions to locate, read, copy, and transcribe original civil case files; legislative debates and instruments; newspaper articles; and other records. There is still a surprising amount of material that has not yet been digitized. I am indebted to the staff of the following institutions for their generous assistance in advising me about their collections and locating relevant and important items: the New York State Archives and New York State Library in Albany; the Georgia Archives in Morrow; the State Archives of North Carolina in Raleigh; the New Jersey State Archives in Trenton; the State Archives and Records New South Wales in Kingswood; the Public Record Office Victoria in North Melbourne; the State Records of South Australia in Gepps Cross; the State Library of South Australia in Adelaide; the National Library of Australia in Canberra; the Parliamentary Archives of the United Kingdom in Westminster; and the Women's Library and Archives at the London School of Economics and Political Science in London.

In mid-2024, I was appointed to a senior lectureship at the University of Melbourne Law School where I re-engaged with the discipline of law. I am grateful for the kind and enthusiastic welcome offered by my MLS colleagues—particularly, Ann Genovese, Jenny Morgan, Anjalee de Silva, Jordy Silverstein, Megan Richardson, and Andrew Kenyon. Their interest and insights have benefited this project in numerous ways. At the University of Melbourne, I have also been part of a supportive American history group, who have offered their thoughts and feedback on drafts of chapters in this book. My thanks to David Goodman, Julia Bowes, Patrick McGrath, Katy Schumaker (now at the United States Studies Centre, University of Sydney), and Clare Corbould from Deakin University.

My thanks, too, to Stanford University Press, to the anonymous readers of my manuscript for their helpful, responsive advice, and to my editor at Stanford, Marcela Maxfield, for believing in this book, offering her keen insights, and keeping the project on track.

Finally, my heartfelt thanks to my family: my sister, Katherine Lake, for her companionship and sharp legal mind; my husband, Lok Tan, for his support of my work and taking care of our children—at home and abroad—when I have been researching or writing; our children—Matilda, Larry, and Henry—whose constant needs, delights, and enthusiasms animate my day-to-day life; my auntie Pam for her generosity and continuing interest in my writing; and my parents, Marilyn and Sam Lake, who have long offered their unwavering support, guidance, and engagement with my interests and ideas. It is to mum and dad that I dedicate this book.

Slain by Slander, by Josephine E. Butler, 1861. Engraving on card.
RECORDS FOR THE ASSOCIATION FOR MORAL AND SOCIAL HYGIENE. THE WOMEN'S LIBRARY. LONDON SCHOOL OF ECONOMICS AND POLITICAL SCIENCE, LONDON, UNITED KINGDOM.

SPECIAL DAMAGE

INTRODUCTION

> He came to see me tonight. He dared to come here in his work-clothes! And to repeat slander to me, vicious stories that he had gotten from you! I gave him his walking papers....
>
> But then he came back.... He implored my forgiveness. But some things are not forgivable. Deliberate cruelty is not forgivable.
>
> —TENNESSEE WILLIAMS,
> *A STREETCAR NAMED DESIRE* (1947)

Blanche DuBois is ruined by slander. Stories about her being a whore, "unclean," and a prostitute are gleaned and shared by Stanley Kowalski, the embodiment of brutish masculinity, causing Blanche to suffer a mental breakdown and be forcibly removed to a lunatic asylum. Tennessee Williams's Pulitzer-winning play depicts how sexual slander is used to harm women and is connected to other forms of gendered abuse: Stanley's explosions of violence, physical intimidation, emotional manipulation, rape. The fact that the slanderous allegations are potentially true does not diminish Stanley's cruelty in wielding them as a weapon, nor Blanche's pitiful plight. Though, what if the figures who appear at the close of the play to cart Blanche away were not doctors, but lawyers? What if they offered Blanche a chance to silence Stanley, vindicate her reputation, reclaim her dignity, and forge a more prosperous path forward?

This book tells the stories of women, many like Blanche, slandered with allegations of sexual immorality who took their slanderers to court seeking compensation and retribution, the difficulties they faced in doing so, and the ways in which their actions permanently altered the development of defamation law. There was young Mary Smith from New Jersey who sued her neighbor Isaac Minor after he spread rumors in the community that she was a fornicator and pregnant with a bastard child.[1] There was governess Harriet Spencer who took a ship captain to court in New South Wales after sailors spread gross talk about her having intercourse with the second mate.[2] There was Frances McBrayer, from North Carolina, called a "dirty, sluttish whore," Nancy Brooker labeled a "a common prostitute," and Elizabeth Bell who had "gross, obscene words" uttered about her by Joseph Allen after she rebuffed his sexual advances while working as a maid at his mother's hotel in Adelaide.[3] There was farming wife Lucy Wilson attacked by neighbor James Goit for having been "screwed . . . under the cherry tree below the barn" and English temperance and suffrage activist Elizabeth Lewis accused by a local publican[4] of having sex in the sand dunes of a popular beach.[5] Such cases are not quaint artifacts of the past, remnants of an earlier time when repressive expectations of feminine chastity and modesty prevailed. They are the direct antecedents to the pervasive trends of gendered hate speech, nonconsensual pornography and deepfake pornography today. They detail stories and slurs of sexual immorality leveled against women to harm, hurt, and humiliate them. They reflect a time—prior to the invention and ubiquity of photography, cinema, and the internet—when words were the primary means of misogynist attacks.

Slut shaming and attacks on women via their sexuality are still rampant. Recent studies indicate that someone calls a woman a slut or whore on X (formerly Twitter) almost 10,000 times per day.[6] In 2024, US Vice President Kamala Harris was subject to a barrage of sexual slander after being nominated as the Democratic candidate for president, such as slurs and accusations that she "slept her way to the top" and gave "blowjobs" to those in power.[7] In May of the same year, boys attending an elite private school in Melbourne, Australia, created a list of female classmates, categorizing them as "wifey," "cuties," "objects," and "unrapeable."[8]

Women have long been denigrated, stigmatized, and attacked via their sexuality. And the law has grappled, from time to time, with how best to address this problem. In the late nineteenth and early twentieth centuries, as my previous book *The Face That Launched a Thousand Lawsuits* demonstrated, it was women bringing cases to protest the use and abuse of their images (often published in sexualized contexts) that led to the first privacy laws in the United States.⁹ In the 1970s, feminists such as Lin Farley and Catherine MacKinnon were central in conceptualizing and introducing sexual harassment laws to combat discrimination against women at work.¹⁰ In recent decades, legal scholars such as Danielle Keats Citron and Mary Anne Franks have successfully led campaigns for the criminalization of nonconsensual pornography and deepfake pornography, particularly gendered phenomena whereby women are degraded, humiliated, and harmed online.¹¹ There have also been calls for and discussion of strengthening anti-discrimination and vilification laws to combat the scourge of hate speech against women online.¹² But in the late eighteenth century and for most of the nineteenth, defamation was the primary mechanism for women seeking justice for words that attacked and denigrated them in sexual terms.

Defamation is a legal doctrine designed to protect a person's reputation. Originating in England, it is one of the oldest areas of law and balances an individual's interest in their reputation against a society's interest in freedom of expression. Defamation can be criminal but is primarily civil: a private action brought by one person against another (or others). It is a notoriously complex area, riddled with doctrinal anomalies and technicalities, largely a result of its chaotic and collated history. It is a legal Frankenstein, a convergence of practice and principle derived from the ecclesiastical courts, royal courts, Star Chamber, local courts, and hundreds of years of transnational common law evolution, constitutional influence, and legislative amendment. It is a product of empire, exported from its homeland of England to diverse British colonies around the globe where it mutated to suit local conditions and circumstances. Such mutations then fed back into the common law ecosystem, influencing the direction and shape of defamation law in the metropole and distant lands. But despite variations and permutations, defamation law—across the United States, Australia, Canada, New Zealand, Singapore and other former British colonies—is still recognizable today, reflecting its shared foundations.

Before defamation law was exported around the globe with the British empire, fundamental doctrinal dimensions and parameters had already been established. Between the sixteenth and eighteenth centuries in England, various gender, class, and jurisdictional distinctions emerged, fostering delineations between "spiritual" and "temporal" offenses, written and spoken words, different classes of persons defamed, and categories of damage or loss. When it came to sexual slander—the focus of this book—such actions were traditionally brought in the English ecclesiastical courts. Early common law held that "where the defamation concerns matters merely spiritual, and determinable in the ecclesiastical court, as imputing adultery, fornication, or heresy, it is no ground of action at common law."[13] The ecclesiastical courts provided a popular and accessible form of redress, where a person could air their grievances, and a defendant might be ordered to provide a public apology (often during a Sunday service) or pay penance.

Several legal historians have explored patterns of English slander actions during the early modern period and beyond. James Anthony Sharpe has documented the steep rise of slander during the sixteenth and seventeenth centuries in England—asserting that "litigation aroused by slander was a phenomenon of the age."[14] Laura Gowing has revealed the degree to which this remarkable rise was due to women crowding the courts with sexual slander suits.[15] Stephen Waddams has shown how the popularity of sexual slander and its pronounced gender pattern continued well into the nineteenth century.[16] Between 1800 and 1855, the church courts of England heard over 3,000 sexual slander cases, of which the vast majority of plaintiffs (over 90 percent) were women. The most common insult was "whore," and the defendants were largely men.[17] For this reason, the ecclesiastical jurisdiction soon became known as the "women's court."[18]

In contrast, the English common law courts were decidedly masculine in orientation. A difference was drawn from 1640 onwards between libel (defamation in material form) and slander (spoken words).[19] Libel—usually affecting the interests of powerful or prominent men—was considered serious and made easier to prosecute (in that damage was presumed and did not need to be proved). Slander actions, on the other hand, could only be brought in the common law courts of England if the words spoken fell into a particular category: "likely to affect the complainant in *his* liberty, office or means of livelihood."[20] These included imputations of criminality, carrying a loathsome infectious disease, corruption, or incompetence. If the allegations did not fall into one of these established categories, and sexual slander generally did not (unless it alleged a crime), plaintiffs faced an additional hurdle. They needed to prove specific economic loss that was the "natural, immediate, and legal consequence" of the slanderous words in question.[21] This was known as "special damage." In 1812, Lord Mansfield confirmed these distinctions: "the law gives a very ample field for retribution by action for words spoken in the cases of special damage, of words spoken of a *man* in his trade or profession, of a *man* in office, of a magistrate or officer; for all these an action lies."[22] The traditional English common law of slander envisaged a man attempting to rectify his reputation as a skilled carpenter, competent physician, or an honest public officer, but for whom sexual slurs were trivial and without serious or material consequence.

But for women, being labeled a whore, fornicator, adulteress, or unchaste could spell ruin. Yet they were barred from bringing slander suits in the common law courts by the largely insurmountable hurdle of proving special damage. And "special damage" was defined narrowly for women via precedent to mean the cancellation of an upcoming marriage.[23] Such circumstances were, of course, limited and left most women slandered—single women without a marriage proposal, married women, and widows—without reputational recourse. In his landmark 1813 textbook, English jurist Thomas Starkie bemoaned this injustice: "The necessity of proving a specific loss, falls with particular hardship upon unmarried females, who are thereby frequently debarred from maintaining actions for imputations most unfounded and injurious."[24] He asked why it was that women should be maligned by their communities and their futures destroyed without redress, when at the same time the law ensured that "the skill and integrity of the lowest mechanic" could not be impugned.[25]

The gender distinctions embodied within English defamation law became glaringly problematic as the British empire expanded. Colonies, such as those in North America and Australia, inherited English common law and civil jurisdictions for determining disputes, but not ecclesiastical courts. Therefore, women subject to verbal attacks on their sexual morality—called whores, fornicators, and unchaste—and facing social and financial ruin, could only obtain legal relief if they could prove special damage. Several scholars have studied the operation of slander across colonial America.[26] Their scholarship indicates how the prevalence and outcomes of women's slander claims varied widely. For instance, while some colonies, such as Maryland, experienced high numbers of women claimants and sexual slander actions, other jurisdictions, such as North Carolina, encountered few. Together, their work suggests that the adherence (or not) by each local court to the strict English rules of slander determined the gendered pattern of defamation disputes—in other words, whether the word "whore" was deemed actionable determined women's reputational recourse. Local conditions and circumstances in each US colonial community pushed and pulled at English precedent, creating widely different standards for the regulation of abusive speech against women.

This uneven and unconnected patchwork became somewhat more uniform after the American Revolution—or, at least, conversations began between jurists in different US states about the demands of English precedent and the preferred directions of common law. These conversations and sharing of ideas were largely the product of better reporting and the establishment of state appellate courts. Prior to the late eighteenth and early nineteenth centuries, local law in the colonies was informed by some British common law textbooks, but not generally by the judgments of superior courts either inside and/or outside each jurisdiction. Local colonial law was also flexible, not pressed to display coherence and consistency, and was sometimes presided over by laymen without legal training. Only in the nineteenth century did systematic reporting of cases and legislative debates allow a body of US jurisprudence to emerge. As Roscoe Pound observed, "[l]egislatures, courts and doctrinal writers had to develop an American common law, a body of judicially declared or doctrinally approved precepts suitable to America, out of the old English cases and the old English statutes."[27] This project of carving a body of American common law from English foundations was also motivated by new ideologies and priorities, such as equal legal and political rights (of course, only for some), economic imperatives, and an emphasis on the republican family.[28] It was also generated by a desire to differentiate new worlds from the old.

It was during this period—the late eighteenth century—a time of American Revolution and Britain's establishment of the first Australian colonies—that cases began to be brought by women challenging the English legal burden of special damage. From New Jersey, to New South Wales, to New York, women in the *new* world sought to obtain compensation for verbal attacks against them, to silence their slanderers, to vindicate their reputations and restore their dignity. Their cases, beginning with Mary Smith's 1788 action in New Jersey, spurred judicial and legislative change—the slander of women acts—abolishing special damage and thus making it easier for women to sue for sexual slander. This book demonstrates that the question of how best to accommodate the slander claims of women became the most pressing and pervasive issue of defamation jurisprudence and reform in the nineteenth-century common law world. It tells the story of the women who brought these suits and the efforts of laypersons, lawyers, and legislators to change the law. It also describes how this short, technical legal phrase—special damage—became the driver of a gendered reform movement rivaling the Married Women's Property Acts in geographic extent and effect.

The term "movement" is used here to describe multiple—interrelated—processes. First, it denotes a group of people who coalesced around similar ideas and worked towards certain outcomes and objectives. As this book illustrates, jurists, legislators, and commentators shared similar ideas about the injustice faced by women needing to prove special damage in sexual slander cases and the urgent need for reform. They communicated with one another on the subject—sometimes across oceans—and pushed for reforms, particularly in newspaper columns and legal periodicals. The women plaintiffs formed part of this movement, as their cases spurred, evidenced, and articulated these arguments. Those involved did not, at the time, identify as being part of a movement, and so this term is applied retrospectively to their activities across the nineteenth century. Second, there was a movement in the sense that there were trends over time whereby people shifted in their perspectives and views. Case arguments, legislative debates, and newspaper/periodical commentary about women and slander law show changes in understanding about the importance of women's sexual reputations for their economic, professional, and social status and the law's inadequacy. In other words, there was a social and cultural movement towards recognizing women's reputational needs and rights across the nineteenth century. Third, in a geographic sense, these reforms "moved" around the common law world, and the word "movement" points to this tide of legal ideas.

Existing scholarship on the history of sexual slander in the nineteenth-century United States is limited. It has shown how some American jurisprudence was motivated by paternalist sentiments, with judges acting to "protect" the sexual purity and innocence of American wives and daughters.[29] It has highlighted how sexual slander cases often reinforced women's place in the private sphere and commodified their sexual virtue.[30] It has demonstrated how American judges used slander law to reinforce cultural stereotypes, tying women to domesticity and emphasizing sexuality as their most important attribute.[31]

However, the story of the global slander of women movement is more complex. The unity and insularity of the common law during the nineteenth century should not be overstated. The common law was both state based and transnational in nature—and largely remains so. Each colony, then state, had different social, cultural, political, and economic conditions *and also* existed within a wider jurisprudential ecosystem. This book demonstrates how the particularities of each locale were fundamental to decisions regarding the sexual slander of women and the enactment of the slander of women acts. Community norms and circumstances affected whom the acts were intended to serve as well as those taking advantage of them. At the same time, individual US state jurisdictions were connected to and influenced by legal ideas occurring outside of national boundaries, in England, but also in other new world offshoots, such as the Australian colonies. Tracking the sharing of ideas and arguments requires a transnational approach. Investigating the precise dynamics of status, speech, race, and gender playing out in each jurisdiction necessitates a comparative inquiry.

Further, understanding sexual slander against women during the nineteenth century and the slander of women acts involves more than an analysis of the words of judges recorded in appellate court judgments. It means digging up the original court documents to read the claims pleaded, the facts submitted in evidence, and the arguments made. It also means scouring legislative debates, examining commentary in newspapers and periodicals, and unearthing the lives and preoccupations of parties and politicians, journalists and jurists, from census and property records, letters, and the accounts of descendants. Doing so illuminates the varied motivations for changing the law, as well as important differences in the types of cases brought and the ways in which judicial or legislative decisions affected the lives of residents in different counties and communities.

It is also not sufficient to dismiss the slander of women cases and the acts as old-fashioned by contemporary standards, as simply reinforcing repressive standards of femininity. For one thing, the instances of slander and verbal abuse documented in this book—"dirty, sluttish whore"—are still leveled at women today to shame and humiliate them. Looking beyond the words of judges and parliamentarians to the voices and experiences of plaintiffs, and between and beyond the United States to other common law locales, offers important insights into the interwoven dynamics of reputation, race, and gender during the modern period, the particularities of what mattered where, and the implications or complexities of legal "progress." There are numerous stories to be told and judgments to be made about these reforms—were they revolutionary, repressive, or a means of extending women's legal rights? The slander of women acts were all these things.

Drawing upon original archival material, this interdisciplinary book is the first to track and trace the passing of the slander of women acts and the cases that spurred them. In doing so, it unearths the stories of the women who brought slander cases and rescues them from historical oblivion. It examines the ways in which women—such as Mary Smith from New Jersey, Harriet Spencer from New South Wales, Lucy Wilson from rural New York, Martha Kelly from Georgia, Suzanna Wishart from South Australia, Mary and Catherine Watts from North Carolina, Elizabeth Albrecht from Victoria, Australia, and Elizabeth Lewis from England, among many others—sought to silence ruinous slurs against them, restore their reputations, and punish their abusers. These cases led to complex debates about the social and economic status of women during the nineteenth century and the duty of men (depending on the rhetoric used) to "protect females" or, alternatively, to advance "women's rights" by addressing their lived experiences and incorporating their distinctive gendered interests into the masculine formulations of English law. These debates linked countries, colonies, and continents, as precedents and parliamentary proposals circulated via transnational common law networks. But while some ideas—such as the need for "gallant" and "civilised" men in the new world to defend the "virtue" of women against sexual slurs—resounded across disparate locations, other dynamics such as anxieties about sexual depravity, racial purity, and arguments about whether the reforms should benefit women in domestic roles or those in paid work played out differently between societies. Such debates forged fundamental and lasting changes to defamation law.

The slander of women movement reflected, reinforced—but also challenged—cultural and social norms about race, femininity, and speech. It tracked shifts in communication, community, and the construction of reputation during the nineteenth century from the milieus of small rural farming towns, where verbal rumors harmed a person's status, to the metropolises of anonymized urban centers where print cultures increasingly became a primary reputational risk. It changed laws that had been entrenched over centuries to privilege men's interests to afford women greater civil rights to sue in response to verbal abuse. It reflected and reinforced shifts in women's status, connected to subjecthood, citizenship, and suffrage. It enabled women in paid work to obtain financial compensation for what we would much later term "sexual harassment."

But, as this book will demonstrate, the slander of women movement also shaped and shadowed the emergence of discursive links between ideas of whiteness, femininity, chastity, and civilization. Not only was an accusation of unchastity ruinous to the respectability and financial security of a white woman, it also threatened her racial status. To lose one's character via allegations of sexual immorality meant becoming "stained," "colored," and thus losing the status of white womanhood. A reputation for chastity was often implicitly or expressly (depending on the jurisdiction) the possession and purpose of white women, and the most damaging imputations leveled in the United States involved interracial sex. Thus legal discourses worked to strengthen racial hierarchies during the modern period. However, as this book shows, the racial and gendered implications of the slander of women movement were not simple, nor straightforward. Black and Indigenous women also used the slander of women acts to publicly call out and punish powerful white men (such as plantation owners) who sexually denigrated and verbally abused them. Their cases challenged the alignment of color with unchastity and demanded recognition of their reputational rights. They fought against the injustice of men abusing them with impunity. This book narrates a fraught and complex story of power, social stigma, and scandalous speech and reveals the costs and compromises of legal progress in a patriarchal and unequal "civilized" world.

There has been surprisingly little writing at the intersection of defamation law and women's or gender history to date. Historical work has tended to focus on early modern England or colonial America, charting and analyzing gendered patterns of slander or gossip as social or cultural phenomena.[32] However, rarely have they interrogated how such claims interacted with or influenced the doctrinal development of defamation law. In other words, the actions brought have been taken as reflecting circumstances occurring outside the courtroom, but not formative in changing the direction or details of the law itself. Some legal historians have sought to explain the evolution of sexual slander and connected it with constructions of femininity.[33] But such studies often treat national jurisdictions as discrete, without asking how ideas informing court cases and debates about slander and its reform traveled and influenced each other within the British common law world.[34] Or they might treat women as a singular group, without investigating the dynamics of race and class that were fundamental to constructions of and stories about status in the nineteenth century. There have been historical studies of "racial misidentification" slander cases in the United States, but few that have connected defamation, race, and sexuality.[35] In mainstream histories of defamation law, sexual slander and women's role in bringing cases that changed the law have largely been omitted or consigned to a couple of footnotes.[36] This book places the slander of women acts and cases squarely within the legal history of race, gender, and reputation.

It also provides a backstory to debates about defamation law's gendered dynamics today. Following the global #MeToo movement, several high-profile cases worked to focus attention on the silencing effects of defamation law. In 2006, the slogan "Me Too" was coined by African American activist Tarana Burke to build community and raise awareness about the sexual assault and harassment of women and girls, particularly women and girls of color. The phrase rose to viral prominence in late 2017, after actress Alyssa Milano responded to the explosive Harvey Weinstein stories by asking followers to tweet "me too" if they had experienced sexual assault or harassment. Within twenty-four hours, Facebook alone had recorded use of the hashtag in over 12 million posts and replies.[37] The #MeToo movement turned sexual misconduct, particularly by high-profile men, into a news topic and offered recognition, an amplified voice, and forms of solidarity to survivors and victims.

However, it also precipitated a spate of defamation claims brought by men against their accusers and media publishers. Prominent examples include proceedings brought by actors Johnny Depp, Geoffrey Rush, Craig McLachlan, and Australian political staffer Bruce Lehrmann.[38] But there were many more involving less well-known individuals as well as cases that never reached the courts. A July 2021 UN Report by the Special Rapporteur, Irene Khan, stated: "In a perverse twist in the #MeToo age, women who publicly denounce alleged perpetrators of sexual violence online are increasingly subject to defamation suits or charged with criminal libel or the false reporting of crimes."[39] Recent feminist legal scholarship has analyzed these trends, pointing out the ways in which defamation law currently protects reputations and prioritizes speech along gendered lines.[40] This book provides a history of the ways in which the law developed to help some and hinder others. Most importantly, it documents women's fights to have their interests and experiences recognized within the masculine mechanics of English defamation law.

The chapters of this book progress chronologically, crisscrossing the common law world to track major developments and arguments occurring about the sexual slander of women and resultant reforms. Each chapter focuses upon a particular state or colony, selected because it represents important moments of change, transnational connections, and/or divergences of perspective or understanding within the slander of women movement. The locales chosen were not the only places that participated in these reforms, but they are the most pivotal to unpacking and detailing this story. The extent to which the slander of women acts had rolled out across the common law world by the mid-twentieth century, affecting nearly all US and Australian states, as well as British India, the Canadian provinces, New Zealand, and Singapore, is detailed in the Conclusion. Further, on another methodological point, the cases detailed within the chapters are those that contested issues of special damage and sexual slander at the appellate level. They thus carry legal significance, primarily adjudicating upon matters of law, not fact. These cases set down precedents and/or had the authority to demand that parliaments must act and pass remedial legislation. The legal legacies of these cases are thus long-lasting. But, importantly, the cases also involved parties with vivid and complex lives—individuals scrambling to restore some equilibrium to their fractured relationships, perilous financial situations, and pained bodies and minds. Each woman plaintiff appealed her case up to the highest court of her state or colony because she was deeply invested in the outcome and reliant upon a favorable result.

This book begins in New Jersey in 1788, where a case brought by young Mary Smith against her neighbor Isaac Minor in Trenton started the global slander of women movement. *Smith v Minor* was the very first sexual slander case to be heard by an appellate court in the new republic and occurred during a unique and significant time in New Jersey's political history. In 1776, New Jersey's Constitution had bestowed suffrage upon "All inhabitants" worth 50 pounds, including women, free people of color, and immigrants. While some other state constitutions in the new nation adopted gender-neutral language, only in New Jersey did the Constitution work to enfranchise women in intent and effect (for the next thirty years). It was the first common law jurisdiction to do so. The sexual slander cases brought by Smith and other women at this time reflect, in their pleadings and arguments, the idea that women were "subjects" and "citizens" of the state, deserving of equal reputational redress. It was during this period—of radical experiments with enfranchisement and post-revolutionary sentiment—that committed Quaker, Chief Justice Kinsey, rejected English precedent, restored Smith's reputation, and kicked off the slander of women movement.

Ten years after Mary Smith brought her case in Trenton, British naturalist and artist John Lewin and his wife Maria Lewin boarded the *HMS Buffalo* in Portsmouth, England, bound for the newly established penal colony of New South Wales. But, as fate would have it, when John stepped off the ship momentarily to retrieve something, it departed without him, causing Maria to embark on the long journey alone, where she was subjected to vicious rumors, slurs, and repeatedly called a whore. In 1799, Maria Lewin brought the first sexual slander case in the Australian colonies. Chapter 2 examines the Lewin case and that of Harriet Spencer, a governess, who sued a ship's captain in 1826 over stories he spread about her being guilty of "criminal intercourse." In the small, largely illiterate, and unstable penal society of Sydney Cove, slander laws played an important role in regulating "savage" masculinity by punishing abusive and provocative speech. But could they also allow women to protect their economic futures in this energetic, egalitarian, and entrepreneurial society? In 1847, New South Wales broke definitively from English common law and made it easier for women to bring sexual slander suits.

In 1808, North Carolina was the first US state to pass a slander of women act. Chapter 3 investigates the circumstances behind the passing of the act, introduced by enslaver William W. Jones, and the ways in which it played out during the antebellum period. Unlike New Jersey, which changed its slander laws judicially and on gender-neutral terms, North Carolina's law reform expressed a legislative motivation to shield and defend the "unsullied purity" of white women as the moral center of the new republic.

This legislation saw discursive connections drawn between enhancing the rights of women to sue for slander and ideas of purity and whiteness. However, despite being passed for the benefit of elite or typical white women, the majority of sexual slander cases heard by the Supreme Court of North Carolina relying on this first slander of women act were brought by women on the margins of this scattered, largely rural society: poor, aging, single, "lunatic," Native American, and/or Black women. Chapter 3 investigates these cases, such as those brought by Cherokee sisters Mary and Catherine Watts, against wealthy white planter, John Greenlee, and how the first slander act offered an opportunity to protest their denigration on the public record and punish their (usually far wealthier and well-connected) abusers, who otherwise felt able to slander them with impunity.

Chapter 4 moves to the neighboring state of Georgia, where agriculture shaped legal culture and color lines, and codification made the state a leader of speech suppression. It examines cases such as *Castleberry v Kelly*, brought by an illiterate farming wife from the Black Belt region, Martha Kelly, against her neighbors, Ezra and Sarah Castleberry, in 1853 for telling Martha's husband in the company of others that "Negroes have been with your wife and I can prove it." The Supreme Court of Georgia held, reluctantly, that such statements were not legal slander within English common law without proof of special damage. Justice MacDonald, giving judgment for the court, stated: "They have in England no inferior race as slaves, as we have here, with whom it is disgraceful to be on terms of social intercourse. Who can say that, there, a case of the sort before us would not be made an exception to this established rule?" In 1859, following outrage over the court decision, the Georgia state legislature acted to make "any charge or intimation against a free white female of having sexual intercourse with a person of color slanderous without proof of special damage." This was the only racially specific slander of women act passed in the British common law world. In 1863, the Georgia code went even further, enacting a broad provision making imputations of "debasing acts" slander *per se*.

In the same year, across the ocean, lauded public singer and performer ("encored at every song") Suzanna Wishart brought an action in the South Australian Supreme Court for comments that she was a "bad woman" who saw many men. As a result she lost all business, "had no other means of obtaining a livelihood," and was left penniless as a young widow. The defense moved to throw her case out of court—arguing that as she was slandered in a "private" or "spiritual" capacity only, not relating to her professional talents or skills, there was no action at common law unless she could prove "special damage" such as a broken marriage proposal. Chapter 5 examines sexual slander cases in the free and mercantile colony of South Australia, where the equal migration of the sexes, marriage, and family formation forged the bedrock of society and lawmaking. If women's honor and prospects could not be salvaged by their "natural guardians" (their husbands), was it up to the state to step in? The South Australian debates—aware of conversations occurring in London and parts of the United States—show a shift in ideas from protecting women's marital security to enabling their economic and legal autonomy.

In his book *The Excellency of the Female Character Vindicated*, published in 1808, American writer and abolitionist Thomas Branagan warned his imagined women readers: "You should compare your character to a clean sheet of white paper, which, if once stained, will be always visibly unclean and unfit for use, unless for the most common purposes." In 1825, a member of the New York Legislative Assembly, John Hulbert, vehemently advocated for slander of women reforms, declaring that once a woman's character was "stained" with slurs of unchastity, it was easier for the "the Ethiopian to change his skin, or the Leopard his spots" or for "the wool dyed with scarlet to become white again" than for her dark "stain" to be washed away. While explicit references to race were mostly absent from the laws of slander in the northern US states (unlike in Georgia), metaphors and discourses of stained and discolored whiteness were pervasive. Detailing numerous cases and conversations, Chapter 6 chapter demonstrates the subtle ways in which ideas about racial purity and sexual morality were intertwined and mutually formative for northern women.

In the self-governing progressive Australian colony of Victoria, in 1887, young hotel owner Elizabeth Albrecht lost her slander action in the Supreme Court of Victoria concerning slurs of adultery and unchastity as she was unable to prove special damage. Justice Williams, forcefully criticizing the English common law upon which the decision was based, stated: "There is a total disregard to the rights of women, and I trust that some member of the Legislature will make it his duty to frame a law to amend such a monstrous state of things." Chapter 7, centering on the gold rush–enriched colony of Victoria, shows how arguments for reforming slander laws focused upon defending the respectability of women engaged in public occupations and trades—as grocery store owners, barmaids, and publicans—and, unlike New York, how the issue was framed as a matter of political equality and the "rights of women." Victoria's slander of women reforms of 1887, though influenced by New York's 1871 legislation, were drafted and debated within a very different social and economic urban landscape as the Woman Movement and calls for suffrage gained ascendancy there.

A year later, in 1888, the British Parliament referred to Victoria's recent slander of women act and questioned whether England should pass similar laws. Since the abolition of the ecclesiastical courts in 1855, English women had been left with virtually no remedy for sexual slander. A bill was soon introduced, by William Gully, Queen's Counsel and member of the House of Commons. Gully had represented numerous women in unsuccessful sexual slander suits, including Elizabeth Lewis, a high-profile temperance campaigner, who sued John Shaw, a publican, for spreading rumors that she had been seen having sex in the sand dunes of a popular beach with her professional assistant. But Gully's Slander of Women Bill faced considerable opposition on two very different fronts. Attorney General Richard Webster and others were worried that words used to casually insult women "when temper gets the upper hand," such as "whore," would become legally prohibited. Such laws, he argued, would place too much power in the hands of vengeful and vexatious women litigants. On the other hand, the bill was opposed by British women's suffrage groups for reinforcing a regressive "double standard of morality for the sexes." They wanted gender-neutral reforms to sexual slander, like those in New Jersey and New South Wales. England, finally, enacted its own Slander of Women Act in 1891. It was one of the last in the British common law world.

Throughout this book, I give little attention to whether the rumors or slurs leveled at women were true. Instead, emphasis is placed on the nature and power of the speech act—the words of gendered abuse and denigration—their effects on individuals, the decisions of women to sue, and their battles in doing so. Whether particular insinuations or vituperative attacks on women—as whore, unchaste, slut, fornicator, incontinent—had a basis in truth, either wholly or partially, is largely irrelevant. Not only is it difficult, near impossible, to determine the facts of the matter over a hundred years later—relitigating the evidence and scrutinizing the fading words of testimony for credibility—but to do so, to probe the truth of the slanderous imputations, positions truth as justifying the abuse. Legally, of course, truth has long been and continues to be a defense to defamation claims. But, here, seeking out whether these women did have various sexual partners and affairs—whether they gave birth to bastards or crippled babies or mulattos, whether they had intercourse in swamps in chicken coops or on public beaches—subjects them to unwarranted judgment and inquiry. It would sanction the idea that it was reasonable to call out or vilify or slander women who engage in unconventional sex. It would sanction the idea that women could or should be shamed for their sexuality, or ashamed of their relations with others. It would shift focus onto the behavior and conduct of the slandered women rather than the acts of their (mostly male) slanderers.

My book uncovers and unpacks the stories and slurs of sexual immorality that were hatched and hurled against women and their resulting harm and humiliation. My primary focus is on women's legal and historical agency, their determination to vindicate their reputations, to reclaim their own life narratives, and to restore their social and economic prospects.

ONE

THE SLANDER OF SUBJECTS AND CITIZENS

New Jersey

On January 1, 1788, in the city of Trenton, New Jersey, nineteen-year-old Isaac Minor made scandalous public comments about Mary Smith, a young unmarried woman in the community.[1] According to court documents, Minor argued that he was simply repeating what someone else told him when he stated: "Mary Smith is with child by Stephen Jones," and "Ezekiel Smith's daughter is like to have a little one."[2] Smith was incensed and damaged by these rumors. According to the pleadings, she felt "hurt, injured and degraded" by his words and her "good name, credit, reputation & esteem" suffered.[3] She had fallen into "public scandal, infamy and disgrace" with acquaintances, friends, and neighbors now wholly refusing to have any "connection or discourse" with her. She was, in sum, "aggrieved and damnified." So, Smith decided to sue Minor in the New Jersey Supreme Court for "trespass on the case for words," being the tort of slander. Minor pleaded not guilty and thereafter the matter went—by consent of the parties—to arbitration where three referees reported that, after hearing and weighing all the evidence, it was clear Minor had indeed spoken the words alleged. They awarded Smith 100 pounds in damages.

But Minor appealed and sought to have the declaration set aside on the grounds that because the words spoken alleged a "spiritual" offense only—fornication—they were not actionable without proof of special damage in the courts of New Jersey. Relying heavily on the technicalities of English common law, Minor argued that only if he accused Smith of being guilty of an indictable offence—that is, giving birth to a bastard child—would his comments be defamatory *per se*. But as it was, his words merely attributed to Smith an act of "moral turpitude."[4] The arbitrators, he submitted, had "clearly mistaken the law."

Smith's lawyers pushed back, stating that Minor's words—asserting the plaintiff was "with child"—put her at "jeopardy of a future prosecution" within the meaning of the relevant statute.[5] Further, they argued, in the interests of "equity and justice," the court should not restrict the law to its "narrower limits." "Redress for malicious defamation," they loftily declared, "should be extended with the utmost liberality, and not frittered away by unnecessary refinements."[6]

The Supreme Court of Judicature of New Jersey faced an important decision regarding women's ability to seek and obtain redress for defamation. It was the first time a case of sexual slander had reached an appeals court in the new republic. If the court strictly followed English law, the defendant was correct: Smith's slander claim and others brought by women involving imputations of sexual immorality should and would be thrown out of court. In 1790, this New Jersey superior court case was deeply influenced and reflective of the state's own immediate history and political moment. It provided an opportunity to communicate the state's views regarding the subjecthood of women and, relatedly, their common law rights to reputation.

This was also the first slander case brought by a woman in New Jersey since Abigail Sharp brought a claim against Abraham Shotwell in 1727 for statements he made about her being a witch: "Sharp is an old witch and had been flying all night and I saw her as she was coming home early in the morning."[7] All other slander cases in New Jersey prior to 1800 were brought by men, alleging false imputations about them including theft,[8] buggery,[9] perjury,[10] professional negligence,[11] being a Tory and aiding the enemy,[12] or being an enemy of the new republic.[13]

Smith v Minor was heard during the post-revolutionary period, just ten years since British forces had been driven out of New Jersey after a series of high-profile and bloody battles. It was a time when Trenton—the location of the sitting Supreme Court—was being proposed and pushed by the northern states as the best location for the new federal capital. Damaged extensively during the war, New Jersey was the center of an industrious process of rebuilding and hosted a reception in 1789 for George Washington on his journey to New York City for his inauguration. It was also experiencing a rapid increase in population, particularly of Europeans. Still mostly rural and agricultural in demographics, the number of white residents in New Jersey doubled between 1790 and 1830.[14] At the same time, the African American population steadily decreased, with enslaved and some free Black residents fleeing to better prospects as the state resisted and delayed the abolition of slavery.[15]

New Jersey was also enjoying a historically significant and unusual period with regard to suffrage, uniquely experimenting with and negotiating the limits and qualifications for state subjecthood and citizenship. At the time Mary Smith instigated her action against Isaac Minor, free single women could vote in New Jersey. The state Constitution of 1776 had bestowed suffrage upon women—as well as free Blacks and immigrants. The article read:

> [A]ll inhabitants of this Colony, of full age, who are worth fifty pounds proclamation money, clear estate in the same, and have resided within the county in which they claim a vote for twelve months immediately preceding the election, shall be entitled to vote for Representatives in Council and Assembly; and also for all other public officers, that shall be elected by the people of the county at large.[16]

Other state constitutions in the United States at the time defined votes and voters as "every man,"[17] "free men,"[18] "male, white inhabitants,"[19] and "male inhabitant."[20] Some, like New Jersey, adopted gender-neutral language.[21] But only in New Jersey did the Constitution work to enfranchise women with intent and effect.

Historians have traditionally treated New Jersey's liberal suffrage provision of 1776 as an accident, oversight, or largely irrelevant aberration. In *Liberty's Daughters*, Mary Beth Norton states that the "constitution's phraseology probably represented a simple oversight on the part of its framers."[22] Linda Kerber omits any mention of it in her foundational text *Women of the Republic*. However, more recent archival work has demonstrated that the decision to extend suffrage was both deliberate and significant. Judith Klinghoffer and Lois Elkis have argued that "New Jersey, rather than representing an anomaly, simply stood at the cutting edge of the political continuum, and its laws represented the furthest reach of possibilities for female citizenship."[23] Similarly, Jan Lewis has written that "New Jersey's enfranchisement of women, along with that of blacks and aliens and its low property threshold for voting, marks it as one of the most liberal jurisdictions at the time."[24]

There is clear evidence, too, that women in New Jersey acted upon their enfranchisement—voting, penning letters to newspapers on political issues, attending protests, and participating in riots—for the next thirty years.[25] They regarded themselves as a rightful part of the body politic. In 1916, historian Raymond Turner wrote of the New Jersey situation: "It is probable that this is the most important instance of voting in government elections by English-speaking women in any early time."[26] This chapter links this political and constitutional history with common law legal history, showing for the first time the productive interaction between a radical redefining of political membership of the new republic and reform of the English common law of defamation. It was no coincidence that the beginning of the global slander of women movement—that would continue to evolve and adapt for more than a century—occurred just as women were first recognized as citizens.

Mary Smith herself, under the age of twenty-one, could not yet vote in state elections nor bring court actions on her own. In order to sue Isaac Minor, she required the consent of her father Ezekiel Smith. This was important because, as the statement of claim makes clear, Ezekiel Smith thus became legally responsible for any costs awarded against his daughter who could not yet herself own property. However, Mary Smith was only a year or so away from property ownership and suffrage in the state, and despite her father's perfunctory signature at the end of the claim, the court documents all represent the action as instigated and driven by her. This was her act of retribution and social restoration in the new republic, not a paternal claim to uphold old world family honor.

The statement of claim clearly recognizes her emerging political and legal status. Mary Smith is referred to repeatedly as a "Subject of the State of New Jersey" previously known by "all other worthy Subjects of the State" as a "person of good name fame and reputation."[27] Until Minor spoke the "scandalous" words about her, she enjoyed the "benevolence" and "good opinion" of all friends, acquaintances, and "*other* worthy Subjects of the State." The careful choice of words in the pleadings—Smith is a "Subject" and not a lady, daughter, virgin, or female—is meaningful. The plaintiff's court papers suggest that gender is largely irrelevant here and so too should be irrelevant to the law of defamation. It does not refer to her lost marriage prospects or dashed hopes of a suitor. It does not describe or position her as a fallen woman in need of judicial protection. The papers state that she is "hurt," "injured," and "aggrieved" by Minor's malicious actions. The pleadings communicate that all plaintiffs—as equal subjects or soon-to-be "Subjects of the State of New Jersey"—who have been injured maliciously by the words of another should receive the same opportunities for legal redress. "All inhabitants" deserved the right to enjoy "the happy state" of a good reputation.[28] "Subject" here seems to infer that Smith is entitled to recourse via legal doctrines in the state, deriving in this instance, from common law. In later cases, women slander plaintiffs shift to being described as "subjects and citizens," and then simply just "citizens."

Prior to almost universal suffrage under the state Constitution of 1776, women in New Jersey had been barred from voting since 1702 by an election law passed under the authority of the Queen of England, Scotland, and Ireland, which stipulated "the Division in which he shall so vote."[29] The reasons for women's radical change in political status in 1776 are still partly unclear, but historians attribute it to elements of revolutionary thought, Quaker egalitarianism, and matters of political expediency.[30] When debates ensued in New Jersey about extending suffrage in 1774-75, the revolutionary elite found their anti-British slogan "no representation without taxation" thrown back at them by various "lower order" and other groups within the population. Why shouldn't women, many of whom were householders and freeholders, have a voice in their government? Further, women in New Jersey were implicated—physically, socially, and economically—in the war, with bloody battles bearing down on them. Many took up arms, led boycotts against English goods, and engaged in fundraising efforts. As tensions rose in the 1770s, New Jersey's population was bitterly divided between loyalists and revolutionaries. One way to shore up women's allegiance was to include them within the body politic.

In 1790, the year of Mary Smith's appeal to the Supreme Court, the state legislature doubled down on women's suffrage, passing an election law that referred to voters as "he or she" in seven counties.[31] This was extended to all thirteen counties in 1797.[32] But this legislative clarification of women's right to vote was perhaps less an ideological embrace of equality and more likely the result of party political strategy. In 1789, a group of conservative men, largely businessmen and Quakers (all destined to be Federalists), pushed for the election of candidates for the first US Congress who would represent their interests—the Junto ticket. Part of this push meant increasing voter turnout in Federalist counties and suppressing it in Republican counties by, for instance, tinkering with the number of days people could vote, placing polling booths in townships, and encouraging women to turn up and vote: hence, why such changes only initially applied to seven Federalist counties. As Irwin Gertzog notes, "the egalitarian motives alleged to have prompted Quakers and others to confer the vote on New Jersey women were probably less important in achieving that result than the struggle for economic and political power within the state."[33]

Nonetheless, in the 1790s, women began participating in political processes in significant and increasing numbers. During this period, Republicans and Federalists waxed and waned in their assessment of whether women voters helped or hindered their bid for power against their rivals. In 1799, Federalist William Griffith, believing that women's suffrage was mostly benefiting Republicans, proposed a constitutional reform to strip women of the vote. The proposal was resoundingly defeated.[34] And in 1800, when Republicans sought to amend election laws to make it easier for more women to vote and not be discouraged at the polls, it was rejected by the legislature as superfluous: "the House unanimously agreed that this section would be clearly within the meaning of our constitution . . . [that] gives this right to maids or widows, black or white."[35] Further, in 1802, an election law seeking to "exclude all persons from voting excepting free white males" was easily voted down.[36] As Lewis has noted, owning property was regarded in the early days of the republic—as across the British common law world—as the main precondition for citizenship.[37] Property ownership seemingly proved an independence of interest and thought. In New Jersey the threshold was relatively low—50 pounds cash rather than land or freehold, as was the pre-revolutionary requirement.[38] Married women were barred (via coverture) from voting, as were slaves (property themselves), but otherwise classifications of gender or race were not essential to one's citizenship in New Jersey at this time. Being a woman or Black did not—yet—make an individual inherently or naturally unsuitable to vote. In the 1802 election, the Trenton *True American* reported that female turnout rose to "alarming heights," possibly making up about 25 percent of the total vote.[39]

Women's centrality to the political fates of candidates and causes in New Jersey during these decades meant that fervent campaigns often celebrated them as independent voters and political beings. And such public discussions reflected and affected wider ideas about women's roles in New Jersey society. In his book *Under Their Vine and Fig Tree: Travels Through America in 1797-1799, 1805, with Some Further Account of Life in New Jersey*, Polish exile Julian Ursyn Niemcewicz observed that in New Jersey, "every young maiden is born a citizen and only becomes a wife later, her country first, husband second."[40] Such observations contrast with accounts from other states in the new republic, as reported by Linda Kerber, where women were positioned primarily as domestic subjects owing duties to their homes and husbands, or exercising their patriotic duties through their family roles.[41]

But in New Jersey, Republican newspapers of this time (trying to appeal to women voters) created a picture of women citizens at odds with the idea of "maids" as dutiful daughters and future wives. A Fourth of July oration by a so-called male citizen, published in the Republican outlet *Genius of Liberty*, declared:

> [O]ur daughters are the same relations to us as our sons; we owe them the same duties; they have the same science, and are equally competent in their attainments. The contrary idea originated in the same abuse of power, as monarchy and slavery . . . the history of women is forever obtruding on our unwilling eyes bold and ardent spirits, who no tyrant could tame—no prejudice enslave. . . . Female Citizens follow examples so glorious; accept the station nature intended for you, and double the knowledge and happiness of mankind.[42]

Poems and toasts abounded in newspapers at this time celebrating the "rights of women" and championing women's choice to reject marriage as their life course. One verse, written by "a lady" and published in the *Centinel of Freedom* in 1800, proclaimed:

> That I hate all the doctrines by wedlock prescribed; Its law of obedience could never suit me, My spirit's too lofty, my thoughts are too free. . . . A vow of allegiance to die an old maid. Long live the Republic of freedom and ease, May its subjects live happy and do as they please.[43]

The discursive similarities in the language of these poems, orations, and newspaper articles and Smith's legal pleadings are striking. As a maid, she sees herself as a "subject of the state," entitled to live "happy" in the republic, enjoying a "good name" for its own sake, not merely for procurement of a suitor or as a precondition for matrimony.

Chief Justice James Kinsey presided over Mary Smith's case. Kinsey was the son of John Kinsey, a Quaker politician, reformer, and earlier chief justice of the Pennsylvania Supreme Court, who was disgraced after his death when it was discovered he had misappropriated thousands of pounds in public funds.[44] James worked as a young law clerk to pay off his father's debts and witnessed the family's fall from honor and the consequent sale of family property, including the extensive estate Plantation House on the banks of the Schuylkill River. He was admitted to the bar in 1753, then became a member of the New Jersey General Assembly. He was also an active member of the Continental Congress and Society of Friends. However, when in 1777, the New Jersey legislature required all attorneys, counselors, and judges to swear an oath of allegiance to the new United States, Kinsey—as a Quaker and pacifist—notably refused. As a result, he was temporarily obliged to give up his extensive and lucrative legal practice. In a history of the Supreme Court of New Jersey, written in 1891, John Whitehead notes, however, that "No suspicion ever attached to him as being disloyal to the cause of the colonies."[45] In 1789, Kinsey was appointed chief justice in New Jersey.

Quakers like John and James Kinsey were a powerful political and cultural presence in New Jersey, and for a long time New Jersey's unique enfranchisement of women was attributed to Quaker ideas and influence, particularly those of Quaker politician and lawmaker Joseph Cooper. Cooper was an influential member of the legislature when New Jersey bolstered its women suffrage laws of 1790 with reference to "he or she," and he authored similar legislation in 1797. In the late eighteenth century, Quakers were a dominant religious group in much of what is now known as southern New Jersey, including counties such as Cape May, Cumberland, Burlington, Salem, Gloucester, and Hunterdon. While conservative in economic and political outlook, they were relatively untraditional when it came to relations between the sexes, believing in at least some measure of social and political equality between men and women. The Society of

Friends was also decidedly abolitionist, pushing consistently for the end of slavery. New Jersey, as a Quaker hot spot in the late eighteenth century, is likely to have been imbued with thought and practice that offered women increased opportunities for forms of authority and agency.[46]

In this climate of revolutionary ideals, surrounded by increasing legislative efforts concerning suffrage and discussion of women's place in society, and as a committed and longstanding Quaker, Chief Justice Kinsey grappled to answer the significant questions posed by Mary Smith's defamation case. At first, his judgment stuck firmly to the technicalities of argument and interpretation: Were words imputing fornication, but not the actual birth of a bastard, covered by the criminal statute in question, and thus actionable as defamation at common law? Kinsey agreed with the defendant that in England, words imputing fornication alone alleged a mere spiritual offense and therefore were not the basis for an action at common law unless special damage could be proved. Mary Smith's courtroom chances dimmed. But Chief Justice Kinsey would not extinguish them. Scrutinizing the exact wording of the relevant criminal statute, he suggested that Minor's words intended to make her an "object of punishment" and so perhaps they alleged a crime.

Chief Justice Kinsey could have stopped there. But he chose to venture further. Even if Minor's words did not allege a crime—it was unclear whether they did—Smith's case was actionable without special damage.[47] At this point, Chief Justice Kinsey's judgment broke decidedly from the traditions and precedents of English common law. The strictures of those old rules were not relevant to this new world society, which was secular in its administration of justice. He stated:

> [A]n action will lie for spiritual defamation in New Jersey, because we have no ecclesiastical courts to punish the offence.... The reason of the English cases is inapplicable here, and the decisions themselves should not, therefore, be regarded with the same technical precision, and applied with the same unbending exactness.[48]

While penned in relatively muted tones, this was a revolutionary judgment.

The chief justice declared that New Jersey, while inheriting and recognizing hundreds of years of English common law, was no longer beholden to it. It is an example of what Roscoe Pound has identified as a post-revolutionary "hostility towards English law."⁴⁹ "Calumny," Kinsey stated, was "so odious and detestable" and "in the present instance" so likely to both injure "the plaintiff personally" as well as "strike at the very peace of society" that the court had "much pleasure" in holding Smith's action maintainable. Further, for defamatory words for which "the laws of England provide[d] a spiritual punishment only," such as those brought by women for adultery, fornication, and unchastity, an action would now "lie here." He confessed that he felt "no small uneasiness to hear it so strenuously contended that, for so atrocious an injury, the laws of New Jersey provided no redress."⁵⁰

Mary Smith, a "Subject of the State of New Jersey," won her slander suit against Isaac Minor in 1790. She also won an almost identical case against John Dye over the same harassing comments.⁵¹ Her reputation was restored, and both men faced substantial economic consequences for their abusive and defamatory conduct. By bringing her action, the first sexual slander case to be heard by an appellate court in the United States, Smith pushed New Jersey to judicially reform the English common law of defamation to include women's interests.⁵² Plaintiffs in that state would no longer face the burden of proving special damage when bringing slander claims relating to sexual immorality. By doing so, she set off the global slander of women movement.

It is notable, however, that the legal changes instigated by Smith's court action and realized by Chief Justice Kinsey's judgment were gender neutral.⁵³ In the nineteenth century, when the slander of women movement gained momentum across US states and then Australian colonies, the changes passed by most legislatures focused explicitly on "females" or women. As I explain in later chapters, the gender specificity of these bills often attracted debate, with various groups in society questioning the benefits and detriments of having different laws—particularly those related to issues of speech and morality—for men and women. Gender ideologies concerning femininity and masculinity relating to men and women's natural qualities, social roles, and obligations were central to these debates. But the gender-neutral changes effected in New Jersey were not discursively based upon the unique needs of women, or on their need for special treatment within the law. Mary Smith was not framed as a wife, daughter, virgin, or maid seeking the paternal protection of the court. Rather, she was positioned as a subject of the state of New Jersey, whose lack of adequate redress under English common law necessitated its immediate reform, even if that meant departing from hundreds of years of established precedent. Such reasoning reflected the historically unique enfranchisement of women in New Jersey at the time. The changes meant that women could now bring slander suits as easily as men in New Jersey.

In September 1805, sixteen-year-old Mary Field Stockton brought a case for slander, via her uncle and attorney Lucius Horatio Stockton, against Thomas Hopkins for the sum of 5,000 pounds in the county of Burlington. In her pleadings, Stockton's lawyers set out that she was an "honest and virtuous *subject and citizen* of the State of New Jersey."[54] She stated that until the "speaking and publishing of the several false, scandalous and defamatory words" by Thomas Hopkins about her, she had, for all her lifetime, "behaved and governed herself" and been "reputed, esteemed and received" by friends, neighbors, relations, parents, and "all other worthy subjects and Citizens of the State of New Jersey" to be "a person" of "good name, fame and reputation." She submitted that she had never been guilty or, until the words complained of, suspected of "fornication." She accused Thomas Hopkins of "contriving and maliciously intending to prejudice, degrade and injure" her and cause her to be "brought into public scandal and disgrace" and disturb her "repose and quiet" by telling people she was a "damned whore" who had a "carnal connexion" with Hopkin's indentured servant, Nicholas Odersook, and was now carrying his "bastard" child. These "false, scandalous and opprobrious" words had been spoken and published by Thomas Hopkins to "divers good and worthy Citizens, Inhabitants and subjects of the State of New Jersey." It is unclear here whether the categories of citizens, inhabitants, and subjects are being distinguished or equated.

The circumstances leading up to and surrounding the case of *Stockton v Hopkins* were complicated, contested, and shrouded in controversy. They illuminate how issues of class and citizenship intersect with political power and the process of conducting defamation proceedings. Mary Field Stockton was the eldest child of Richard Stockton, a leading lawyer and politician in New Jersey, and the grandchild of Richard Stockton Sr. (1730-1781), signatory of the Declaration of Independence, and Annis Boudinot Stockton (1736-1801), one of America's earliest published women poets. The Stocktons were a prominent and powerful New Jersey family, early graduates of and closely connected to the College of New Jersey (later,

Princeton University), and owners and residents of Morven, a slaveholding estate and plantation.⁵⁵ The Morven estate now stands as a museum, gallery, and garden that recounts the history of the Stockton family.⁵⁶ However, no mention is made of the sexual scandal that engulfed them in the early 1800s.

Mary Field Stockton, born in 1790, was a student at an esteemed boarding school run by Thomas Hopkins (a recently arrived English immigrant) and his wife Elizabeth, in Bordentown, southeast of Trenton. But in August 1805, Richard Stockton received a seemingly anonymous letter informing him that "a bound fellow of Mr. Hopkins," Nicholas Odersook, was making Mary "the constant subject of ridicule all over this town" by telling people he had had relations with her and other matters "of a much grosser nature."⁵⁷ Odersook also apparently brandished handkerchiefs embossed with Mary's name as proof of their connection. The original author of the letter, Henry Sibart (a German gardener), when tracked down and confronted by Richard Stockton, also elaborated that Odersook had told people that Elizabeth Hopkins (the school mistress) had seen Mary and him coming out of the "ice house" together. When asked about the matter, fifteen-year-old Mary Stockton confessed to gifting Odersook her handkerchiefs, and Odersook admitted that he had talked about her. But neither confirmed that they were engaged in a sexual relationship.

After receiving the letter, Mary's parents remonstrated with their daughter about "the impropriety of making free with such people."⁵⁸ Circulating rumors of unchastity clearly had the capacity to wound Mary's reputation, but this was doubly so where such rumors connected her with someone who was both a "foreigner" and an indentured servant. But her humiliation was as much caused by the content of the speech as by the characteristics of the speaker. Odersook had taken "shocking liberties" with Mary's name, displaying a freedom of expression he had no rights or worthiness to enjoy. At the time, indentured servitude was common in New Jersey, and as with adjacent Pennsylvania, the vast majority of indentured servants in the eighteenth and early nineteenth centuries were European, often German.

The circumstances were further complicated by the fact that some months earlier, Mary Stockton had begun circulating a story through the school that she had recently been married—in a lavish ceremony—to Biddle Wilkinson, son of General Wilkinson, an upstanding New Jersey gentleman.⁵⁹ She elaborated and gushed upon the details to her schoolmates, noting that "after the ceremony was performed, her father blessed her in a manner so peculiarly affecting, that it drew tears from her eyes."⁶⁰ She also informed students and maidservants at the boarding school that she had afterwards "slept four nights with her husband" and was now pregnant. One of Hopkins's servants, Alice MacNally, gave evidence that Mary Stockton told her she was "with child" to Biddle Wilkinson and that she had "milk in her breasts."⁶¹ During the same encounter, Mary also told MacNally that another girl had recently left the boarding school as she was pregnant by Thomas Hopkins.

Stockton's propensity for telling stories, described as of "dangerous and iniquitous invention" by Hopkins, soon led to her expulsion from the boarding school.⁶² As a consequence, Mary Stockton's parents declared that if she were to be expelled, they would make the allegations of sexual misconduct against Thomas Hopkins public. On September 3, 1805, Richard Stockton wrote to Elizabeth Hopkins: "Madam, I will never in silence submit to your bringing home my daughter in the manner you have, which, without explanation, will enable you to cover the follies of your husband by her disgrace."⁶³ By that time, the combined effect of salacious stories spoken about town by Odersook, Mary's own fabrications about getting married and becoming pregnant, and her dismissal from the boarding school combined so that the "whole of Trenton was buzzing with a variety of reports relative to Miss Stockton."⁶⁴ So began a fight to save Mary Stockton's reputation from disgrace and put down a furiously spreading scandal. At the same time, respectable families, hearing that Thomas Hopkins was implicated in fathering the child of a pupil, pulled their daughters from the school.

The slander trial instigated by Mary Stockton against Hopkins, which commenced in October 1805, pivoted on the evidence given by indentured servant Nicholas Odersook. In one deposition, he swore that his master, Thomas Hopkins, had bribed him to spread rumors about Mary being a "whore," having a sexual relationship with him, and becoming pregnant.⁶⁵ Specifically, Hopkins told Odersook that Stockton was "with child" and that she would "charge the said child to him" (identify Hopkins as the father). According to Odersook, Hopkins then ordered him—given he was a "young man"—to "own it himself," meaning for him to go town to town and confess to being the father of Stockton's unborn child. In exchange, Hopkins reportedly promised Odersook seven months of time off his term of indenture—as well as a coat, a pair of shoes, and "five collars"—and threatened that if he did not spread the rumor, Odersook would land in the state prison where he would be "fed only once per day, have no clothes and be whipped." Odersook testified that the stories he was forced to tell about Mary Stockton being pregnant with his child and having intercourse with him were "utterly false and untrue" and that he always "behaved to her as a servant ought" and in no other way.

Mary Stockton won her case and was awarded 5,000 pounds in damages plus costs—a sizable sum.[66] Whether the fifteen- or sixteen-year-old had become pregnant at any time, or whether and with whom she had had sexual relations while residing at the boarding school, were not matters raised at trial. Stockton accused Hopkins of defaming her, and Hopkins simply denied (without success) that he had spoken the words. After a jury of twelve men decided the fate of the parties, Hopkins attempted to appeal the decision to the Supreme Court of Judicature, partly on the basis that Mary had suffered insufficient damage. During trial proceedings, Richard Stockton had admitted on the stand that his daughter "had sustained no injury" from Hopkins's words.[67] However, Hopkins's attempt at an appeal was unsuccessful. Such failure rested upon the earlier victory of Mary Smith against Isaac Minor in 1790, when Chief Justice Kinsey had judicially removed the barriers within English common law faced by women bringing sexual slander suits. No longer did women, such as Mary Smith or Mary Stockton, need to satisfy the onerous condition of proving economic loss. Rather, they could recover damages, exact retribution, and regain community respect simply by showing that slanderous words had been spoken about them. Like words denigrating a man in his occupation or trade, damage was presumed to flow. Such changes put women, technically, on the same footing as men when it came to defamation law in New Jersey, recognizing their new status—repeatedly emphasized in Stockton's pleadings—as citizens and subjects of the state.

But court actions were not the only way to correct the public record. Thomas Hopkins, outraged over his courtroom loss to Mary Stockton, set about in appealing to "the only sure friend of the unfortunate, the most sacred and faithful ally of impartial justice"—the press.[68] On October 15, 1807, Hopkins published an open letter and an "Advertisement" in the *United States Gazette* (aligned with the Federalist Party) and the next day in the rival *Philadelphia Aurora* (connected with the Democratic-

Republicans).[69] In it, Hopkins positioned himself as the victim of great injustice, occasioned by the use of the law by those in positions of status to shape the narrative and punish the weak. "I am the injured party, and you are the aggressor," he declared.[70] In his Advertisement, Hopkins expressly referred to himself as a "mediocritist in society," hopelessly up against opponents who were "opulent and influential."[71] The only remedy, he considered, was to "submit to the public simple and unexaggerated narration of the whole transaction." Soon after, in February 1808, he penned and self-published, in Philadelphia, his side of the story, titled *An Appeal to the Tribunal of Public Justice; Being a Concise Statement of the Facts Which Led to the Extraordinary Case of Stockton Versus Hopkins*.[72]

In his book, Hopkins charged the Stocktons with deliberately damning his character and pursuing defamation proceedings against him as a way of vindicating their wayward daughter's reputation and deflecting attention away from the salacious stories circulating about her. However, the most interesting element of his account is his acuity to the classifications and connections of those embroiled in the scandal. Odersook, as a German indentured servant, is denounced and punished for "his base conduct" and is characterized as vulnerable to corruption, exploitation, and manipulation. The letter of the German gardener, Henry Sibart ("written by a foreigner"), which originally set off the controversy, is discredited, and he is "discharged" from his service. Mary Stockton is framed as a privileged but pathetic creature, with a propensity for lying and a dangerous and dubious sexual morality. The Stockton parents are frequently framed as figures of power, largely due to their combination of wealth, professional status, "local" political connections, and longstanding citizenship of and residence within New Jersey. In contrast, Hopkins paints himself as an upstanding but naïve "stranger": "My talents, my character, were my all; and perhaps what was equally fatal, I was a stranger of only a few years standing in the land."[73] He goes on: "it would have been but poor policy for an insulated stranger, as I was, to go to law with a man who is not only a Lawyer, in the habits of intimacy with the whole Bar and Bench, but also possessed of unbounded influence in other respects."[74] As a foreigner, Hopkins regarded the press as his only viable method for reputational recourse.

The case of *Stockton v Hopkins* underscores the extent to which slander proceedings and the right or ability to silence speech were riven with jostling local dynamics of subjecthood, citizenship, and social status. The enfranchisement of women that shaped the content of the common law in *Smith v Minor*—allowing women to bring cases for sexual slander without the burden of proving special damage—led to the success of Mary Stockton's action and the futility of Hopkins's appeal. But at the same time, the process of instigating, pursuing, and defending defamation proceedings in New Jersey was inseparable from hierarchies of power that clustered along lines not only of wealth and property, but also immigration status, political loyalties, character, and community embeddedness. To be a "stranger" meant vulnerability, not only to be disbelieved and manipulated by others with greater connections, but to be charged and convicted of committing slander.

Of course, slander proceedings also intersected with issues of race. Since the eighteenth century, many in the colony, particularly the Society of Friends, had advocated for the end of slavery and pushed for their members to free their enslaved workers. Such calls increased in the context of the Revolutionary War and calls for freedom from the oppression of the British. In addition, resistance by enslaved peoples was increasing, with thousands fleeing during the conflict to join the British loyalist forces, the biggest act of emancipation prior to the Civil War.[75] In 1783, at least 240 formerly enslaved persons from New Jersey departed with the English for other British lands, including Australia, choosing the possibilities of British subjecthood under a constitutional monarchy over being objects of property in a republican state. But despite these upheavals, the Stocktons (descendants of Quakers but later Presbyterians), like much of white New Jersey, held on to their property. In many counties of New Jersey, the number of people enslaved grew after 1790, and most Blacks remained enslaved after the passage of the New Jersey Act for the Gradual Abolition of Slavery in 1804.[76] In September 1806, a year after the slander trial brought by Mary Field Stockton, Richard Stockton placed an advertisement in the *Federalist* newspaper offering a $20 reward for the return of his runaway "Negro Man slave, named Sampson," described by Stockton as "about 30 years of age, five feet six or seven inches high, very black, of good countenance, but awkward in appearance when spoken to; his knees knock, and his legs are remarkably small, compared to his body."[77]

To understand the ways in which sexual slander actions intersected with race in New Jersey, it is useful to briefly compare the lives and circumstances of Mary Field Stockton and her contemporary (and perhaps cousin) Betsey Stockton. Betsey was born into slavery at Hayridge Farm (later known as Constitutional Hill), the home of Major Robert Stockton, a cousin of Richard Stockton Sr., Mary's grandfather. She was likely eight years younger than Mary and probably the daughter of an enslaved woman in Stockton's household and a white man, "whose identity is as yet unknown."[78] She was given the name Betsey, a diminutive form of Elizabeth, which was the name of at least two white women in the Stockton family. Before the age of five or six years old, Betsey was taken from her mother and placed in the household of Robert Stockton's daughter, Elizabeth, and her husband, the Reverend Ashbel Green. There, she was both tutored and held in bondage, enslaved then indentured, until she was almost twenty years old. In 1813, when Betsey was approximately fifteen years old, Green, judging Betsey "wild and thoughtless, if not vicious" and apparently seeking to "save her from the snares and temptations of the city, which I feared threatened her ruin," sold three years of her service to Nathaniel Todd, a relative and fellow Presbyterian pastor.[79]

The context of Betsey's birth and her treatment as a seeming spirited teenager underline the stark differences in approach to white and Black women's sexual and social lives. Betsey's birth signified sexual relations between a Black enslaved woman and a white man in authority, but such matters were suppressed and tacitly accepted. They were not the foundation for a controversy. Further, Betsey's alleged wayward behavior as a teenager was addressed by selling her into the service of another household. By contrast, suspicion that Mary, or any other white student at the boarding house, was implicated in a sexual affair with the schoolmaster was scandalous, and the forces of law were employed to protect and defend her. The abusive treatment of white women, as subjects and citizens of the state, was deemed a problem that required legal intervention and correction. But for Black enslaved women, as non-subjects and non-citizens, exploitation was commonplace, unremarkable, and written into the law itself.[80]

Race was also relevant to marking the types of accusations leveled against white women. In September 1808, unmarried woman Sally Stillwell brought a case for slander against James Syme.[81] The pleadings state that she was a "good, true, honest, virtuous and faithful *citizen* of the State of New Jersey," and since her "nativity" had always "carried, governed and behaved" and been taken by friends, neighbors, acquaintances, and other worthy citizens to be "a woman of good name, fame, credit," and reputation.[82] Note the shift in description occurring across these three cases between 1790 and 1808. Mary Smith was a "subject of the state of New Jersey," Stockton was a "subject and a citizen," whereas Stillwell was simply "a citizen."

Stillwell alleged that on May 12, 1808, in the city of Newark, Syme had conversations with "divers good & worthy citizens of the State" wherein he "proclaimed openly and loudly":

> "She is a damned whore, and Moses" (meaning a certain negro man, named Moses) "and Nicolas" (meaning a certain other negro man, named Nicolas) "and Tone" (meaning a certain other negro man, named Tone) "have fucked her" (meaning the said Sally had committed the crime of fornication with the said negro men). "And I" (meaning himself) "can prove it by two respectable witnesses."[83]

On other occasions Syme told people he had seen Moses in bed with Sally, alleged another man, John Baird, had "fucked her," and stated loudly to people that "she was the damnest whore in Hackensack," and "every negro in town has fucked her." As a result, the pleadings stated that Sally Stillwell had been "injured, degraded and damnified in her good name, fame, credit and reputation," causing her to be "abhorred," "disrespected," and shunned by the community. She pleaded that "still daily do more and more refuse . . . from having any manner or conversation with her."

An accusation that an unmarried white woman had voluntarily had sex with numerous Black men was perhaps the most serious sexual slander that could be uttered in early republican New Jersey. But it was not simply the meaning but the language that stung her. The words "fucked" and "whore" were abusively and repeatedly hurled at and about Stillwell, to damage her dignity as well as her reputation. She won her case and was awarded 1,000 pounds in damages and court costs. The Stillwell case played on anxieties of racial mixing at a time when the proportion of free to enslaved Black persons was increasing in New Jersey, especially in the northern counties such as Hackensack, and when matters of citizenship were once again being anxiously debated—and restricted.

In the early 1800s, disagreements and rifts developed within the Jeffersonian Republicans. Moderate Republicans, who split from the party and located themselves as a third centrist party, wished to confine voting to those who held land. Liberal Republicans responded that every "black, white, yellow or red" individual "holding stocks in the funds of the community . . . [was] a member of the community" and should be allowed to vote for public office.[84] Further, a corrupt referendum regarding the location of a new courthouse and jail in either Newark or Elizabethtown inflamed intra-party tensions. Some counties received outrageously high voter turnout: 279 percent. Voter fraud was pinned on enslaved Blacks and married women frequenting the polls, women casting multiple ballots, and white men dressing up in petticoats or blackface.[85] Such was the perceived ballot box chaos that, in October 1807, the Republican Party reunited over the issue of suffrage. To placate moderates, liberal Republicans agreed to restrict voting to taxpayers and to exclude aliens. But since both excluded groups—the poor and the newly arrived—traditionally voted Republican, their loss had to be offset by disenfranchising Federalist-leaning groups: women and free Blacks. The white, male political class thus struck a deal, restricting the vote to "free white male citizens" and disenfranchising the poor, women, Blacks, and aliens with one swift motion.[86]

It was only after the constitutional change or "clarification" that ideological justifications followed, explaining disenfranchisement based on supposed inherent qualities connected to race and gender. Legal scholar Jacob Katz Cogan has argued that increasingly voters were identified during the nineteenth century by who they were, rather than by what or how much they owned.[87] And the privileged identity was that of the white American male citizen. New Jersey witnessed this transition from early citizenship based on allegiance and property, to citizenship based on gender and racial classifications. As Jan Lewis has noted, in the early nineteenth century, "the perimeters of the republic were pulled in, and New Jersey's brief experiment in an inclusive franchise was redefined as a bad interpretation, and a piece of its history reimagined as nothing more than a bad dream."[88]

But, as this chapter has shown, the legacy of expanded enfranchisement had already opened further possibilities and left its mark on the common law, especially for women. As "subjects and citizens," their interests and experiences were incorporated into defamation law, leading to the judicial removal of the burden of proving special damage in cases of sexual slander. Such changes began a slander of women movement that would spread to other places in the British common law world, each with its own unique contexts and catalysts. In fact, the year Mary Smith brought her groundbreaking slander case against Isaac Minor—1788—the British sailed into Botany Bay in New South Wales, establishing a penal colony that became plagued with its own sexual sandals, anxieties about "civilized" speech, and debates about women, slander, and special damage.

TWO

SAVAGE SPEECH AGAINST CIVILIZED FEMALES

New South Wales

"In this country more particularly, the calumnies circulated against the plaintiff, could admit of but one construction, and that construction could not fail to sink her in the estimation of the world," declared Chief Justice Stephen when summing up an 1826 case brought by English governess Harriet Spencer against Captain Robert Jeffery in the Supreme Court of New South Wales.[1] Spencer had accused Jeffery of spreading rumors about her engaging in "criminal intercourse" and other acts of impropriety with a sailor during the long, arduous sea voyage from England. Spencer's case—filled with debate about class and respectability, race and reliability of evidence, sex and suspicion—also became plagued with problems of proving special damage and contributed to the first slander reforms in the Australian colonies.

This chapter locates New South Wales within the global slander of women reform movement and examines how discourses about the meanings and functions of reputation changed in the penal colony. Initially, slander worked to defend feminine "respectability" by stating or reinstating a person's colonial class categorization (convict, free, married, servant). In addition, it punished certain types of speech and played a vital role in prescribing ideas of "civility" and regulating rude or "savage" manifestations of masculinity. In a precarious and isolated society based on dubious moral and legal grounds—that advancing civilization justified the violent dispossession of Indigenous peoples—depraved or disrespectful conduct was deeply threatening. As historian Penny Russell has noted, the question as to who was "civilized" and who was "savage" acquired new significance. Speech, particularly in a predominantly illiterate populace, had the power to disrupt and derail rules and undermine fragile authority. Publicly calling a woman a whore or spreading vicious rumors of sexual impropriety about her was doubly dangerous as it questioned "civilized" gendered ideals on both fronts: feminine virtue and proper manly restraint. However, by the 1820s, the doctrine of slander took a decidedly commercial turn, becoming emmeshed with emancipist motivations to build an egalitarian market society. Slander became entwined with defining gendered ideals of conduct and less connected with a person's origins. Motivations for respectable reputation became practical and pragmatic—necessary for securing employment and attracting capital for entrepreneurial success. The slander cases, debates, and reforms examined in this chapter—by contrast with those in New Jersey—highlight the ways in which gendered ideas of reputation, social status, speech, and their regulation developed and diverged across the world during the nineteenth century.

The American Revolution spurred New Jersey to break from the English common law of slander and protect the reputations of women as equal subjects and citizens of the state, as detailed in Chapter 1. But the Revolution also pushed Britain to find new locations for the convicts housed within its overflowing jails and to secure its economic and geographic dominance in the Asia-Pacific. Indeed, it was an American—a British loyalist, James Mario Matra—who first seriously proposed the idea of settling New South Wales with convicts.[2] But despite becoming another English common law colony, the new penal society became home to distinctive norms of gender, race, authority, and status. When Governor Arthur Philip steered the first fleet to Botany Bay in 1788, the area that subsequently became Sydney was home to approximately thirty different Aboriginal clans. Together, the Indigenous peoples of the region far outnumbered Europeans during the first few decades of settlement.

The First Fleet comprised between over 700 convicts (less than 200 of them women) and around 550 sailors, government officials, marines and their families, and some free settlers. Seven of the convicts were African Americans, formerly enslaved, who had been promised freedom in exchange for loyalty.[3] Perhaps some hailed from New Jersey. It was an intimate, isolated, and inhospitable place in which the new arrivals built a society. By 1800, the year the first sexual slander case was decided, the European population was estimated at 3,000, with women in a clear minority. Two thirds of the population were free, with the majority former convicts or emancipists. It wasn't until the 1820s that free immigrants began arriving in any substantial number and a more fluid market society emerged.

From the outset, New South Wales was intended as an agrarian settlement, rather than an urban center.[4] Though penal in purpose, it presented first as a military camp and later as a scattered English village. Convicts did not reside in jails initially but worked mainly outdoors. It was far from idyllic; rather it was a place of "contrariety," promising unique hardships as well as fresh starts, at the "ragged edge of empire."[5] Ruled by an autocratic governor, whose orders were enforced by ever-present soldiers and marines, governance was direct and the administration of justice generally *ad hoc* and rudimentary. The first courts were established via a ceremony on February 7, 1788, when David Collins became the first judge-advocate to preside over disputes and the English common law was adopted, so far as it was relevant and convenient. Housing and provisions were basic, food was scarce sometimes to the point of starvation, and the work was physically arduous. Male convicts were forced to labor in sawpits, quarries, and brickfields, and female convicts in domestic service, and both were subject to forms of severe punishment. The settlement offered only basic pleasures to its residents: gambling, drinking, fighting, sex. As James Dunk has noted, many early arrivals went mad, and without asylums, wandered the bush or were imprisoned.[6]

Due to these harsh and isolated conditions, distinctive social norms, expectations, and gendered dynamics developed within early colonial Australia. Russell has highlighted how the idea of "civilization" became a source of anxiety and significant preoccupation: "here in the wilderness, the power of civilisation as an idea, a habit, a way of being, faced its most dangerous test." Not only did rough conditions and extreme distance from the metropole of Britain make cultivating "civil" society difficult, but justifications for dispossessing and enacting brutal violence against Aboriginal people and assumptions of *"terra nullius"* were based on an imagined dichotomy of "savage" and "civilised." Degradation and depravity within the European settlement threatened to undermine the premise of superiority on which the dubious moral equation of colonization rested.[7]

The presence, play, and predilections of female convicts also fueled anxieties about gender, sexuality, and social disorder.[8] The "visibility" of feminine promiscuity and appearances of depravity and chaos were highly offensive to officials and authorities. Great emphasis was thus placed on maintaining a "decent exterior," controlling perceptions of pollution, and pressing the importance of civilized manners and conduct. In this fledging penal colony, concerns about legal, political, and gender order plagued the minds of officials, and regulating the boundaries of status, sexual morality, and speech was central to this mission. It was into this masculine and makeshift place, stalked by anxieties and uncertainty yet offering possibilities of redemption and future prosperity, that Maria Lewin disembarked and initiated the first sexual slander case in Australia.

In 1798, English artist and naturalist John Lewin and his wife Maria Ann Lewin planned to travel to New South Wales on the *HMS Buffalo* so that he might study, collect, and paint Australian birds and insects for British patron, silversmith, and passionate entomologist Dru Drury. Drury financed Lewin's voyage and supplied him with insect-catching apparatus, guns for game hunting, copper plates, and a pair of gold scales. In return, Drury expected a "Collection of Insects of equal value from Port Jackson in New South Wales as soon as possible."[9] Lewin also attracted the support of Lady Arden, Margaretta Elizabeth Perceval, a naturalist and collector with a particular interest in exotic fungi. Lewin, Drury, and Perceval were members of a complex network of English natural history artists, authors, publishers, collectors, financiers, and amateur enthusiasts who crossed continents and class lines during the late eighteenth century. Joseph Banks, who had accompanied James Cook on his scientific exploration of the Pacific in 1768 on the *HMS Endeavour*, was perhaps the most prominent and well-connected expert and patron of the natural sciences. On February 6, 1798, the colonial secretary, the Duke of Portland, wrote to Governor Hunter in New South Wales: "Mr Lewin is a painter and drawer in natural history and being desirous of pursuing his studies in a country which cannot fail to improve that branch of knowledge, you will allow him the usual government rations during his residence in that settlement."[10]

On June 8, 1798, the Lewins boarded the *HMS Buffalo* for their much-anticipated departure for New South Wales. As they waited on board, John suddenly realized he had left an item in London and left hastily to retrieve it. In the meantime, however, fair winds picked up, and the ship set sail without him. John Grant recounted the incident some years later in 1805:

> Mr Lewin married before he came, but by a fatality which has made them prize each other more since, Mrs Lewin was left on board at Portsmouth, while he foolishly went back to London for something; in interim a wind sprung up, and he was left behind, and did not arrive here till 12 months after her.[11]

Maria Lewin, distressed and in tears, was forced to embark upon the long journey to the colony alone. John managed to follow her on the next available ship, the *Minerva*, a convict transporter, but it wouldn't arrive until eight months after the *Buffalo*. In his biography of Lewin, Richard Neville writes that, in contrast to John Lewin, nothing much is known about Maria Lewin and that there was no record of her birth or their marriage in England. However, her petition to the Colonial Office for a pension in 1822 and her death certificate in London in 1850 register her birth date as 1765, making her thirty-three years old at the time of travel to New South Wales and five years older than John.[12]

The *HMS Buffalo* was captained by forty-three-year-old master mariner and merchant William Raven. On board was his wife, Frances Raven (whom he married in Barbados in 1780), as well as several free settlers. The *Buffalo* was a storeship, carrying stock, provisions, and tools for the struggling colony and a handful of free emigrants. Many of the passengers would soon be subpoenaed as witnesses at the Lewin defamation trial.[13]

Despite its name, the bow of the *Buffalo* featured the carved wooden figure of a kangaroo, highlighting the significance of the Pacific's natural wonders for imperial minds. George Barrington's *History of New South Wales*, printed in London in 1808, observed: "the natives appeared very much pleased, not expecting to see the animals of their country represented by us in wood."[14] But he also noted: "The natives still hostile to the settlers, speared one of those at George's river so shockingly that he died of the wounds."[15] Lewin and the other free settlers disembarked into a tense community, wedged between day-to-day deprivations and frontier conflict.

The voyage from England appears to have been fraught with rumors and innuendo. Gossip and slurs about Maria Lewin having sexual relations with men onboard washed about the ship. Without a husband to "protect" her and unconnected to the other families, she had few allies. In the months after arriving, Maria Lewin chose, with the help of the first chaplain in the settlement, Reverend Richard Johnson, to put an end to the insults and gossip by suing George Thompson, in the Court of Civil Jurisdiction, for slanderous allegations of sexual immorality.[16] Little is known about the defendant Thompson. Unlike others on board, such as the Grono, Bean, and Anson families, there are no records of his passage, no indication that he worked as a sailor on the ship, and little evidence of his activities in the colony thereafter. The only clue is a civil case relating to a promissory note that was brought by a George Thompson against Dennis McCarthy in 1804, concerning three years of imprisonment suffered by Thompson as a result of a 30 pound debt.[17] Newspaper reports of the case describe Thompson, at one point, as owning a farm.[18] Given the small settler population in New South Wales at the time—only in the thousands—it is probably the same George Thompson. He was likely not a man of notable means or social prominence.

Far from being an objective adjudicator, Reverend Johnson ran the case on behalf of Lewin. Numerous persons were called as witnesses, and the hearings were held on three days: November 4 and November 30, 1799, and February 4, 1800. John Lewin arrived on the ship *Minerva* in the middle of proceedings, on January 11, 1800. The defendant contended that the allegations of sexual impropriety against Lewin were true. Elizabeth Grono, wife of Captain John Grono, testified on behalf of the defendant that she saw Maria Lewin standing at Second Mate Hugh Machin's cabin door at an "unreasonable hour of the night" and that on another occasion she and Maria had some "private little conversation" about Mr. Lewin being sexually "deficient" or "impotent."[19] Lieutenant Thomas Hobby, then twenty-five, also testified for the defendant, stating he remembered overhearing a "quarrel" between Maria Lewin and Machin in Rio de Janeiro and a rumor that Machin "upbraided" Maria for being on shore with Captain Callender "at a great many bawdy houses."[20] Hobby also stated that he "often thought her conduct very improper as a married woman," and Mrs. Raven had reported to him that she had seen "Mrs. Lewin go out of Captain Callender's cabin in a bed gown at a very early hour, at day-break in the morning."[21] This rumor was confirmed by Hugh Machin, who testified that he overheard Thompson say to others that Lewin had come out of Callender's cabin "half-naked" and was seen sitting on his bed "drawing on her stockings."[22]

These rumors continued to circulate after the ship arrived in Sydney Cove, and particularly during an occasion at Captain Raven's house, where Thompson, apparently "using a great deal of gross language," called Maria Lewin a "whore" before a dozen witnesses. Machin testified for the plaintiff that William Frazier (a convict or former convict) had been pressured by both Thompson and Frances Raven into spreading rumors about Maria. Machin described Thompson to the court as a "great rascal" and agreed with Reverend Johnson's assessment that Frazier was "dependent" on the good graces of Captain Raven. Furthermore, he judged that Frazier, Thompson, and another man called Dusty were all "under the influence" of Mrs. Raven. Frances Raven and Thompson appeared to be close, allied for strategic and/or personal reasons, and seemed to have a joint interest in injuring Maria Lewin.

The *Lewin* case highlights the ways in which women of unclear class background, traveling alone, were vulnerable to verbal attacks on their sexual virtue. English ideas of class intermingled with intimate and inhospitable conditions. During the trial, it was revealed that the respectable Grono family told others on board that Maria Lewin had been "a kitchen maid and a kept mistress" in London.[23] This story likely worked to cause and compound the allegations about Maria's adultery and "very improper conduct."

English attitudes about servants and convicts—both lower class—as sexually available and lacking civilized feminine virtue were reinforced by onboard antics. Joy Damousi has highlighted how prostitution and sexual activity were common aboard vessels transporting female convicts at this time, generating anxieties among colonial officials about promiscuity, pollution, and social disorder.[24] An entangled culture of intimate relations between servants, convicts, sailors, and captains pervaded. Damousi's work focuses on convict transport ships, but Lewin's case demonstrates that cultures of chaos, sexual disorder, and gendered power plays were also a salient feature of merchant vessels carrying free settlers. Status was fragile and in flux, and gendered leverage was complex, particularly for those in fluid social categories. Alliances—strategic, intimate—gave those of lower rank like Maria Lewin and George Thompson a way of advancing or protecting their interests. But such private alliances did not equate with public repute. Perhaps Mrs. Lewin did find comfort, security, or passion with Hugh Machin or Captain Callender on the long, grueling voyage. But once she disembarked, reinstating her respectability required appealing to official and written processes. Bringing a "civil" slander action worked to move Lewin from one vulnerable status category—sexually promiscuous servant—into a more secure one: free, white married woman.

This case also highlights the fundamental role of speech—gossip, whispers, abuse—in shaping status within the isolated, illiterate penal colony of Sydney Cove. This was a largely oral culture where information and insults traveled via tongue and voice, not ink and paper. In 1800, in England, approximately 40 percent of men and 60 percent of women were illiterate.[25] Literacy rates were likely lower in the colony of New South Wales due to the large number of convicts from lower classes being transported. For instance, between 1815 and 1819, only 18 percent of female convicts could sign their names upon marriage.[26] Verbal abuse was common and constituted a threat to order, as well as official authority. Clashes and negotiations between the "weighty, broad and permanent conversations of pen and paper" and "the narrow and ephemeral conversations, the living, burning, sharp-edged exchanges of individuals face to face" were constant.[27] The doctrine of slander arose from such collisions: between local insults, remarks, and rumors and the written laws and authority of the British empire.

Underlining the importance of slander in regulating community order, until 1810, all defamation claims in New South Wales pertained to slander, not libel, and they were relatively common.[28] Of the 292 disputes heard by the Court of Civil Jurisdiction between 1788 and 1809, the vast majority concerned debt or succession (inheritance), but slander came in third place, ahead of shipping, sale of goods, assault, land titles, or seduction. In a profoundly unbalanced gender demographic, women constituted a minority of all plaintiffs, only 6.5 percent. They usually brought actions for debt, succession, and slander.

Slander actions in New South Wales played a vital part in policing masculine manners. Russell notes the degree to which language marked out modes of respectability in early colonial communities.[29] Coarseness, swearing, cursing, and licentious speech were associated with forms of "savage" masculinity and posed a threat to authority and attempts to cultivate more refined manly attributes of restraint, respect, and self-control.

In *Lewin*, participants in the trial frequently commented not just about the allegations of immorality against her, but the method of their delivery: "a great deal of gross language," "threaten and speak abusive language to her," "frequently heard the defendant abuse Mrs. Lewin."[30] In England, the common law of slander focused expressly on individual reputational injury and did not censor "mere abuse."[31] But in New South Wales—where the future settlement rested on the discipline and reformation of male convicts—slander was also used to punish forms of disruptive and "uncivilized" speech.

The preoccupation in slander actions with masculine manners is well illustrated in another action brought by Richard Atkins, retired military officer and judge-advocate, against surgeon John Harris the same year as Maria Lewin's case.[32] The court documents state that Harris had publicly accused Atkins of being a "swindler." However, reading the court minutes, it is clear this defamation claim was not simply, or even primarily, a dispute about reputation. Rather, it was a forum for performing and imposing civilized masculine conduct and language. As in *Lewin*, references abound to "very unbecoming language," "improper manner," "very improper language," "language and manners," "make use of improper Language to me as a Gentleman," "rudeness and contempt," "infamous and diabolical language," "grossly insulted in my official Capacity as a Magistrate," "envenomed Tongue," and "such opprobrious and high disgraceful Expression." In fact, Atkins expressed being more offended by Harris's disrespectful behavior and his uncivilized abusive speech than he was about its content. In his opening statement to the court, he pleaded that he was "not accustomed to be spoke to in such a manner for, Gentlemen, the mode of expressing words are often more insulting than the words themselves."[33] He appealed to the members of the court in their "cool manly and firm conduct" as "Gentlemen" and the "Coolness and Deliberation" of judicial proceedings. Slander, in early New South Wales, was as much about proscribing savage masculinity—hot-headed, impulsive, vulgar, and unrestrained—as it was about prescribing ideals of feminine modesty.

After her case, Maria Lewin's respectability was vindicated, and Thompson's abusive and barbaric speech punished. He was ordered to pay her 30 pounds in damages plus costs. If this case had occurred in England, Lewin would likely have initiated it in the ecclesiastical courts. In England an action for sexual slander at common law required proof of special damage—an almost impossible task. But in early New South Wales, such legal technicalities were not raised, likely due to ignorance and the need to reinforce standards of civil behavior. The colony inherited English common law, but it applied only so much as suited local conditions. Much of the arcane complexity was left behind as the colonial courts—with wide powers—determined what aspects to observe and what to ignore. Without a local legislature, ecclesiastical courts, or an accessible right of appeal to the Privy Council, the New South Wales Court of Civil Jurisdiction had almost complete and ambiguous autonomy over private disputes. This was a plural legal culture and in the early years, the empire's concern was for an efficient, inexpensive, and orderly penal colony, not a strictly legal one.[34] Much of the court's decision-making accorded more with notions of "common sense."[35] Such a rudimentary and flexible legal system, and anxieties about feminine sexuality and masculine manners, allowed women like Lewin to more easily bring slander cases. This changed, however, with the arrival of English-trained lawyers, the establishment of the Supreme Court of Civil Judicature in 1814, and the Supreme Court of New South Wales in 1823. An increasing adherence to British common law worked to disempower and disappoint defamed women in the next decades.

On June 9, 1825, the *Sydney Gazette* published a verse condemning the sexual slander of women in the colony:

> Viler far the wretch, whose aim,
> Is worth and beauty to defame;
> With innuendo, hint and sneer;
> To wound of modesty the ear;
> Raise on her cheek the burning blush
> Bid the indignant tear to gush
> And, at her mild, ingenuous heart,
> To level slander's barbed dart![36]

It asked could "no remedy be found" to stop those who "raise[d] a glow on virtue's cheek" and "wound[ed]" the "innocence" of women in ways that were presently "beyond the law"? The following year this injustice was highlighted by the high-profile case of *Spencer v Jeffery* (1826), which like *Lewin*, involved allegations of impropriety by a woman who had recently voyaged from England.[37] But New South Wales had changed significantly since 1800. After the end of the Napoleonic Wars, free migration rapidly increased, as did convict transportation to fuel the labor demands of a growing entrepreneurial population. The rudimentary, intimate, and rather chaotic penal community structured along particular social categories—"savage," convict, free settler, and "civilized" gentleman—was being transformed into a more self-sustaining, fluid, and egalitarian market society. As Stuart Macintyre noted, "a social order based in rank and station, in which relationships were personal and particular, yielded to the idea of society as an aggregation of autonomous, self-directed individuals, everyone seeking to maximise their own satisfaction or utility."[38] Spencer's slander case was intertwined with commercial concerns and a desire for prosperity in the new world.

Harriet Elizabeth Spencer, a young single woman and governess to Margaret and Robert Campbell Jr., sued Captain Robert Jeffery for slanderous allegations that she had been guilty of impropriety on board the merchant ship *Toward Castle*. To understand this case we need to read it alongside another occurring simultaneously involving the same individuals and voyage: *Campbell v Jeffery*.[39] This latter suit was brought by Robert Campbell Jr., Sydney entrepreneur and husband of Margaret Campbell, also against Captain Jeffery as an action of *assumpsit*, that is, breach of implied promise to provide his wife, their child, their governess (Harriet Spencer), and their maid with "proper accommodation aboard the vessel, a sufficiency of provisions and kind treatment." According to newspaper reports, Campbell's action in part arose over a dispute between Campbell and Jeffery about the amount to be paid for the passage of his family and employees. In London, they had agreed upon the sum of 150 pounds for the journey, but then Jeffery demanded 200 pounds on arrival in Sydney, for additional living expenses incurred when the ship stopped over at the Cape of Good Hope. The newspaper reported that "the causes of disagreement were simply an unsettled demand for living at the Cape."[40] However, it seems tensions between the Campbells and Jeffery ran deeper.

In early 1825, Spencer had been working as a governess for George Henry Law, Bishop of Bath and Wells in England, and his wife Jane, when she came across an advertisement for a governess placed by Mrs. Margaret Campbell to look after the Campbell children in Sydney. Spencer applied for the position as she thought the cold climate of Wiltshire had affected her lungs and hoped a change would cure her ill health and offer a fresh start. Campbell offered to pay Spencer 50 guineas for the first year and 60 pounds for each following year. This was a good rate. The average wage for governesses in this period was between 20 and 45 pounds per annum.[41] Arrangements were then made for the voyage of Campbell, her children, Spencer, and a "female servant" on the *Toward Castle*. One imagines that Spencer must have regarded the impending journey with some degree of trepidation: many months spent at sea in cramped quarters sailing to a far-off colony would have posed an "endurance test," a "harrowing experience," or at the very least "a long and dreary monotony."[42]

The ship departed London on August 17 and reached Madeira, Portugal, on September 15, where Captain Jeffery exhorted Campbell to leave the ship (without her servants) and join the other passengers at a hotel on shore. But Campbell refused, stating that she had promised to treat her governess as family, and Spencer's situation entitled her to "be treated with respect." The court file relays that Campbell "looked upon Miss S. as her second self and wished her to be treated with equal respect."[43] Jeffery responded angrily: "Oh governesses are not considered on that footing in England!"[44] They continued to argue, with Campbell resisting going on shore while Jeffery declared that the girls left alone on board would "be perfectly safe!" The exact reasons why Mrs. Campbell refused to abide by the usual convention of leaving the ship at port are unclear, but it was probably due to a perceived threat to either Spencer's physical safety, her reputation, or both.

It is significant that Jeffery and Campbell's dispute turned upon Spencer's class status, as governesses did indeed occupy, as historian M. Jeanne Peterson has described, "a situation of conflict and incongruity" in England.[45] A governess was expected to be a "lady in every sense of the word," derived from a good family, well-educated, and able to teach skills and observe social conventions. But due to circumstance, she was also forced to work and earn money, rather than remain idle in the house of her father or husband. In 1848, Lady Elizabeth Eastlake described the status of the English governess in stark terms: "[o]ur equal in birth, education and manners but our inferior in worldly wealth."[46] Being paid a wage was an insult to social rank and placed governesses below the ladies and children they served, although they still hovered above other household servants and maids. The situation of class ambiguity was exacerbated when traveling to an increasingly egalitarian antipodean colony. But as will be explored below, being consigned to a servant class no longer aligned with presumptions of promiscuity in New South Wales.

Soon after departing Madeira, according to the testimony given by Campbell in *Spencer*, Jeffery took Campbell aside to say that he had seen Spencer and the maid on the ship's deck late at night and that "people, females more especially, should be particularly cautious in their conduct on board of a ship."[47] Campbell reported his comments to Spencer, who was "much distressed" and said she had been feeling unwell due to the hot weather and needed fresh air. Soon after, Spencer reportedly suffered a fainting fit in her cabin and was attended by Mr. Simmons, the third mate, as well as the maid. The doctor was called and testified during the slander trial that Simmons's prompt attendance to Spencer had been "indelicately discussed" amongst crew members the next morning. Sometime later, near the Cape of Good Hope, Jeffery reported to Campbell further rumors about the improper conduct of Spencer, including that Simmons had visited her cabin inappropriately. Campbell testified at trial that it was clear Jeffery was expressing his belief that "a criminal intercourse had taken place" between Spencer and Simmons.[48]

The source of such rumors was a point of much contention. On board, Jeffery at first refused to "give up" or identify the "undoubted authority" behind the observations. Then when pressed by Campbell, he put forward Mr. James, first officer of the ship, and Mr. Scriven, a "passenger" and "gentleman." Scriven forcefully denied being the source of the rumors, and James had already disembarked for ill-health. Jeffery then denied nominating them and instead identified his steward, named as William Thomas from Jamaica in the *Campbell* proceedings, but identified only as Sambo in *Spencer*. The court records described him as having "a countenance as black and shining as the lacquered part of a tea tray."[49] Campbell again denied the allegations put by Jeffery and defended Spencer's virtue. There were numerous conflicting arguments on board and in court about who was responsible for promulgating and circulating the ruinous slurs against Spencer. Simmons was questioned by Jeffery on board about reports he had been visiting Spencer's "bed," to which he replied: "It is false. I understand your black steward has been propagating malicious reports respecting Miss Spencer, and I must insist upon putting him to his oath."[50]

The court found on the evidence that Captain Jeffery had no proof of the veracity of the allegations about Spencer and should not have spread them, particularly if they originated with the "black steward." The court asked: "Was it not the business of a captain to prevent slanders going forward from a common steward, against a young lady, who was under his protection, and which might have the effect of banishing an amiable young female from society?"[51]

In summing up judgment for the plaintiff, Chief Justice Stephen awarded Spencer 50 pounds and declared:

> A woman's feelings, the feelings of a tender female, are in general of too sensitive a nature to be lightly sported wi[t]h. In this country more particularly, the calumnies circulated against plaintiff, could admit of but one construction, and that construction could not fail to sink her in the estimation of the world—to a civilized female, in any part of the globe, a fair reputation is an inestimable possession. It is a jewel, whose lustre should not be sullied by the blighting breath of calumny, nor parted with on trifling terms.[52]

Race, respectability, and one's pecuniary prospects were important dynamics within this trial. Chief Justice Stephen seemed to consider the evidence of a "black steward" inherently unreliable and emphasised the importance of a "fair reputation" to a "civilized female" in any "part of the globe." Feminine virtue or propriety was a possession of civilized peoples, to be neither enjoyed nor undermined by "savages".

Such ideologies also accord with the civil court records. No Aboriginal or Black litigants took defamation actions in colonial New South Wales during this period. Kirsten McKenzie suggests that this was likely a consequence of their absence from the professional and commercial community.[53] Macintyre notes that they could not testify under oath and so were limited in their ability to participate in judicial proceedings. Kercher argues that the doctrine of *terra nullius* should have meant that Aboriginal people became British subjects and were thus able to press their rights in the civil courts, but this seldom occurred. Apart from one action for debt initiated by a member of a seal-catching vessel in 1814, Aboriginal people did not appear as witnesses, plaintiffs, or defendants for any civil actions. Within this colonial society, racial ideologies linking honor and civilization with whiteness and savagery with blackness also worked to deny Aboriginal people individual reputational rights protected via defamation. Indigenous Australians were considered to live a degraded existence. Liz

Conor has suggested that Aboriginal women—as a group—were routinely insulted and dismissed by colonizers as both uncivilized and sexually available "gins" or "lubras."[54] Their own systems and codes of honor, respect, and reputation were largely disregarded.

This trial also demonstrates the degree to which a person's material prospects became intertwined with reputation in New South Wales. During the trial, William Moore, the counsel for the defendant and first free solicitor in the colony (meaning he migrated as a free person, not a convict), argued that Spencer's case should be dismissed as she had not pleaded or proved special damage.[55] This legal issue, which *The Australian* newspaper called a "striking anomaly," was also plaguing the cases of numerous women in the United States at the time.[56] It had been ignored during the *Lewin* trial in Sydney due to lack of concern with legal niceties, anxieties about sexual disorder, and a desire to sanction men's uncivilized speech. But things had moved on since 1800. The plaintiff's lawyers argued that even though the words were not in themselves actionable, "they became so when spoken of a person in the occupation of an office of profit."[57] The finesse of this argument demonstrated significant legal expertise. It relied on the idea that the English common law of defamation primarily protected men's hip pockets—their standing as middle-class traders and professionals. So, if a woman was also engaged in paid work, why shouldn't she be entitled to redress when an allegation of sexual immorality threatened her job?

The Supreme Court of New South Wales initially agreed. While imputations of adultery or unchastity were treated as spiritual in England—and matters for the ecclesiastical courts—Spencer would, if unsuccessful with her case, lose her job as a governess in the colony, blighting her economic survival. Thus, Chief Justice Stephen overruled the defendant, declaring that "the words, as applied to the plaintiff, if true, would disqualify her from holding her situation" and therefore "were actionable."[58] His ruling would have heralded a stunning new shift in slander law for the young colony, but it was appealed—successfully—and a new trial ordered. There is no record that the trial went ahead.

Spencer's case highlights the centrality of reputation to women's and men's economic prosperity in the colony during this time. Mr. Campbell was a successful Sydney entrepreneur, Jeffery was the captain of a merchant ship, Miss Spencer was trying to further her occupation as a governess, and Mr. Moore was pursuing professional success as the first free solicitor in the colony. They were all on the make in a place that was experiencing rapidly changing demographics, governance structures, and social dynamics. Free migrants were arriving in ever-increasing numbers, gender imbalances were correcting, and the population was exploding (to approximately 30,000 colonists by 1820). Pastoral exploration and agricultural economies expanded, further violently encroaching on Aboriginal lands. Transported convicts now experienced harsher penalties and fewer casual work opportunities and their labor was more regulated. Inhabitants' lives—their marital arrangements, labor conditions, and social positions—were subject to greater judicial and bureaucratic surveillance. Bustling urban centers of social fluidity, money exchanges, and connections thrived.

New social categories emerged that reflected a commercial emphasis, evidenced for example by Robert Wilmot Horton's Third Report from the 1826-27 Select Committee on Emigration that encouraged the assisted emigration of "labourers" who could ultimately transform themselves into "capitalists and colonists."[59] A self-sustaining and free trade society developed, governed by a legislature and more assiduous and professional judiciary. Such shifts were, in large part, also a result of Commissioner John Bigge's reports, published in 1822 and 1823.[60] Within this context, a popular movement of emancipists also gathered force asserting the rights of all colonists, regardless of their origins, to pursue and accumulate wealth.

Within this more democratic market society, where status became unmoored from old class hierarchies, proper conduct became vital to enterprise and employment. Whereas class status designated quality of character in the old world and new colonial categories—convict, servant, free, gentleman—mattered in 1800, by the 1820s manners and behavior could sink or save you, irrespective of rank or origin. Captain Jeffery and Margaret Campbell's dispute about Spencer coming on shore displays these shifts in perspective. To Jeffery, Spencer was merely a servant and thus was available for intimate relations with sailors and subject to moral suspicion. To Campbell, on the other hand, Spencer was domestic labor, but still able to retain respectability. For women, performing feminine sexual virtue was just as important as one's position as maid or governess. At numerous points in the *Spencer* trial, participants assessed Spencer's conduct, habits, and whether she acted with propriety. For middle-class men, however, attributes annexed to their occupational or professional status—hard work, creditworthiness, skill—became more central to identity than previous ideas of gentlemanly refinement or aristocratic honor.[61] These gendered manifestations of reputation reflected business and economic imperatives. In this mercantile society, reputation had practical uses and pecuniary ramifications. Manners, conduct, and behavior were crucial to perceptions of status and material prospects. Social relations and status were based on what was visible on the surface.[62]

During this period, the number of libel actions (brought by men) grew as the press began covering the activities of public, political, and professional life more assiduously. Some legal historians have suggested that the broader term "defamation" might be used to describe cases concerning expression and reputation in this era, rather than the distinct legal categories of slander and libel.[63] But negating the difference between libel and slander misses a vital distinction, one with profoundly gendered and cultural consequences. Men, not women, brought libel claims in early New South Wales. Both men and women brought slander claims. But only women brought *sexual* slander claims and thus were confronted by the consequences of the common law distinction between spiritual and material matters. The English legal rule that "whore" and other sexual slurs were not actionable slander at common law without proof of special damage was a direct impediment to women's prosperity and respectability in the colonies. This law overturned Spencer's initial victory. And it would lead New South Wales to break definitively from the English law of defamation in the 1840s and carve its own unique path. It was the first Australian colony to do so.

Between the 1810s and 1840s, the British Parliament debated and formulated various proposals to reform the law of defamation and, in particular, to abolish the distinction between libel and slander. In 1843, Lord Campbell launched the most determined effort, moving for a Select Committee of the House of Lords to investigate the issue, and telling their lordships that "on this important subject the law of England is more defective than that of any other civilised country in the world."[64] The Select Committee heard from a wide range of witnesses and reported that while at present there was a remedy for "any words reduced into writing" via libel law, words "publicly spoken" and "falsely and maliciously" imputing "a Want of Chastity to a Woman" or "Want of Veracity or Courage to a Gentleman" cannot be sued upon under slander. They noted contemptuously that, in contrast, any "action may be maintained for saying that a Cobbler is not skillful in mending Shoes." With the demise of the doctrine of *scandalum magnatum*, only tradesmen and professionals could bring slander cases in the common law courts. It was outrageous to the Select Committee that a lady of "high station" or a "gentleman" was not adequately protected by English defamation law because they could not prove "special damage," but a mere cobbler could.[65]

However, while the Select Committee's recommendations were initially received positively, and a bill incorporating them sailed through its first and second readings, it ultimately failed. The British attorney general, Sir Frederick Pollock, disagreed vehemently with the proposed changes and only allowed a bill reforming the defense of truth. The distinction between slander and libel remained unchanged. Women subject to slurs of unchastity, prostitution, or adultery in England continued to be barred from bringing claims in common law courts by the almost impossible burden of proving special damage. As Chapter 8 of this book details, the situation became even more desperate in 1855 when the ecclesiastical courts were abolished, leaving women with no viable avenues of redress.

The legal minds of New South Wales were very much aware of the debates in London about defamation reform. In 1823, the New South Wales Act established the first Legislative Council, and in 1842 convict transportation ceased. The colony was now partly self-governing and imagining itself anew. In 1846 and again in 1847, a bill was introduced by Richard Windeyer—journalist, barrister, and elected member of the Legislative Council—copying almost exactly the recommendations of Lord Campbell's Select Committee. Windeyer arrived in the colony as a free migrant in 1835 and was a believer in progressive law reform and advancing the interests of the colony. He believed that despite the reform proposals failing in the House of Commons, "the state of circumstances of this colony" meant they might be "advantageously adopted."[66] To Windeyer, defamation unfairly dredged up long-forgotten private details of people's previous lives—such as their convict or class background—subjecting them to embarrassment and distress that undermined the "sociality of the community."[67] During his election campaign, he spoke of protecting "all men in equal enjoyment of their social rights."[68] Defamation reform, as Paul Mitchell has observed, would allow every white man—convict or gentry—the promise of a fresh start in a new world.⁶⁹ It put down savage abuse and encouraged an egalitarian merchant community.

But importantly, Windeyer's bill also significantly enhanced the reputational rights of women. Conduct displaying "civilized" feminine virtue was central to women's economic prospects in the colony, either via marriage, occupation, or both. Paradoxically, removing the almost impossible burden of proving economic loss (special damage) allowed women greater economic mobility. Reporting on the bill, the *Sydney Morning Herald* attributed the abolition of the slander/libel distinction directly to the sexual slander of women:

> By the first clause . . . the same law is made applicable to oral as to written slander, thus doing away with the absurd distinction which now exists between these two classes of cases. By the present law of libel, to call a respectable woman unchaste is not actionable—to write of her the same thing is a libel, and actionable. . . . This absurdity is put an end to by the clause above mentioned.⁷⁰

The Act to Amend the Law Respecting Defamatory Words and Libel 1847 (NSW) was passed, representing a radical departure from British precedent. By abolishing the distinction between libel and slander and thus scrapping the burden of special damage, it established New South Wales as at the forefront within the global slander of women reform movement. Section one of the act stated: "that the right of action for oral slander shall extend to all defamatory words for which an action might now be maintained if the same were reduced to writing."⁷¹ Ordinary women—former convicts, current servants, and workers—in New South Wales, unlike those in England, could now bring actions for sexual slander in the common law courts without the burden of proving special damage.⁷² They could silence "savage" speech, they could press their rights to respectability, they could obtain compensation, they could keep their jobs.

Under these reforms, Harriet Spencer would have won her civil suit. In 1851, Mrs. Canavan, a widow and dressmaker, sued for slander that accused her of running a brothel and her four daughters of being whores.⁷³ The defense questioned whether sufficient damage had been suffered. But the 1847 act (cited in court) stopped them from advancing lack of special damage as a legal argument, and as a result Canavan and her daughters won their case.

THREE

UNSULLIED PURITY AND THE FIRST SLANDER OF WOMEN ACT

North Carolina

North Carolina, like New South Wales, inherited the strict rules of English defamation law. "The Common Law is the Law of the Land simply," stated a 1774 legal textbook for the colony of North Carolina.[1] In this setting, sexual slander claims could only be brought by women if they imputed an indictable offense or, of course, included evidence of special damage. Few such suits were pursued, leading legal historian Donna Spindel to surmise that in colonial North Carolina most conflicts over vituperative speech or heated words were settled privately, within families and communities, without resort to the courts.[2] It is also likely that the colony's adherence to the common law—deeming "whore" not actionable *per se*—acted as an interlocutory hand brake on slander suits. Women appeared as litigants in 25 percent of defamation suits in colonial North Carolina, as opposed to 54.5 percent in the nearby colony of Maryland, where a local ordinance in force for a few years relaxed rules around actionable words and incidentally prompted an explosion of women's sexual slander suits (until 1671).[3]

No equivalent legal innovations or experiments were attempted in colonial North Carolina. It did not pass any statute altering the substance or status of English defamation law. Accounts of scant sexual slander suits in the colony are consistent with adherence to old world precedent: plaintiffs consistently pleaded special damage in the form of a lost marriage proposal.[4] But in the early nineteenth century, North Carolina took a bold step, passing an act that enabled women the ability to sue for sexual slander without proving special damage. Unlike New Jersey, it did so via the legislature rather than the judiciary. The act, the first of its kind in the new republic, had the (unintended) consequence of benefiting women on the margins—those who lacked access to the traditions of private dispute practices that rested on privilege and patronage. It also reflected increasing concerns about men's power to persecute and harm women—as a group and as individuals—via speech.

In 1806, the *Raleigh Minerva*, a North Carolina newspaper, published an article titled, "On the Frequent Satire upon Women," chastising men—"from the libertine to the rake"—for their present-day looseness in tongues and morals when it came to discussing women.[5] Woman, the author contended, was "the tender flower of society" with "inestimable and indispensable delicacy" whose "protection and support the God of nature intended Man." In particular, women required urgent protection from the "unrestrained licentiousness" of "confident calumniators," as "the breathe of slander shakes a woman's reputation, on which is her whole dependence for esteem, and her sole claim for respect." The article concluded by appealing to the sentimentality of men's familial ties:

> Do these manly and spirited gentlemen recollect, when they indiscriminately implicate the sex, that their mothers are women, that their sisters are women, and that their wives are, or will be, women? And is there on these accounts, no gratitude; no respect; no affection? Or are these old-fashioned emotions?

Perhaps one man was stirred by these old-fashioned emotions. On December 10, 1808, William W. Jones, then representative for New Hanover in the North Carolina House of Commons (and later a delegate from the town of Wilmington), introduced a bill to enable women to bring actions of slander in certain cases relating to unchastity.[6] Jones is an obscure figure, largely undocumented and unaccounted for in newspapers of the time, apart from introducing or supporting a couple of minor bills.[7] However, it is possible to piece together some bare details of the man who introduced the first slander of women act in the common law world. By researching property details, census records, legislative archives, and wills, the sketch of a figure becomes clearer.

In 1800, seven years before becoming the delegate for New Hanover

County in the North Carolina legislature, Jones, then between the ages of twenty-six and forty-five, lived in New Hanover with his wife (also between twenty-six and forty-five), teenage daughter, younger daughter under ten years, two sons under ten years, and ten enslaved persons.[8] In a will written in 1802, Jones does not mention his wife (who had likely passed away) but names his four children as beneficiaries: Elizabeth, Ann, David, and William. At that time, none had yet reached legal capacity.[9] But in 1808, when Jones introduced the Slander of Women Act, he had two daughters coming of age. Ann was a teenager, and Elizabeth was marriageable, between eighteen and twenty-three years old. While there was general discussion and debate about the slander of women occurring in North Carolina at the time, no case in New Hanover County or the surrounding region explains Jones's urgent and individual motivation for the bill. Perhaps a private matter involving his daughter Elizabeth moved him to act. Or perhaps he was aware of cases in other states, such as the New Jersey matter of *Stockton v Hopkins*, reports of which circulated in the national newspapers in 1808: the *Aurora General Advertiser* and the *United States Gazette*.[10] Jones's bill sought to better protect women in North Carolina—those idealized as "the tender flowers of society"—from the "unrestrained licentiousness" of calumniators.

Titled "Slander of Women," the bill introduced by Jones stated in its preamble that it was of the first importance in a "free and well-regulated government" that laws that secure to individuals the "enjoyment of private character" should be "plainly defined and clearly understood."[11] It went on to observe that doubts had arisen whether actions for slander could be maintained in North Carolina against "persons who may attempt, in a wanton and malicious manner, to destroy the reputation of innocent and unprotected women, whose very existence in society may depend on the unsullied purity of their character." The act stipulated that "any words spoken of a woman which may amount to a charge of incontinency shall be deemed and held to be actionable."

Unlike New Jersey, which changed its slander laws judicially and on gender-neutral terms at a unique time of women's suffrage and ideas of equal citizenship, North Carolina's law reform expressed a legislative motivation to shield and defend the "unsullied purity" of women as the moral center of the new republic. Feminist historians such as Linda Kerber, Ruth Bloch, and Jan Lewis have shown how domestic life—embodied by women as wives and mothers—was regarded as inextricably linked to the health of America's political and civic life during the early republic period.[12] Women were positioned as responsible for nurturing the virtue of male citizens—both their children and husbands—and thus as the custodians and cultivators of civic morality. Ruth Bloch writes that "as mothers, young social companions, and wives, women came to be idealized as the source not only of domestic morality but also of civic virtue itself."[13] The roles of republican mother and wife simultaneously enabled women greater presence and participation within political discourse and placed upon them significant pressure to perform and personify virtue. A perceived slip in standards—sexual, maternal—was not simply a matter of interpersonal grievance or financial consequence but a crisis of national character. North Carolina's slander of women law reforms expressed a collective legislative motivation to shield and defend the so-called unsullied purity of women as the moral center of the new republic.

But of course, only particular women were envisaged as suitably qualified for upholding civic virtue. Native American women were increasingly pushed to the fringes, regarded as impediments to the nation-building project. And African American women, largely enslaved, were violently and legally deprived from forming and maintaining their own families, let alone embodying republican ideals of domestic purity. Further, as Deborah Gray White has argued, Black women were regarded and characterized, particularly by southern whites, as sexually voracious and naturally promiscuous. This ideology was used to justify their systemic rape and exploitation by white men (who lost no social prestige doing so) and simultaneously worked to define the sexual purity of white women.[14] However, being European in itself was no defense to accusations of depravity. While white women enjoyed a greater presumption of purity, it could easily be sullied by poverty and precarity. And as Milton Ready notes, "women on the bottom rungs of society, whether free whites, blacks, or slaves," who either withdrew from "respectable society" or who suffered ostracism and isolation because of sexual liaisons or pregnancy, formed an increasingly larger biracial grouping in antebellum North Carolina.[15]

The slander cases brought by women in North Carolina following the 1808 act highlight increased and interlinked anxieties about race and sexual purity, particularly within poorer segments of society. Of all the slander of women cases appealed to the Supreme Court of North Carolina between passage of the act and the Civil War, many related to accusations of interracial sex and many were either brought by women of ambiguous racial status or those struggling on the precipice of respectability. And for many of these women, vindication would prove elusive. Quoting the act, one judge commented that these were not the "innocent, chaste" women of society, whose "unsullied purity" was intended for protection.[16] Slander actions in North Carolina marked out racial and class boundaries, reflecting and determining rightful claims to chastity and hence to white womanhood. Several of the plaintiffs were also, however, Native American, who used slander claims to protest their social and sexual disparagement by powerful local planters.

Those envisaged by the language of Jones's 1808 act—unsullied by poverty—rarely, if ever, prosecuted slander claims in court in North Carolina. It is likely that such scandals were settled privately. In her work on speech and the courts in colonial North Carolina, Spindel notes that the small proportion of such cases—in comparison to other nearby colonies—suggests that "most conflicts leading to or resulting from heated speech were settled privately."[17]

The tradition of resolving such matters within families and immediate communities would also have been helped by the passage of the act, as it gave women a legal advantage and thus made such actions harder to defend. But defendants did staunchly and persistently fight slander claims brought by plaintiffs they regarded as vulnerable or beneath them. Often, defendants who were well-connected and propertied displayed indignation and rage for being taken to court by such lowly women. The women who brought and appealed sexual slander actions all the way to the Supreme Court needed legal standing, some financial means (though not substantial), an investment in fighting for their reputation, and a precarity that necessitated public pronouncement of their purity as the only option. They also required bravery to confront and punish those who subjected them to sexual verbal abuse. Neither enslaved nor slaveholding (whose sexuality was governed and regulated privately by masters and husbands), slander plaintiffs attempted to use the mechanisms of civil law to articulate their status. Victoria Bynum has demonstrated that women on the margins, whom she labels "unruly women"—being free women of color and poor whites—regularly showed up in the civil and criminal court system of North Carolina.[18] My research accords with her findings, as marginalized women formed the greatest proportion of slander plaintiffs during the antebellum period. But protecting these groups was not the purpose of the 1808 act. And so, over time, the judiciary progressively read down (meaning tightened and narrowed the interpretation) of the Slander of Women Act, relying upon legal technicalities to curb its application.

In the early republic and antebellum period, North Carolina comprised a scattered rural population where a person's social standing was as much entangled with local talk, grudges, and relationships as it was with broader shifting ideologies about race, gender, and class. Unlike Virginia or South Carolina, the state—due to the absence of large towns and a staple crop—did not develop an extensive plantation society and resembled more of a frontier settlement spread out across a vast wilderness. By 1850, only one town—Wilmington—comprised a population of over 5,000. Within the white population, there were generally three social classes—the planters, the yeomen or subsistence farmers, and the poor. Sprawling plantations were uncommon compared to neighboring states; most white residents either owned small farms or worked on them. Black residents, who comprised 25 to 28 percent of the total population, were mostly enslaved on properties where masters owned fewer than five slaves and often labored alongside them.[19] Approximately 2 percent of the North Carolina residents were free non-white persons, about double the proportion in nearby South Carolina. County and neighborhood also mattered substantially to the dynamics of social interactions and determinations of status. Slavery was more entrenched in the Piedmont and coastal regions, which produced large crops of tobacco, cotton, and rice. By 1860, nineteen of those counties had more enslaved persons than free white residents, whereas in the western counties—such as Burke, Surry, Wilkes—the percentage of African American enslaved people ranged from 2 to 25 percent of the population.

In many areas of North Carolina, less systematic slavery arrangements led to more arbitrary, tighter, and individual—though not necessarily less brutal—relationships between Europeans and African Americans. As demonstrated by slander actions heard by the Supreme Court, social attitudes about interracial sexual relations were not uniform, and they were largely bound up in perceptions of a woman's place in society and her entitlement to presumptions of purity and credibility. Martha Hodes has demonstrated that attitudes towards interracial sexual liaisons in antebellum North Carolina, and even accusations of rape by white women against Black men, were highly influenced by community perceptions of the woman's class and character as well as anxieties about mixed race children. Southerners considered that poor white women, who often worked as servants in the homes of others alongside enslaved persons, were prone to sexual depravity and dishonor, and the stories of these poor white women were often discounted and doubted, especially when there were rumors of them consorting with Black men.[20] The free children of white mothers and Black men were unsettling to the patriarchal and racial order. Slander claims, made easier by the 1808 act, were an important vehicle for demarcating gradations of class in North Carolina and articulating exactly what kind of women were entitled to presumptions of purity and credibility. The judicial elite, who sat on the Supreme Court bench, used legal rules and technicalities to express skepticism and resistance to saving the reputations of poor or marginal women. Nonetheless, as this chapter shows, even when women did not legally win, they succeeded in other respects. Court cases enabled them to publicly press their side of the story and push back against verbal abuse.

As well as civil cases, there were also state prosecutions for sexual slander. In 1818, the state of North Carolina prosecuted a farmer, Sampson Neese, of Orange County, for maliciously and unlawfully contriving to injure the "good name, fame, credit and reputation" of twelve-year-old Elizabeth B. Holt, described in the documents as "a good worthy, virtuous girl."[21] Neese wrote a note and nailed it to "a tree on the side of the Public Road leading from Trolinger's Bridge to Hillsborough," stating:

> Notice to all Persons Jentlemen I have taken it upon myself to inform yo of A sircumstance that occird Latterly between John Holts and Benjamin Whitbys as I was going on I discovered A man and woman along the field side and after standing a while I discovered that on was a Negro Seeing that they were so busily engaged I lit of and made towards them I got within About twenty yards of them and Behold it was Betsy Holt the daughter of Miss Holts and a Negro boy I Beleaf belonging to Mr Whidbey...[22]

But despite the serious aspersions cast upon young Elizabeth Holt's character, the state's case failed, with Judge Henry Seawell ruling that the note written by Neese was ambiguous, and therefore it was for the prosecution to plead and prove its precise meaning or construction. He declared that the note "represents that Elizabeth Holt was seen busily engaged with a negro boy," but that "these words themselves import no criminality, nor do they represent Elizabeth Holt in a ridiculous light, except by understanding them to mean something not expressed." In other words, the prosecution needed to stipulate that these words were understood by the "whole world" as meaning Elizabeth Holt was seen having sexual intercourse with a "negro boy." Only then, stated the court, could the jury agree, and the court inflict punishment on Neese.

By applying strict rules of pleading, the court declared that the meaning of the note was ambiguous and thus needed to be clearly articulated to the jury to convict Sampson Neese of criminal slander. It is difficult to see, however, how any local would be confused as to what the words "busily engaged" meant regarding the activities of Elizabeth Holt and the boy, especially if such activities were worthy of a public notice nailed to a tree. But vindicating Holt's reputation was not a priority of the North Carolina Supreme Court. Census and land grant records show that the Holts were mere tenant farmers, with no land nor any enslaved African Americans as property.[23]

In 1818, a civil case came before the Supreme Court of North Carolina involving aspersions of interracial sex. Gideon and Dolly Horton (unpropertied and undocumented by the 1820 census), from the County of Granville, sued local planter and slaveholder William Whitfield Reavis after he told people there was a report in the neighborhood that Dolly "had had a communication with a man of the wrong color" before she was married.[24] The pleadings stated that on the day Reavis uttered the words, Dolly was a "virgin and chaste woman" and since her "nativity" had been "esteemed and respected as such by other good people"; she had never been suspected of "adultery or fornication," and many people desired to take Dolly as their wife, particularly a man named James Waddy.[25] But Reavis, "contriving maliciously and wickedly to injure" Dolly in her "good name and reputation [and subject her to] disgrace and infamy," told people: "Harris Austin (meaning a negro man named Austin) kept her . . . they were caught together." The pleadings stated that this meant "Dolly King the Plaintiff and a negro man Austin did cohabit together and were caught on that day and had carnal knowledge of each other." Thereafter Dolly was "injured, degraded and damnified in her good name, fame, credit and reputation" and lost the marriage proposal of Waddy.[26]

However, evidence during the trial revealed that at the time when Reavis told people about the rumors, he was asked whether he believed them to be true, and he replied that "he did not know well how to do so, as she was a clever, smart ingenious girl." Again, Judge Seawell (who also presided over the previous case of *State v Neese*) was a stickler for observing the common law rules of defamation. He advised the jury that there was a difference between stating the existence of a fact and stating a report of the existence of such fact. The former imported guilt, the latter did not. As a result of these instructions, the jury found for the defendant. Dolly King appealed but was unsuccessful, with Chief Justice John Louis Taylor—British-born and the first chief justice of the recently established Supreme Court of North Carolina—holding that "the proof is that [Reavis] said there was such a report in the neighborhood, and that he expressed, at the time of speaking the words, his difficulty in believing them."[27] Despite the apparent seriousness of the rumors, allegations of interracial sex involving a white woman, and the passing of the Slander of Women Act in 1808, neither Dolly King's slander action nor the state's defamation case concerning Elizabeth Holt succeeded. The reputations of both lowly white women could not be protected by the legal remedy of slander. The Supreme Court of North Carolina was careful to adjudicate the limits of the 1808 act and did not vindicate those deemed unworthy.

However, in 1821, the *Hillsborough Recorder*, a North Carolina newspaper, did observe an increasing trend of women across the country appealing to courts when slandered by men in the community. By this time, slander of women laws had been reformed either judicially or via legislation in several states.[28] The article recounted that "some of our slandered females seem to have found, of late, a remedy, for that not uncommon malady of male tattling, coquetry, or defamation."[29] It elaborated: "It has of late become the fashion (and we are glad of it) to appeal to the law, from the decision of these Schools of Scandal; and the law has afforded in recent instances, honourable redress." It concluded that several recent verdicts had been obtained that they hoped would prove exemplary.

Perhaps they were referring to events in nearby South Carolina, where in 1818 the Constitutional Court of Appeals gave judgment for a woman and her husband, Mary and James Wood, after she was publicly called a "mulatto."[30] In finding for her, Justice Nott declared that if true, the words would reduce the plaintiff "to the state and condition in which that degraded class of people is placed."³¹ He conceded that there were "no foreign authorities" on point but was certain the decision came within the "principles of the Common law," which—established in the most "barbarous ages" of England—now needed to adapt to the "modern state of society [and an] age of refinement and civilisation."³² Calling a white woman a mulatto in South Carolina became actionable defamation. Then, in 1824, the state's legislature passed its own Slander of Women Act equivalent to North Carolina's 1808 statute.³³

During the 1820s, a series of cases brought in North Carolina (lasting almost a decade) tested the limits of the 1808 law and its application to Native American women. Mary and Catherine Watts sued their neighbor, John Mitchell Greenlee, in Burke County, North Carolina.³⁴ In 1822, Mary Watts pleaded she was "a person of good fame and reputation [and] esteemed by all persons" and had never been guilty of any of "the infamous acts imputed to her." She stated the defendant, being an "evil minded person," falsely and maliciously published the following words: "She the said Mary is big (meaning big with child) to negro Ben. That all Watts girls (meaning the plaintiff as one of said girls) is with child to negro Ben. She (meaning the plaintiff) is incontinent (with all the various legal modifications charging said words)."³⁵ The reference to legal modifications related to the 1808 Slander of Women Act that made imputations of incontinency slander *per se*. Mary claimed $5,000 in damages. However, the defendant pleaded not guilty, and the matter lapsed (likely due to unpaid court fees).

But in 1824, Mary Watts married Daniel Hollifield, and her case was revived with the necessary bond paid. She also made an application to amend the pleadings to join her husband, but the court refused on the basis that Mary was a *feme sole* when proceedings were first issued.³⁶ In March 1827, the matter was finally heard before Judge Strange and a jury of twelve men, who found for the plaintiff and awarded her $600 in damages as well as costs. However, Greenlee, dissatisfied with the verdict, then appealed the matter to the Supreme Court of North Carolina, based on errors within Watts's pleading.

In the complaint, Watts had claimed that the defendant spoke the words, and during the trial some witnesses testified to this fact: "that the defendant at certain time said that Watts' daughters were all with child by his negro man," and "Poll, Bets and Kate are big by negro Ben."³⁷ However, other witnesses deposed that the words were spoken by another person:

[A]t various times a certain man by the name of Asa Martin, being an idle, drunken, vagabond who at that time resided at Greenlee farm as his tenant was requested by Greenlee to tell that story or was asked what is that story about old Watts' daughters and negro Ben . . . whereupon Martin stated that all old Watts daughters were with child to negro Ben, at which the defendant laughed and was much pleased.

The credibility of witnesses testifying to Greenlee speaking the words himself was doubted by the judge, and he thus instructed the jury to disbelieve them. But he counseled that if Greenlee procured the words to be spoken by another, he "was as guilty as if he himself had uttered them." Hence, Greenlee appealed the decision on the basis that the pleadings (stating that Greenlee spoke the words) were contradicted by the evidence (that Martin in fact spoke the words). He won, with Judge Leonard Henderson agreeing that "the charge in the declaration must correspond with the proof."[38] A new trial was ordered.

In September 1828, the matter began again, and the jury found for the plaintiff a second time. However, Greenlee yet again appealed, this time arguing that the actual words proven to have been said—"all Watts' girls are big"—were not themselves actionable, and the plaintiff needed to show that they actually meant something defamatory, that is, "big with child to negro Ben." This, the defense argued, Mary Watts had failed to do. The defendant also argued that "incontinent" was not specific enough as an imputation and did not necessarily convey a want of chastity.[39] Now chief justice, Henderson gave judgment for the case again, holding that words not in themselves actionable, such as 'all Watts' girls are big," may be rendered so by "innuendo." In other words, other extrinsic facts needed to be put to the jury so they could determine if the words were defamatory in their context. Otherwise, he held, "juries would be quite arbitrary in giving to words such a meaning as they pleased."[40]

But extrinsic innuendo had not been introduced into evidence at trial, and therefore the court quashed the verdict as defective. On the point regarding the word "incontinent," however, no extra material was needed to show the meaning was defamatory as it was "the word used in the statute" of 1808 and "cannot be understood, when generally applied to a female, to mean anything else but that she is unchaste."[41] The Watts daughters had clearly been unlawfully slandered—this much Henderson conceded—but it held that the errors in the lower court reasoning were fatal and dismissed their case. Despite winning the sympathies of multiple juries, Mary Watts and her sister Catherine Watts (who launched a court case in 1829) both lost.

It is likely that the social and racial status of the sisters counted against them in the minds of the judiciary. They were the granddaughters of John Watts Jr. (1746–1808), also known as Young Tassel, a leader of the Chickamauga Cherokee during the Cherokee-American wars and who (as chief of the Chickamauga towns) played a decisive role in the Treaty of Tellico Blockhouse with Governor Blount in 1794 that marked the end of those wars, as well as the Treaty of Tellico in 1805.[42] Young Tassel was described as "the Nation's greatest warrior and ... the most influential of the chiefs ... whose views always prevail in council."[43] He was the son of a British trader, John Watts, and a Cherokee mother, Oousta White Owl Carpenter, and was raised within Cherokee culture.

Historian Theda Purdue discusses the Watts family in her work, noting that "a trader and interpreter named Watts married a sister of Old Tassel, the principal chief of the Upper Cherokees."[44] She points out that southern Indians, such as the Cherokee, considered the children of white men and Indian women to be Indian, not white or "mixed blood" or "half-breeds," as European Americans referred to them.[45] As well as acquiring tribe belonging, the children of Indian women and white fathers often also transitioned easily to situations as planters and entrepreneurs. Young Tassel had several wives and children, including son John Joseph "Ches-too-lee" Watts (the plaintiffs' father), born in 1765. Joseph married Elizabeth Lydia Ann Cargile in 1795, and the family operated a ferry in Burke County, North Carolina. Between 1811 and 1814, Joseph Watts received several land grants around the North Fork of the Catawba River. Watts and Cargile had at least eleven children, including Mary Polly (also known as Poll) in 1795, Patricia Elizabeth (known as Bets or Betsy) in 1798, and Catherine (known as Kate) in 1802.

In 1885, Catherine Gains (née Watts), a plaintiff in the *Watts v Greenlee* cases, then eighty-two years old, gave an affidavit stating that the family were "all Cherokee Indians by blood and descent," members of the Cherokee Nation, and that her father, Joseph "Ches-too-lee" Watts spoke both English and Cherokee languages fluently.[46] It was part of an 1907 application by her great-niece, Cynthia A. Brought, and her three children for a share in money that had been appropriated for the Eastern Cherokee Indians by Congress on June 30, 1906.[47] In the application, Brought claimed to be a member of the Cherokee Nation, with her grandfather being Pleasant Watts, the eldest brother of the slander plaintiffs Mary and Catherine Watts, and that her great-grandfather, John Watts or Young Tassel, was a signer of the 1805 treaty. She attested that her grandparents, Joseph Watts and Lydia Cargile, resided on the Cherokee reservation in Georgia. In the late 1820s, having lost their decade long slander cases against John Greenlee, the Watts extended family had relocated to Rabun County, Georgia. One of the affidavits in the 1907 application states that Joseph Watts and Lydia Cargile avoided being forced out, onto the Trail of Tears in 1835-36, due to their old age.[48] However, there were Watts family members documented among those forcibly removed.[49]

The Watts' daughters failed slander actions could also be due to the defendant being wealthy and well-connected. John Mitchell Greenlee was a member of the expansive Greenlee family, born in 1775 in Burke County, North Carolina, to James McDowell Greenlee and Mary Mitchell McDowell, who had migrated from Ireland.[50] The Greenlees owned large tracts of land in the nineteenth century, on which they primarily drove cattle, along the Catawba River. Land grant details show that John M. Greenlee, alone, acquired 1,190 acres between 1814 and 1818 that neighbored the Watts family—with both Joseph Watts and John Greenlee holding land on the North Fork of the Catawba River.[51] The Greenlee family also owned large plantations, such as The Glades near Old Fort, and enslaved many Black women, men, and children on those properties. In 1820, census records show that the five Greenlee brothers owned 184 slaves between them. John Mitchell Greenlee was the largest slaveholder, enslaving forty-nine persons on his properties. Among those enslaved on Greenlee's property was "negro Ben"—the man referred to in the *Watts v Greenlee* cases. Greenlee's large slaveholding was unusual and notable for Burke County, where (in 1830), only 98 households owned more than 10 slaves, 375 owned fewer than 10, and 1,888 owned none.[52] The Greenlees were also closely engaged in local politics and held positions of public office, with James Greenlee (John Greenlee's father) representing Burke County at Hillsborough when the State Convention of 1788 sought to ratify the newly proposed federal Constitution. A book on the genealogy of the Greenlee families, authored by descendants Ralph Stebbins Greenlee and Robert Lemuel Greenlee, published in 1908, stated that John M. Greenlee—the defendant in the slander case—was "a Whig, then Democrat" and "a member of the Legislature."[53]

During the first trial, evidence was also given that there was "enmity" at the time between Greenlee and Joseph Watts, as well as between Asa Martin and Joseph Watts.[54] This could have arisen from tensions between local Native American populations, which included the Watts family, and the settlers increasingly taking over their lands.[55] The Greenlee genealogy records that David Washington Greenlee (the defendant's brother) had a large plantation along the Catawba River, "beautifully situated," and that "Indians were not troublesome then though they often came through in large numbers."[56] John M. Greenlee chose to slander the Cherokee Watts daughters as unchaste to denigrate the family's social status within the Burke County community. He delighted in doing so, with evidence given that he laughed when spreading the slurs about them. He no doubt regarded the Watts sisters as well beneath him in social standing. Purdue notes that during the first few decades of the nineteenth century, white Americans increasingly saw individuals as fixed in their cultures and were convinced of racial ordering whereby inferior races submitted to superior ones. "Mixed bloods" like the Watts family may have dominated "full blood" Indians in the eyes of white residents, but "Anglo-Saxons dominated those of less than pure racial lineage."[57]

The fact that Mary and Catherine Watts launched and fought not just one, but multiple slander suits (lasting almost a decade) against a prominent and established slaveholder such as John M. Greenlee, and won those suits in the eyes of white male juries, is remarkable. For them, the courts and the 1808 act offered an opportunity—perhaps the only one—to protest their denigration and punish Greenlee for his verbal abuse. But it is also telling that they ultimately lost their cases due to judicial determination and were soon motivated to leave the county. Perhaps it was also a matter of geography. The juries giving verdict in the trials comprised white men from the local area, who would have known the individual parties and relationships involved. The appellate judiciary, on the other hand, sitting on the bench of the North Carolina Supreme Court, was in Raleigh, some 200 miles to the east. The appellate judges would have only known the racial and economic status of the parties and the legal details of the dispute.

It is important to note that during the decade-long cases between the

Watts daughters and John Greenlee, no mention is made in the court documents about their Cherokee ancestry and identity, even though John Watts (their grandfather) was a significant figure in Cherokee-European negotiations. In fact, the racial background of plaintiffs is not discussed in any North Carolina Supreme Court jurisprudence. On paper it is deemed irrelevant, even though it was likely highly relevant in practice. This can be contrasted to cases in neighboring South Carolina where a plaintiff's racial status was often contested within slander suits. In 1856, the Court of Appeals of Law of South Carolina heard a case brought by twenty-five-year-old Narcissa Smith against her much older neighbor Samuel Hamilton after he told people she was "the mother of a mulatto child."[58] Smith succeeded, with the jury awarding her the sizable sum of $3,000 in damages. But the defendant then moved for a nonsuit, arguing that Smith needed to prove "she was a white or unmarried woman; since she might be a free negro, or married to one; in either case of which to have a mulatto child was only natural, and ... would not be slanderous." However, Justice Munro was unconvinced. The fact that Smith sued in her own name was evidence she was *feme sole*, and he declared: "a plaintiff need not aver herself to be white, for that the law presumes." He further commented that "the plaintiff's color might, and doubtless would have made, a material difference in the estimation of the jury," but the court would presume a party's whiteness, unless proved otherwise.[59]

In North Carolina, the Supreme Court progressively read down the 1808 Slander of Women statute, narrowing its application overtime. In the 1840s and 50s, the court held that the legislation did not cover slander about a woman having a lascivious disposition. The words needed to impute that she had illicit sexual intercourse. In 1840, Robert and Frances McBrayer, farmers in Rutherford County, just northwest of Charlotte, North Carolina, brought a slander suit against their neighbor, Abel Hill, for accusing Frances of incontinence.[60] This was also a bitter family dispute. The plaintiff and defendant were cousins: Hill's mother was Margaret McBrayer, sister of David McBrayer, Robert's father.

A witness for the plaintiff testified that Hill had told him he went to the plaintiffs' house and that Frances asked him to go into a room to see some carpenter's work that had been done. Then, as Frances began sweeping the house, Hill put his hands upon her and she "rose up and kissed him." At that moment, her children appeared at the door of the room, and she declared: "Lord, what have I done!" The witness reported that Hill then told him: "you may depend on it she is such a woman." Another witness for the plaintiff told the court that he had frequently heard Hill say of Frances that she was "a dirty, sluttish woman" and that she would "put a saucer of molasses down to the children at one end of the house" while she had illicit sexual relations at the other end. A third witness swore that there had been an indictment against Hill for assault and battery on Frances, and that the reason Robert McBrayer had not summoned witnesses to prove his wife's good character was because "the general impression in that neighborhood was, that he, the defendant, kept the plaintiff's wife."[61] The defendant argued that the words, as set out in the pleadings, were not actionable, and the trial judge agreed. The plaintiffs were nonsuited and appealed to the North Carolina Supreme Court.

Chief Justice Thomas Ruffin gave judgment for the court. Ruffin, a once-lauded jurist who sat on the North Carolina Supreme Court and resided as chief justice from 1833 to 1852, was described by Roscoe Pound in 1936 as one of the top ten judges of American history.[62] In present times, he is most known as the judge who penned the 1830 North Carolina Supreme Court decision of *State v Mann* that declared: "The power of the master must be absolute, to render the submission of the slave perfect."[63] Via this case, Ruffin, an extensive slaveholder himself, created for slave owners a complete immunity from criminal prosecution for the physical punishment of their enslaved people, no matter how brutal or cruel. The facts of the case concerned the shooting of an enslaved woman, Lydia, in the back, while she attempted to flee violence inflicted upon her by a man who had hired her services, John Mann. He was initially convicted but then acquitted on appeal by Ruffin's judgment. Sally Greene and Eric L. Muller have described the decision as "undoubtedly the coldest and starkest defense of the brutality of slavery ever to appear in an American judicial opinion."[64] In July 2020, with the re-examination of *State v Mann* and Ruffin's slave-owning activities, the statue of Ruffin that had stood at the entrance of the North Carolina Court of Appeals building in downtown Raleigh since 1915 was removed.[65] Months later, his portrait was taken down from the Supreme Court courtroom.[66]

In *McBrayer v Hill*, Chief Justice Ruffin read down the 1808 Slander of Women Act. It gave a woman an action for words that amounted to a charge of incontinency, which meant in his view not merely imputing to her "impure desires" or a "lascivious disposition," but the criminal act of adultery or fornication.[67] He declared that the legislature could have gone further and made the act more expansive, but they chose not to do so. Therefore, he regarded himself as bound by a narrow construction, even though he conceded that an accusation of "propensity" could be as "destructive to the reputation of a woman, as the most explicit charge of personal prostitution." According to Ruffin, the words reported to have been spoken by the defendant by the first two witnesses were not actionable. They only imported "evil thoughts in the heart" of Frances McBrayer, not yet "open lewdness." However, the accusation by Hill that he "kept" McBrayer was caught by the 1808 act. According to Ruffin, the "common and well-established sense" of the word "kept" "when used in reference to connexions between the sexes" was to "denote habitual and criminal carnal conversation, amounting to cohabitation."[68] This was not the act of "maintaining a virtuous lady in her innocence" but the "vicious one of having a wanton at his command for carnal gratification—of keeping her for sensual uses." On this point, judgment was reversed and McBrayer won. Legally, the reasoning in this case was very similar to *Watts v Greenlee*. In both cases, the appeals judge found only some of the words actionable: "incontinent" in *Watts*, "kept" in *McBrayer*. But whereas the Native American Watts daughters lost, the propertied white farmer's wife Frances McBrayer won.

The next two cases for sexual slander in the North Carolina Supreme Court contested the defense of truth when it came to the 1808 act. In 1847, Huldah Snow, a young, unmarried woman working as a servant in the household of farmers Joseph and Temperance White, brought a case against her much older and wealthier neighbors: farmers and enslavers Judith Witcher (referred to as Julina Wilcher in other records) and her husband William Witcher.[69] Snow pleaded that Judith had been spreading rumors about her being "lewd and incontinent in habit and character," and more particularly that she had "brought forth a bastard child," was a credit to Zilpha Sims (a woman known as a "notorious prostitute"), had a shape like "a big bellied negro woman named Luce," and there were reports given by Judith Witcher's "negro woman" of Huldah having lost a child.[70] Snow claimed $2,000 in damages. The defendants pleaded justification—truth—and introduced a witness at trial who swore that he had had "criminal intercourse" with the plaintiff on several occasions. The jury found that the defendant had proved some of the accusations true, but not others, and awarded the plaintiff $100 in damages.[71]

The defendants appealed arguing that they had proven the main charge of the declaration true, and the plaintiff—unrepresented at this point by an attorney—did not respond. Justice Richard Mumford Pearson agreed with the defense, stating that the declaration primarily alleged a "charge of incontinence," which was proved by the evidence of the Witchers' witness. He stated that this (unnamed) man's testimony, if true, showed that Huldah Snow "was not one of those 'innocent' chaste women, whose 'unsullied purity' the recital declares it was the intention of the Act to protect."[72] In other words, Huldah Snow—as a poor white woman—fell outside the scope of the Slander of Women Act. Justice Pearson followed Ruffin's decision in *McBrayer v Hill* by holding that the plaintiff's plea that Judith Witcher imputed her to be "base and lewd" was not actionable, as it simply meant "lustful, libidinous." He declared that the "gravamen of the action is a false and malicious charge of incontinence and a want of chastity," and Huldah Snow had been sufficiently proved to be sullied. Huldah Snow—a poor, unmarried white woman without legal representation—lost her case on the basis of the testimony of one unnamed man.

One year later a similar case was heard in Wilkes County. John Waters and his wife (sometimes spelled Watters in the court records) sued fifty-eight-year-old farmer George W. Smoot for accusing Mrs. Waters of having intercourse with another farmer named Nelson Haggins.[73] According to court documents, Smoot told people that "the lunatic (meaning Mrs. Waters, one of the Plaintiffs) was caught in the swamp with Nelson Haggins with his arms around her neck . . . and that he had her down (meaning that the Plaintiff Mrs. Watters [sic] was incontinent)."[74] As in *Snow v Witcher*, Smoot pleaded justification and introduced evidence to show the plaintiff had had criminal intercourse with various other men. He won and the plaintiffs appealed. Pearson referenced *Snow v Witcher* but distinguished it on the facts, stating that whereas it had contained a general charge of incontinency (and so could be proven with general evidence of unchastity), the imputations about Waters were specific and referred to one named man: "here, the charge is particular—The defendant, at the time he spoke the words, selected Nelson Haggins as the man, and he cannot be allowed, in his plea, to shift his ground."[75]

In 1850, according to US Census records, there was only one man named John Waters living in Wilkes County.⁷⁶ Property records also show two land grants in Wilkes County to a John Waters in 1854. In 1850, at age twenty-one, John lived in a house with his parents, Wesly and Martha Waters, and five other Waters between the ages of four and twenty-seven. It is likely that Nancy Waters, aged twenty-seven at the time, was his wife. In the census, there is a mark next to her name in the column "Deaf and dumb, blind, insane, idiotic, pauper, or convict." This may be why Smoot referred to her as a lunatic.

John Waters, co-plaintiff, was the grandson of John P. Waters and Elizabeth Cullom, who were indicted in 1809 for cohabiting in "the manner of husband and wife" and fined 50 pounds. In his petition to the General Assembly of North Carolina in response, John P. Waters conceded that "about forteen years ago [he] did take into his house a Certain Elisabeth Culms [*sic*] a woman of colour, and . . . he became attached to the s.d. Elisabeth in such a manner that, [he] did Intend to make her his lawfull wife." He swore that "from the love he bares his said little children and their kind mother, still desirous to keep them together to do a fatherly and Husbands part by them."⁷⁷ Elizabeth was Cherokee. In 1909, Linville Waters (John Waters's little brother, who was four years old in 1850) filed Eastern Cherokee applications with the US Court of Claims, also known as the Guion Miller Roll, swearing to be Catawba Indian through his grandmother Elizabeth Cullom.⁷⁸ Numerous affidavits included within the application state that Wesly Waters and his family were "recognised as Eastern Cherokee Indians."

They were clearly regarded within the local Wilkes County community as non-white. In 1843, William Watters [*sic*] (the uncle of John Waters, the plaintiff) was convicted of unlawful fornication with a white woman, Zilpha Thompson. He argued that she was his lawful wife and that he was European—that his grandfather, John P. Waters, was a white man. One witness for the defendant testified that he knew Watters's [*sic*] parents: his mother, Elizabeth Cullom, was a "bright mulatto with coarse straight hair," and his father, John P. Waters, was "a white man but of a dark complexion for a white man."⁷⁹ But another witness, for the prosecution, declared that he knew Watters's [*sic*] grandparents and both were "coal black Negroes." The court held there was sufficient Black ancestry for Watters [*sic*] to be defined as "a person of color." The Waters/Watters family in Wilkes County was clearly regarded as of mixed race and/or persons of color. This made them especially vulnerable to slander and slights in the community.

Miscegenation—and slander cases concerning it—were common in antebellum North Carolina, especially between lower status classes. In 1859, Candance Lucas, a single woman of twenty-eight living with her parents and siblings in Montgomery County, sued her neighbor Gilbert Nichols for slander.[80] She pleaded that Nichols told others that Lucas "had got a new sweet-heart, Wesley Dean's Pete; it used to be Ben Lucas and sometimes Jake Calicoat" and that "all three of these persons, Pete, Ben and Jake, were slaves, belonging to persons of the surnames attached to them, and lived in the neighbour of the plaintiff." Nichols reportedly also said he "would give any one twenty-five dollars that would get her a young one," meaning get Lucas pregnant.[81] After Lucas brought her slander claim, Nichols doubled down, telling people that she had "had two or three black children" over the years.[82] At trial, the defendant did not seek to prove the accusations true, and the court instructed the jury to determine whether the words had been spoken, and if so, whether they imputed incontinence to the plaintiff, that is, "charged the plaintiff with having had sexual intercourse with the said slaves."[83] The jury found for the defendant and Lucas appealed.

Following and citing Ruffin in *McBrayer v Hill*, Justice Matthias Manly held that the malicious words uttered by Nichols did not charge incontinency and therefore were not actionable under the 1808 Slander of Women Act. "Incontinency," he declared, "means a want of restraint [with] regard to sexual indulgence, and imports, according to our statute, definitive, illicit, sexual intercourse."[84] "The worst interpretation that can be put upon the words," he went on, "is a charge of wanton or lascivious disposition." The words spoken by Nichols after Lucas brought her case—that she had delivered two or three Black children—could not be admitted as evidence of meaning, as they occurred after pleadings were filed.

Victoria Bynum has argued that Lucas lost her case due to her father's troubled social and financial standing in the community (bankruptcy) and personal loyalties and grudges surrounding the case: the Lucas and Nichols families were in bitter conflict that ran deeper than the case at hand.[85] These factors no doubt made Lucas vulnerable to slanderous attacks and affected courtroom dynamics during the trial. However, it is unlikely that Justice Manly, sitting at the bench of the Supreme Court of North Carolina in downtown Raleigh three years after the words were spoken, knew or cared about intimate squabbles in the Little River community of northeastern Montgomery County. More likely, he felt compelled to follow the precedent set down by then-Chief Justice Ruffin and keep the scope of the 1808 act narrow, particularly when it came to the claims of women like Candance Lucas. On the edge of financial precarity, unmarried, aging, and rumored to be consorting with slaves, Lucas's unsullied purity was not to be protected by the 1808 act.

North Carolina's Slander of Women Act—the first legislation in the common law world, introduced by planter, enslaver, and father William W. Jones—sought to protect "the reputations of innocent and unprotected women" whose very presence in society rested upon the unsullied purity of their character. The language of the act and its preamble connected with articles in newspapers that chastised men for their "unrestrained licentiousness" in slandering women who could not defend themselves due to their "inestimable and indispensable delicacy." The act and the related debates envisaged white women, entitled to presumptions of purity, and who were yet to be sullied by poverty or precarity, as their targets for protection. In other words, it sought to uphold and define elite white women's reputations for sexual and moral superiority. These intentions became clear as the North Carolina judiciary read down the act over time, limiting its application via technical rules so that it did not work to vindicate the wrong class of persons—Justice Pearson making this explicit in his *Snow v Witcher* judgment.

Nonetheless, most sexual slander cases brought under the 1808 act that appealed to the North Carolina Supreme Court were not instigated by elite white women as the "tender flowers of society." They were in fact pursued by women on the margins: poor, servants, aging spinsters, "lunatics," Native American, and African American. And sometimes unrepresented by legal counsel. And it is important to understand that these were plaintiffs in civil suits, not complainants in criminal proceedings, and so were in control of filing the claims and weighing the risks of a court case (the slander being repeated in court, the costs of appealing) against the benefits of pursuing the matter. They attempted to use the act to vindicate their reputations, defend or elevate their social standing, and punish their slanderers. Their agency and strategic decisions in doing so should not be discounted.

Often—but not always—their cases were legally unsuccessful, due to the resistance or hostility of the judiciary. But winning or losing a case is only one marker of victory. Defamation is about public perception and belief, and the 1808 act allowed women (without access to the private power of privilege and patronage) to refute slander and proffer their side of the story—especially within their local communities. Being awarded a large sum of damages is one way of vindicating a reputation, but even an unsuccessful case can throw doubt upon circulating rumors and punish a slanderer. Defending a civil claim is expensive, inconvenient, time-consuming, and emotionally taxing—something to be avoided if possible. For the Watts sisters and many others in antebellum North Carolina, the 1808 Slander of Women Act offered an opportunity—perhaps the only one—to protest their denigration on the public record and punish men like John Greenlee for their verbal abuse. Without it, no writ could have been filed. The act made marginal women's resistance visible and held their slanderers accountable. It provided them with a mechanism—a legal cause of action—to confront and push back against their (usually far wealthier and well-connected) abusers who otherwise felt entitled to slander them with impunity.

FOUR

FREE WHITE FEMALES AND SOCIAL INTERCOURSE WITH BLACKS

Georgia

No state went further. In fact, no other common law jurisdiction in the world went further in fortifying its laws against slander during the nineteenth century than Georgia. By criminalizing sexual liaisons outside of marriage (adultery, fornication), codifying slander imputing "debasing acts," and enacting laws proscribing accusations of white women having sex with Black men, Georgia clamped down on the tongues of its residents when it came to discussing women's sexuality. In 1872, adjudicating upon a case wherein a man had slandered a widow, telling people he saw her having sex in a chicken coop, the Supreme Court of Georgia took pride in its leadership of speech suppression:

> Whatever may be the rule at common law, or in the other States, in Georgia it is actionable, orally to impute to another a crime punishable by law.... But our law goes further than this, and further, I think, than has been gone in any other State or country adopting the common law.[1]

Georgia led the common law world in limiting what could be said about white women and sex.

The story of slander in Georgia is one of color lines and codification. Georgia's relatively late but energetic economic embrace of slavery fostered the rapid growth of a Black enslaved population during the nineteenth century to work the dispossessed lands of the Creek and Cherokee

Indians. The exponential expansion of slavery in the state, especially into the interior, fueled a system of hardening segregation and white supremacy. This was coupled with a lagging institutional legal system, originating with Georgia's founders' suspicion of lawyers and their paternalistic commitment to fostering a utopia for the white working man. But this resistance to jurists and jurisprudence paradoxically turned Georgia into a leader of the US codification movement. Faced early on with a chaotic and undecipherable mass of local ordinances and decisions, a group of secessionists—future Confederate colonels and captains—remade and rewrote the state's laws during the first half of the nineteenth century. They produced a document, the 1863 code, that reflected the aspirational character of Georgia on the eve of civil war: a slaveholding democratic society for the everyman embodying an "epoch distinguished above all others for sound thought, self-judgement, and vigorous common sense."[2] Included within this code were the only racially specific slander of women laws in the English common law world. This chapter explores how Georgia's unique legal and social history—a commitment to equality for whites and to making law accessible and understandable to them—produced such distinctive slander laws.

Envisaged by British social reformer James Oglethorpe as a refuge and new beginning for the debtors who crowded London's prisons, Georgia (named after King George II) was the last of the thirteen British colonies to be founded in North America and was ruled by a London board of trustees for its first twenty years between 1732 and 1752. Attempting to create a society of diligent yeoman farmers, merchants, and artisans from England's "worthy poor," the trustees initially and unusually prohibited rum and slavery and strictly limited the size of land grants to 500 acres. England's plebian class would be reformed by "unwearied Industry" and diverted from lives of "idleness and vice."[3] Whereas bans on rum and limits on land tenure were either ignored or successfully opposed by early waves of settlers, the trustees held firm on the prohibition of slavery. This was not motivated by concern for the humanity of African Americans. As Betty Wood notes, the trustees were not abolitionists or pre-abolitionists.[4] In fact, prior to his Georgia plans, Oglethorpe held high office in the Royal African Company. Rather, the trustees believed that the institution of slavery would defeat the goal of rehabilitating the poor through hard work. They argued that if slavery were permitted, the English laboring classes would no longer labor: they "would be unwilling, nay would certainly disdain, to work like negroes."⁵ For this reason, the trustees also purposefully avoided the introduction of a cash crop in Georgia (otherwise dominant in plantation societies of British North America and the West Indies), preferring to encourage a boutique economy based upon the production and export of luxuries: silk and wine. This would be a utopian white workers' paradise where the British poor could make good.

For those who queried these justifications for Georgia's establishment and its bans on slavery, the trustees also argued that the colony would offer a strategic port against Spanish expansion and aggression. Worries about the Spanish and their luring of escaped enslaved persons away from British colonies such as South Carolina, as well as their ability to fan the flames of plantation insurrections, also hardened attitudes against the introduction of slavery in Georgia. But on January 1, 1751, with the British defeat of the Spanish and the failure of Georgia's economy to thrive on the proceeds of silk and wine, the trustees relented to pressure from fervent pro-slavery advocates. The colony's prohibition on slavery was repealed, and a large-scale rice industry was quickly established in the low country surrounding Savannah. Georgia's previously plummeting population rebounded, and by the 1760s newcomers flocked to the colony and began importing slaves directly from Africa to work on plantations in the coastal mosquito-ridden malarial swamps.

The introduction of plantation slavery and rice cultivation in Georgia brought about a profound economic and political transformation. Enormous wealth produced off the backs of enslaved people was siphoned into the hands of a small minority of landowners, creating a planter elite who took over from the trustees to rewrite the first laws to suit themselves. Whereas the initial slave code of 1750 regulated enslavers (for example, by restricting their means of disciplining enslaved persons) and criminalized interracial sex, subsequent slave codes of 1755, 1765, and 1770 worked to increase enslaver liberties (including by not punishing them for sexual relationships with Africans).

Further important shifts in power occurred in the late eighteenth and early nineteenth centuries, as immigrants pushed into the fertile interior, violently dispossessing and forcibly displacing the Creek and Cherokee peoples as they went. And in 1793, after the invention of Eli Whitney's patented cotton gin, Georgia became the hub of the Black Belt region.

Between 1820 and 1840, the white population exploded, doubling from 189,570 to 407,695.[6] Although some of these new arrivals came as families, most were single, landless men looking for opportunity. It was during this era that slavery democratized in Georgia, as an ideology and a practice. Between 1810 and 1840, the Black population of Georgia—the vast majority enslaved in the interior—grew from 60,000 to 280,944, and then to 436,631 by 1860.[7] Cotton cultivation required less of an initial financial outlay than rice crops and so allowed more commoners to partake in its farming. Young white men without means, hoping one day to preside over their own land and human chattel, could also grab positions as overseers as the cotton industry boomed.

This growing group also had a keen interest in differentiating their skills from the menial work of enslaved persons. The cotton kingdom created a labor regime that deliberately deskilled and demoted Blacks and collapsed distinctions between peoples of African descent. Blacks as a group were defined and subordinated, their work tasks restricted, to create status for nonelite whites. Color lines, somewhat ambiguous and indeterminate in eighteenth-century Georgia, crystallized and calcified, as every white man saw the economic and political benefits of white supremacy and aspired to plantation prosperity. As Watson Jennison argues, "nonelite whites in Georgia not only benefited from the rise of white supremacy but pushed hardest to enact legislative changes to make Georgia conform to the tenets of the ideology."[8] Enslaved persons were also put to work constructing the railways transporting cotton to ships waiting to sail it across the world. By the 1850s, Georgia claimed more miles of rail line than any other southern state, and by 1860 it was the most populous southern state. By then known as the Empire of the South, Georgia had the largest number of enslavers and enslaved persons in the United States, outside of Virginia.

In Georgia, agriculture begat legal culture. This occurred both in content and form. Whereas the introduction and expansion of plantation slavery wrote color lines into the laws of the state in increasingly darker ink, an early and persistent commitment to the interests of the common white man influenced the ways in which the legal system was organized and expressed. In the eighteenth century, trustee hopes for "a happy, flourishing colony" necessitated, in their minds, a society "free from that pest and scourge of mankind called lawyers."[9] The trustees—in a unique and bold move—banned the immigration of lawyers to the colony. This was because lawyers threatened to disrupt and sow discontent amongst commoners with their irritating challenge to and questioning of regulations and governance. The trustees established some rudimentary courts, but they appointed laymen, often illiterate, to preside over them. However, after becoming a royal province in 1752, the ban on lawyers was lifted, and English-trained lawyers, joined by American-born ones from neighboring colonies, soon started migrating. Nonetheless, lawmaking, the bar, and jurisprudence were slow to come to Georgia. The state did not set up its first state appellate court until 1846.

Georgia's commitment to educating laymen as their own advocates led it to initiate several important law reforms. It was the first state to simplify rules of pleading so that anyone could bring an action in the civil courts, and the first to neatly and comprehensively codify its criminal laws in 1811 and 1816 into the Penal Act.[10] Writing in 1850, Joseph Henry Lumpkin, the first leading justice of the Georgia Supreme Court and brother of Governor Wilson Lumpkin, remarked on the state's achievements in codification that put it ahead of England and New York:

> Lord Brougham, and those associated with him, in re-modeling the English Law, received the most extravagant praise, for recommending to the British Parliament things, as new, which had been in successful practice in this State for thirty years. And even New York, which is supposed to have gone a whole bar's-length and more beyond any other State in the Union, in the work of progress and reform, is content to end pretty much where Georgia started, half a century ago.[11]

The early codified criminal laws—which intended to soften the rigor of the penal code by replacing public hanging, whipping, branding, ear-cropping, and the pillory with fines and prison sentences—came into effect with the building of the state's first penitentiary in Milledgeville in 1816. Lucius Quintus Cincinnatus Lamar I, a Georgia-born lawyer, was commissioned to compile the laws into a volume.[12] The ninth division of the volume, "Offences Against Public Peace and Tranquillity," proscribed public affrays and challenges or duels as crimes.

Defamation also featured prominently, in the form of libel: "A libel, is a malicious defamation, expressed either by printing or writing, or by signs, pictures and the like, tending either to blacken the memory of one who is dead, or the honesty, virtue, integrity or reputation of one who is alive, and thereby exposing *him* to public hatred, contempt or ridicule."[13] Anyone committing libel faced a sizable fine of $1,000 as well as "imprisonment in the penitentiary, at labour or hard labour" for up to three years. The same section also set out that calling a man a coward in writing for refusing to duel constituted a libel. White men, those likely to be subject to written attacks on their reputations or called cowards in "any newspaper or hand bill," were well protected by such laws.

The criminal code, while not dealing with slander expressly, contained provisions that supplemented its common law regulation in certain important respects. The tenth division of this volume set out all "offences against the public morality, health and police," including incest, adultery, fornication, cohabitation, open lewdness, and keeping a lewd house. For example, the sixth section declared that "any man or woman who shall live together in an open state of adultery and fornication . . . shall be severally indicted" and subject to a fine, as well as imprisonment for repeat offending.[14] The criminalization of these liaisons and activities also occurred in some other states such as Pennsylvania and Connecticut, though not so explicitly and extensively.[15] In Georgia, it had pronounced consequences for slander law in the state. It meant that much (but not all, as we will see) sexual misconduct slander was caught by the common law exception of charging someone with committing an indictable offence. Thus, if a man or woman was accused of adultery or fornication in Georgia, in most instances they could sue for slander without the burden of proving special damage. Early criminal law codification in Georgia worked to expand the scope of slander law, especially for women.

The effect of these criminal codes on slander law came before the Supreme Court of Georgia in its very first year of operation. In 1846, the court heard a case brought by James E. Pledger and his wife Matilda Pledger (née Rheedy) against Middleton Hathcock.[16] The parties were from Floyd, a county nestled snuggly in the Black Belt, on Cherokee land, bordering Alabama. The pleadings stated that Matilda was a "good true just and virtuous woman," received and accepted by all her neighbors and acquaintances and who had never been guilty nor suspected to have been guilty of "fornication, whoring or adultery."[17] She claimed that Middleton Hathcock—"falsely and wickedly and maliciously" intending to injure and "damage" her "good name, fame and credit," bring her into "public scandal, infamy and disgrace," and subject her "to the pains and penalties of the laws of the State"—had a loud conversation with someone within hearing of other persons wherein he stated: "Have you heard of Matilda Rheedy and Micajah C. Martin whoring of it?" During the trial, Hathcock's attorneys demurred, arguing that the words charged in the declaration were not actionable without proof of special damage.[18] As a married woman, Matilda Pledger could not—by definition—show she had lost the hand of a prospective suitor. Hathcock was successful, the court ordering that the plaintiffs pay his legal costs of $9.50.[19] Matilda Pledger appealed, seeking justice from the newly minted Supreme Court. Citing the New York decision of *Brooker v Coffin*, the Pledgers' lawyers argued that the rule for actionable slander was words imputing "a crime involving moral turpitude" or one that would subject the plaintiff to "infamous punishment."[20] They submitted that in Georgia adultery and fornication were punishable at law. The defendant's attorneys stuck to the common law rule regarding sexual slander: that it was not actionable *per se* and thus needed proof of special damage.

The matter was heard by the first three Supreme Court justices in Georgia: Joseph Henry Lumpkin, Hiram Warner, and Eugenius Aristides Nisbet. Justice Warner penned the judgment, providing an emphatic rejection of the defendant's argument and lower court's legal reasoning: "If the laws of the country did not protect female character from such slanderous imputations," he thundered, "we should deeply regret it."[21] Referencing English jurist Thomas Starkie, he declared that the law presumed loss from the publishing of scandalous words when a person is charged with the commission of a crime. And in Georgia, *unlike* New York and other US states, such activities were clearly criminalized: "By the 5th section of the 10th division of the penal code, it is declared, any man or woman who shall commit adultery or fornication, or adultery and fornication, shall be severally indicted and punished by fine or imprisonment."[22] Justice Warner went on to explain that the reason why sexual slander was not actionable in Great Britain was that it was adjudicated in the spiritual courts. But London, he pointed out, was the exception to the rest of England. There, a woman could be "carted for the offence" of incontinency, and therefore slander imputing incontinency was actionable. He concluded: "As we have seen by the penal code of this State, the offence of adultery and fornication is indictable and punishable in the temporal courts, and consequently to charge a person with either offence is actionable."[23] Judgment was reversed in favor of the plaintiffs. Early codification of the criminal code removed the immediate need for a slander of women act. Special damage was not necessary because the state had already transformed much sexual conduct outside of marriage into criminal offenses, and thus most forms of sexual slander became actionable under traditional English common law.

But though extramarital sexual liaisons between white persons were criminalized by the code and thus caught by slander laws, there was some confusion as to how such laws applied within a slave society with rigidly drawn color lines. In 1852, the General Assembly of Georgia enacted legislation, an amendment to the penal code, relevant to sexual slander. It clarified that "Any white man, and woman of color, of any shade or complexion whatever, free or slave, who shall live together in a state of adultery or fornication, or of adultery and fornication, such white man shall be guilty ... and indicted of the same."[24] The act made clear that it was criminalizing the same conduct between a white man and woman of color as that constituting criminal adultery and fornication between "free white persons." According to the same code, a person was defined as "not white persons" if they had at least one-eighth "negro or African blood in their veins."[25] This amendment was intended to plug a hole in the criminal code that only seemed to apply to sexual relations between white persons. It reflected a society where, for white men, sexual liaisons with Black women were frowned upon and discouraged. But interestingly, it did not criminalize sexual relations between Black men and white women. The reason for this asymmetry is unclear. Perhaps such relations were so inconceivable they did not warrant regulation. The implications of this omission for slander law soon became a subject of judicial controversy.

In 1858, the Supreme Court of Georgia heard a case that exemplified aspects of Georgian life and markedly changed the law of slander. Samuel and Martha Kelly, from the rural Black Belt county of Warren, sued their neighbors Ezra and Sarah Castleberry for slander after Sarah made public comments imputing that Martha had sexual intercourse with various Black men and had given birth to a Black child.[26] At the time the words were spoken, in April 1853, Samuel and Martha, then ages forty-two and thirty-two, respectively, were illiterate farmers, parents of five children, and did not own any enslaved persons.[27] It is worth noting that in their census record, they were initially described as "farm labourers" before the word "labourer" was manually crossed out and an "er" added to "farm."

The annotation reveals their wish to be known as farmers, not merely workers.

The nearby Castleberry family occupied a higher echelon of society. Ezra and Sarah were older, fifty and forty-six years old, respectively; were able to read and write; had two children; and enslaved a family of six (two adults, four children) in a cabin upon their land.[28] Their combined property and personal wealth was notable: $14,450. At the time, 44 percent of Warren County was white, 55 percent were enslaved, and 1 percent were free persons of color. This breakdown was largely representative of Georgia as a whole, though statewide the demographics were reversed (enslaved persons comprised 44 percent of the total population). In 1860, less than a third of Georgia's adult white male residents owned slaves. The Castleberrys were part of this minority, and the Kellys aspired to join it.

In July 1853, the Kellys filed a claim against the Castleberrys in the Superior Court of Warren County for $500. The complaint set out that the Kellys had always been "good and respectable" persons who enjoyed the "good opinion and esteem" of the neighborhood until Sarah Castleberry had conspired to injure and destroy Martha's reputation.[29] On April 25, 1853, Sarah Castleberry, in conversation with Samuel Kelly and others, reportedly said that Martha "had a negro child and that is not all. . . . Negroes have been with your wife and I can prove it." The pleadings set out that this meant that "Negro men had carnal communications with the said Martha." For reasons unspecified—perhaps unpaid court fees—the case took several years to come to trial and was not heard until October 1857 when a jury of twelve men gave verdict for the plaintiffs for $500. However, the Castleberrys appealed and sought to "arrest judgement" on the basis that no cause of action had been articulated. They argued that the words spoken by Sarah did not impute a crime under Georgian law and therefore Martha needed to prove special damage, which—as a married woman, like Matilda Pledger before her—she could not do.

The Superior Court of Appeals in Warren overruled their application, with Judge James Thomas declaring that when Georgia adopted English common law it adapted only such that was "suitable to our condition."[30] Whether or not it was technically a crime for a white woman to have intercourse with a Black man was irrelevant, he surmised, because in Georgia "the offence here alleged stands on a different ground." He commented that in England, if a woman of "royal blood" had illicit intercourse with "servants," "the issue" (child) of that union would be considered royal blood and "might wear the crown of England." But here, in Georgia, "the offspring of illicit intercourse with a negro is branded with infamy and disgrace [with] his or her position in society infinitely below that of the slave father."[31] Enslaved Blacks in Georgia were not equivalent in status to white servants in England, he stated. The mother of a child born from such a union would not just be "excluded from all good society but she would be banished from a brothel." Interracial sex produced offspring that represented, to the court, a gross blurring of the racial boundaries of Black and white society. Such offspring occupied a lower status than their enslaved father and made the mother less than a whore. Alleging such a scandal must be actionable slander, Judge Thomas concluded. The Castleberrys, dissatisfied with this decision in Martha Kelly's favor, took the case to the Supreme Court of Georgia.

Justice Charles James McDonald gave judgment for the Supreme Court. Citing *Pledger v Hathcock*, he stated that the "general rule in respect of actionable words was established": they must impute either a crime or an infectious disease.[32] This, of course, was not strictly accurate. There was a third category—words affecting a man in his office or profession—that was proving important for women in the Australian colonies at this time but was regarded in Georgia as irrelevant. Justice McDonald stated that in these circumstances, the question was whether the words set forth in the declaration imputed an indictable offence. Now came an exercise in statutory interpretation concerning the question of whether a white woman having sex with a Black man was a crime in Georgia. Two of the three justices on the bench believed that the penal code provisions concerning adultery or fornication only applied to intercourse between free white persons. This is because the provision in question required them to be severally indicted, and "a negro man who commits the act with a white woman" could not be indicted under the code because he was not considered a legal person.[33]

Justice McDonald went on to state that this interpretation was supported by the legislation passed in 1852 (described above) that deemed it necessary to enact a provision criminalizing cohabitation, adultery, or fornication between a white man and "woman of color." Such an enactment would have been superfluous if the original proscription of adultery and fornication applied to interracial sex in Georgia. Therefore, if fornication between a white woman and a Black man was not a criminal act, then words imputing that act to Martha Kelly were not slanderous *per se*, and she needed to prove special damage.

McDonald expressed his deep dissatisfaction with this construction of the law, but reluctantly acquiesced. He was "strongly of opinion" that the "Court of common law" had the same power in Georgia to determine what are remediable wrongs in new types of cases "which could not possibly occur in England."[34] Here was such an opportunity, he thought. This racially segregated plantation society based upon extensive slave labor was a far cry from the conditions of eighteenth-century England. "They have in England," he reasoned, "no inferior race as slaves, as we have here, with whom it is disgraceful to be on terms of social intercourse." "Who can say that there," he asked, "a case of the sort before us would not be made an exception to the established rule?"[35] McDonald, sixty-five years old at the time, was a former governor of Georgia, avid secessionist, and pro-slavery advocate. Upon his death two years later in 1860, he owned fifty-three men, women, and children (enslaved on his plantation in Cobb County) and had amassed assets worth $127,800.[36] McDonald thought the outcome of the *Castleberry* case an outrage but felt unable to alter the common law on his own. As no special damage had been proved, judgment was reversed and the Castleberrys won. Martha Kelly—denigrated to lower in status than a whore by scandalous rumors of interracial sex—would not have her name vindicated by the courts.

Castleberry v Kelly was reported by local newspapers, who noted that "to charge a white woman with having had carnal connection with a negro man is not slander in Georgia."[37] And the following year the Georgia legislature changed the law, prescribing:

> That hereafter, any words falsely and maliciously uttered, which impute to any free white woman of this State, carnal knowledge and connection with a slave, negro, or free person of color shall be held, deemed and adjudged actionable, per se, and without allegation or proof of any special damage.[38]

The act noted below this provision that it was necessary to overcome the result in *Castleberry v Kelly*. This was Georgia's own distinctive Slander of Women Act, the only one in the British common law world to mention race. It expressly restricted reputations for chastity to white women and cast aspersions of interracial sex as the most damaging kind of imputations, requiring their own specific law. It was a law, like many others, enacted by the elite to reinforce sexual and social color lines, particularly between ordinary white non-slaveholding Georgians and Blacks (free and enslaved). It demonstrated, as Timothy Lockley argues, anxieties that miscegenation would lead to class alliances between common whites and Blacks against the interests of the elite that would threaten the social foundations of southern plantation society.[39] Strict slander laws sent a message that certain things could not be uttered about white women. Even at the level of language, miscegenation was intolerable. Many of the plaintiffs who brought slander claims under North Carolina's 1808 Slander of Women Act, being Black or Cherokee, would have found it difficult, or impossible, to do so in Georgia.

But Georgia judges also made clear there were degrees of whiteness for women plaintiffs. Some were less deserving of protection due to loose behavior and dubious social company, and this would be reflected in the amount of damages awarded. In mid-1857, fourteen-year-old Josaphine Croft brought an action for slander via her father, a brick mason, against their neighbor Clark Beggarly for his accusation that: "She is a girl of bad character; she is a whore; I believe her to be a whore; she keeps the same kind of company that such women keep."[40] The Crofts and Beggarlys were neighbors in the city of Atlanta. Neither family was particularly wealthy, though the Crofts enslaved one fifty-five-year-old woman. Sarah and George Croft had four children, and Josaphine was the eldest.[41] Clark Beggarly was married with an infant child. According to evidence at trial, the words were spoken by Beggarly to the landlord of the house where the Croft family rented in an effort to have them evicted. In a fit of "violent passion," he shouted that the whole family were whores and Josaphine a "damned whore."[42] In defense of Croft's claim, Beggarly argued truth. He pleaded that the plaintiff's "character for chastity was not good," "her associations were not good," and "her house was a place of resort at late and unusual hours of the night for men."[43] He also asserted that in August 1857 she had "carnal connection and sexual intercourse" with a man named Cranford.

At trial, numerous witnesses were heard for both sides of the dispute. Some testified for the plaintiff that they had known her and her family for some time and that her "character for virtue was good," that they had "never heard anything against her," and that "her general reputation was that of a chaste and virtuous girl."[44] Others appeared for the defendant and painted quite a different picture. They stated that "common rumour" held that she was a "bold, fast, impudent, forward and suspicious girl," "loosely raised," who was often seen on the streets and public walks of Milledgeville and Atlanta either unattended or in the distasteful company of Lucy Dean, a free "negro woman."[45] Witnesses relayed that Josaphine Croft "hired" Lucy Dean to find her men. A man called Cranford answered in interrogatories that he engaged the plaintiff as a prostitute in August and September 1857. Croft's attorney objected to this evidence, arguing that as it occurred months after Josaphine's slander suit was filed, it could not be used against her. Judge Bull agreed and instructed the jury that as the word spoken— "whore"—was actionable *per se*, the plaintiff was *prima facie* entitled to recover, and no special damage need be proven. Despite the extensive evidence of "bad character," the jury gave verdict for Josaphine Croft, awarding her the sizable sum of $4,250 plus costs.[46]

But Clark Beggarly appealed. His lawyers set out numerous grounds to the Supreme Court of Georgia for consideration, but the primary submission argued that the damages awarded were excessive. Justice Joseph Henry Lumpkin, Georgia's first chief justice, gave judgment for the court and clearly expressed his disapproval of the plaintiff and his sympathies with the defendant. Clark Beggarly's "intemperate" shouting at Croft that she was a whore in front of her landlord was not "excusable," as such.[47] But here was a man "actuated alone from a desire to protect his family from an unworthy neighbour." Beggarly was motivated by concern, Lumpkin counseled, not malice. His words—while "wholly unjustifiable"—nonetheless demonstrated the "earnestness and strength of his convictions." They came not from "the slimy tongue of a slanderer" but were "spoken in a strictly business transaction."[48] While the law, Lumpkin noted, cannot necessarily forgive such slander, it can treat the circumstances with "indulgence."

For, on the other hand, here was the plaintiff, a "bold, fast and forward girl of doubtful or suspicious character," who while not proven to be a prostitute, had a "general reputation" that was "not very good." She was seen about the streets at "unseasonable hours" in the company of "a negro woman ... by the name of Lucy, of notoriously infamous character." During one of these outings, Lucy approached a "group of young men ... conversed with them," and then one of the men went off with the women. Lumpkin commented that Beggarly heard or saw things that understandably "alarmed his fears and justified him" in denouncing the plaintiff.[49] The evidence might not have proven the slander true, that Croft was a whore, but according to Lumpkin, "in all the circumstances" the verdict could not be justified. Women and girls like Josaphine Croft did not deserve vindication by the courts, and to do so would "confound all distinction between the pure and the impure."[50]

Chief Justice Lumpkin then launched into a treatise on the limits of slander law in regulating the conduct and reputations of young women. "Slander verdicts, however enormous," he declared, could not "preserve the reputation of our daughters" if they grew up without parental restraint. "Governments may enact salutary laws," he admonished:

> [T]he ministry may thunder weekly from their pulpits the lessons of the Law, Courts may execute judgment in righteousness, but, unless family discipline be enforced, all other efforts will be in vain, to save the rising generation from ruin and wretchedness, and the land from destruction.

To Lumpkin, slander of women laws were a limited tool for cultivating and securing purity and chastity in young women, and thus for saving the morality and future of the republic. Parental, or rather paternal discipline, was the preferred method for stopping young women from playing "wanton" in the streets with dubious characters—that is, free Black persons—for company. Slander laws could, at best, only hope to remove, after the fact, some of the "taint of pollution."[51] Despite no evidence showing Croft was a prostitute, her association with Lucy Dean in public places led Chief Justice Lumpkin to reverse the lower court's decision vindicating her name.

Even though the Supreme Court expressed reservations about the function and utility of protecting women's reputations, the same year as the *Beggarly v Craft* [sic] decision, Georgia strengthened its slander laws even further.[52] Georgia's 1860 code, which came into effect in 1863, was the first comprehensive code in the United States and made it a leader in the codification movement—though this leadership was not acknowledged at the time. The US codification movement was begun by English reformer Jeremy Bentham in 1776 when he anonymously published *A Fragment of Government* and then entreated President James Madison from 1811 onwards to reject the common law (uncertain, arbitrary, technical) in favor of a code than Bentham himself would draft. He instructed Madison and other officials in the United States to "shut" their ports against the common law as they would against "the plague."[53] Bentham is credited with coining the term "codification."[54] Madison rejected Bentham's proposition, but it inspired Edward Livingston (once mayor and US attorney in New York, who later moved to New Orleans) to draft various codes for Louisiana, which were adopted in 1825.

A major driving force of the US codification movement of the early nineteenth century was rejection of the common law for its undemocratic (and therefore "barbaric") Englishness. One layman, writing an open letter in 1832 to a Massachusetts lawyer, stated that the legal profession,

> [b]y adopting the Common Law of Great Britain, the customs of the most barbarous ages, and of a nation whose principles of government are totally abhorrent to our own, customs contained in a thousand different books so intricate, so ambiguous, so contradictory that no man ever yet understood them . . . [had] heretofore contrived to exclude everyone.[55]

Codification promised accessible and locally appropriate rules for new democratic societies. From the 1820s to the 1850s, several states such as New York, Pennsylvania, Massachusetts, and Ohio enacted statutes partially codifying formal rules of practice, and to a lesser extent, substantive areas of law. Efforts by reformists were persistent, but due to fierce conservative opposition, state codification results were patchy and incomplete.

Georgia's codification occurred alongside, but was unconnected with, that which was going on in the rest of the country. Digests were commonly published in the state (to make sense of local statutes) but struggled to cleanly encapsulate all laws. One early "digester," Oliver Prince, remarked in 1822 that due to so many statutes being chaotically enacted and recorded, "the law on most subjects is utterly beyond the reach of the people at large."[56] But the frequent digests themselves also proved problematic—they overlapped, each was uniquely organized, and they were inconsistent in whether they covered general statutes, local laws, and/or cases. In 1847, the General Assembly requested three judges of the Supreme Court to report upon any defects in the laws of Georgia and give their opinion on the expediency and practicability of condensing and simplifying the laws of the state. Chief Justice Lumpkin's report was published in the *Western Law Journal*. He surmised that it was an "imperative duty to bring the law, as far as is practicable, within the reach and comprehension of the people."[57] "All men here," he wrote, "are by birthright hereditary lawmakers, and judges upon the *reputation* and lives as well as the arbiters of the property of their fellow citizens."[58] The law should be understandable by "every man" and "divested of all technicality and intricacy as far as it is possible." Directing his attention at the legacies of English common law, he pointedly remarked that the "sooner it is emancipated from the cumbersome appendages of the scholastic and feudal ages, the better."[59] Lumpkin's treatise about the merits of codification echoed the trustees' early desires to free the law of technicality and make it the tool of the commoner.

Though speaking of emancipation and throwing off the shackles of the past, Lumpkin was quick to reject any notion of being a revolutionary. Earlier in his essay, he assured readers: "We are decidedly opposed, however, to *revolution*."[60] He proposed simply to retain all present law "in its fundamental features" and to "lop off only its excrescences, to winnow away the rottenness which the mildew of time has produced, and engraft on the main stock such new provisions as will accommodate the whole to the present state of society and of the world."[61] Lumpkin advised the legislature to appoint three commissioners to revise, amend, and consolidate Georgian jurisprudence.

The General Assembly acted on Lumpkin's recommendation, authorizing the creation of a single code that would "embrace in condensed form, the Laws of Georgia, whether derived from the Common Law, the Constitution of the State, the Statutes of the State, the Decisions of the Supreme Court, or the States of England of force in this State." The General Assembly elected three commissioners to the task: Hershel V. Johnson, Iverson L. Harris, and David Irwin. However, Johnson and Harris declined, arguing they did not believe it was possible or preferable to codify the whole of the common law. Two further commissioners were subsequently appointed: Richard Clark and Thomas Reade Rootes Cobb. The latter, an energetic lawyer, wealthy slave owner, and secessionist, was also the son-in-law of Lumpkin, having married his daughter some years earlier.

Lumpkin and Cobb, connected by marriage, both had an outsized impact on slander law in Georgia and were also passionate advocates of slavery. In 1849, Lumpkin, an evangelist, pronounced that the institution of African slavery, despite attacks on it from abolitionists in the north, would exist in "perpetual duration" because it was ordained by God and "subserve[d] the best interests of both races."[62] He affirmed that "we will persevere and defend it from any and all hazards." Lumpkin also asserted that according to the Book of Genesis, Blacks were "cursed" and "judicially condemned to perpetual bondage."[63]

As the nineteenth century advanced, religious justifications were accompanied and bolstered by new scientific theories. Cobb believed that biological differences distinguished the races and that Africans were mentally inferior and thus suited to slave labor. He pronounced: "the physical, intellectual and moral development of the African race are promoted by a state of slavery and their happiness secured to a greater extent than if left at liberty."[64] He further mused that if one were to remove the restraining and controlling power of the master, "the negro becomes, at once, the slave of his lust, and the victim of his indolence, relapsing, with wonderful rapidity, into his pristine barbarism."[65] Such views, held by two of Georgia's prominent jurists—the first chief justice of the Supreme Court and the lead author of Georgia's 1863 code—were written into the law.

One early issue for Cobb and the other commissioners when drafting the code was to what extent it should supplement or alter existing law. During a meeting in Atlanta in 1859, they decided just to "reconcile, harmonize, render consistent the body of the Law, so as to give shape and order, system and efficiency, to the sometimes crude, and often ill expressed, sovereign will of the State."[66] The commissioners then divided the work between themselves, with Cobb assigned the civil code, containing the laws of slander and libel. Cobb sought to include all Georgia statutes dealing with civil rights and duties and then "fill out and make perfect the body of our laws" via the incorporation of principles from standard legal texts concerning common law and equity. But despite intending to gather and set out existing laws on each topic as historian Jefferson Davis argues, Cobb's civil code added a significant amount of new material.

The 1863 Georgia code was unique: in its origins, formulation, and extent.[67] No other US states had, or have since, accomplished the task of so comprehensively codifying their laws. But its significance has often been dismissed and minimized. Roscoe Pound, for instance, stated: "The code has had little effect. For the most part the courts treat it as declaratory of the common law."[68] But this was inaccurate. The code was important in several respects. First, it accomplished Lumpkin's goal of making the law accessible to all literate laypersons in Georgia—bringing it "within the reach and comprehension of the people."⁶⁹ Five thousand copies of the code were printed for state use, and editions were available for purchase by members of the public for the small price of three dollars. Second, it worked not simply to declare but to fundamentally alter certain common law principles. Its impact upon slander and libel was profound. In the late nineteenth century, the Georgia Supreme Court acknowledged this fact, noting: "While the changes in the law made by this codification were probably more numerous than was at first supposed, yet these changes generally, instead of marring the symmetry or detracting from the splendor of our system of laws, add to its luster and its excellence."⁷⁰ And in stark contrast to Pound, the court praised the 1863 code as "the most perfect system of codified laws then existing in any country on the globe."⁷¹ They credited Cobb and "his masterly intellect" as its primary author.⁷²

In setting out the laws of libel and slander under "Injuries to Reputation" in section 1 of article 2, Cobb introduced an entirely new and broad category of slander *per se*: charging a person with a "debasing act which may exclude him from society."⁷³ This was a legal "catch all," a way of making all imputations of sexual immorality defamatory *per se*, that is, without proof of special damage. Previously, there needed to have been an accusation that alleged a person committed a crime or suffered an infectious disease, or that a white woman had had sex with a Black man. But now, all slander actions relating to allegations of sexual misconduct were actionable without proof of special damage. However, Cobb did not live to see his code or its amendments come into effect. In 1862, he died fighting for the Confederate Army after he was hit by a Union shell that severed his femoral artery. The Civil War reshaped the 1863 code in obvious ways, making those parts related to slavery void. But the slander provisions, protecting white women from aspersions of interracial sex, lived on well into the twentieth century.

In 1870, Cobb's catchall slander amendment was recognized for its audaciousness and was applied successfully to protect a white woman's virtue. Evaline J. Lewis, a forty-nine-year-old white widow and housekeeper, brought a case for words against A. M. Hudson (spelled Ammon Hudson in the 1870 census), a fifty-nine-year-old wagonmaker, after he told various stories about her in the community.⁷⁴ According to the pleadings, in May 1869, Hudson told people "Mrs Lewis would not suit me" for a wife because "she was too thick with" Henry C. Kellogg. He went on to say that "some time back" he had seen Lewis "with her clothes up with a man" at the McAfee and Kellogg chicken coop and that Lewis had employed him to procure her a "magnetic conception preventative," and when he did, she seemed very familiar with it.[75] Hudson also apparently communicated to people that he had witnessed Lewis being affectionate with and going into bedrooms with various men, including Kellogg. Kellogg was a forty-year-old married man who had been a colonel in the Confederate Army but now ran a country store. Lewis argued that the words spoken by Hudson conveyed she was guilty of the debasing acts and claimed $10,000 in damages.[76]

However, Ammon Hudson demurred to the complaint, submitting that it disclosed no cause of action. His lawyers argued that for words to be actionable *per se*, they must impute a crime and that the words spoken by Hudson were too imprecise and ambiguous to do so. He did not explicitly tell people Lewis had illicit sexual intercourse, Hudson's lawyers cautioned. Judge Knight of the Forsyth Superior Court agreed, and Lewis's case was dismissed.[77] She appealed to the Georgia Supreme Court.

Judge Henry Kent McCay, who studied law under Lumpkin and served as a Confederate Army captain, gave judgment for the court. He opened by noting that it was actionable to orally impute to another a crime punishable by law. "But," he noted, "our law goes further than this."[78] He ventured that on the topic of slander, Georgia went "further... than any other state or country adopting the common law."[79] McCay was correct. Georgia was a British common law outlier when it came to actions for words. Its codified laws made all sexual misconduct slander actionable *per se*. The unique catchall added by Cobb in 1860 was cited: "In this State it is actionable to charge one with being guilty of any debasing act which may exclude him from society." On the basis of this new addition, the Georgia Supreme Court held that Lewis had been defamed by Hudson. His slander depicting her "with her clothes up with a man" in a chicken coop would be regarded as debasing even among the "low and vicious" since even they, McCay admitted, have some remains of decency. He concluded: "If an act so debasing as this is not covered by the clause of the Code we have referred to, it would seem difficult to say what act is."[80] White women in Georgia could now more easily protect their reputations—from aspersions of criminality, accusations of interracial sex, and rumors of debasing acts—as long as they (unlike Josaphine Croft) respected the proper racial boundaries of social and sexual intercourse.

The women who brought and fought sexual slander cases in the Georgia Supreme Court were uniformly white, hailed from the Black Belt interior, and occupied lower to middling economic positions. They were not poor, but neither were they elite, nor, in most cases, slave owning. These characteristics made them especially vulnerable to aspersions of interracial sex that threatened their enjoyment of the social privileges occasioned by whiteness and made legal redress—as opposed to leveraging private social power—their only option for reputational vindication. But while common white women wielded slander law as a weapon to defend their status and standing (which rested on the legal and social subordination of Blacks), the laws themselves were enacted and adjudicated by elite plantation owners with financial interests in laws that wrote and reinforced the color line. Such laws were framed by a discourse that biologically and evangelically justified slavery and a commitment to codification for its promise of democratic accessibility. By simplifying rules of pleading and neatly containing all the state's messy laws into one or more codes, the elite class encouraged common whites—as "hereditary law-makers"—to go to court and utilize the legal system for resolving their private disputes. By doing so, they—case by case—embodied, entrenched, and defended the ideologies of white supremacy underwriting such laws. Of course, they could argue in court, it was defamatory to say a white woman had had a sexual relationship with a Black man. Of course you could not say that a white woman had engaged in fornication or committed a debasing act. Certain subjects were not permitted as matters of public discussion or speech. It was now written clearly in the code.

FIVE

"DEPRIVED OF HER NATURAL GUARDIAN"

South Australia

And so it wanders round
From ear to lip, from lip to ear
Until it reached a gentle heart,
And that—it broke...

When first that word
Her light heart heard
It fluttered like the frightened bird,
Then shut Its wings and sighed,
And, with a silent shudder, died.
—FRANCIS S. OSGOOD, "SLANDER,"
EXAMINER (SOUTH AUSTRALIA, JULY 8, 1853)

In the late eighteenth and early nineteenth centuries, slander laws—in their functions to prohibit certain speech and privilege the moral reputations of some groups of people—were intricately bound up in the project of state building. In New Jersey, they worked to protect the sexual reputations of women as newly emerging citizens. In New South Wales, they prescribed the limits of civilized expression and enabled emancipist hopes of escaping one's class and convict background in an egalitarian market society. In North Carolina, slander laws enacted to protect elite women as unsullied and innocent were in fact used by plaintiffs marginalized by poverty, precarity, and race to protest their denigration and ostracism. In Georgia, codified slander laws rested on increasingly strict color lines and defined the limits of public talk about white women's sexuality. And in South Australia, British plans for a new colony founded upon marriage, family formation, and procreation influenced legislative debates and judicial reasoning about the direction of slander law.

In 1829, English political economist Edward Gibbon Wakefield, residing in a London prison (in consequence of a sexual scandal) and theorizing the optimal conditions for setting up a new colony in Australasia, explained that in selecting British emigrants, an absolute preference should be given to "equal numbers of both sexes, and to persons between the ages of eighteen and twenty-four."[1] This would not only discourage "the many evils" attendant in a disproportion of sexes (namely, "the general corruption of females") but cause a "very rapid increase of people in the Colony." Jeremy Bentham suggested this imagined place be named Liberia or Felicitania, but the proponents instead chose to call it South Australia.[2] Envisioned and modeled in opposition to previous colonial experiments, such as New South Wales (that had been built precariously on convict labor and seemingly plagued by social and sexual depravity), the future prosperity and character of this self-conscious new society would rest on respectable and stable foundations of marriage and procreation. Privileging the equal arrival of young men and women, fostering and protecting their romantic unions, and encouraging the production of offspring would become a cornerstone of much policy and lawmaking in South Australia for decades to come.

With the energetic and persistent advocacy of Robert Gouger, founder of the South Australian Association, and others, Wakefield's musings finally became a reality when the South Australia Act was passed in 1834. The province was the product of numerous compromises between its promulgators and the British Colonial Office concerning the form and functions of its planned system of government—the price to be paid for land, the place of state-aided religion, and proposals regarding the treatment of Aboriginal peoples—but an emphasis upon the importance of populating it with young couples remained central. Slander of women legal cases and reform debates occurring throughout the common law world at this time would become emmeshed here with rhetoric and frameworks that prioritized and privileged marriage and family formation more explicitly than any other jurisdiction investigated by this book. Arguments about the scourge of slander and its remedies also became entangled with projects of early self-government and paternalist ideas of societal improvement.

In South Australia's first decades, the founders' designs for equal migration of the sexes were soon realized. As Paul Sendziuk and Robert Foster note, between 1847 and 1851, over 20,000 people were provided free or assisted passage, 34 percent of whom were men and 39 percent women (the remainder were children).[3] Most of these migrants were agricultural laborers and domestic servants, products of nineteenth-century England. This system to regulate migration ensured a greater parity of men to women than any other Australian colony at this time.[4] In 1878, when Catherine Spence—prominent and prolific South Australian author, commentator, and reformer—penned an article titled "Some Social Aspects of Early Colonial Life" in the *South Australian Register,* she reminisced about the unique intimate and familiar relationships fostered by the colony's migration system and local economic conditions.[5] "Perhaps never in any human society," she mused, had the "equality of sexes" been so fully realized as in South Australia in its early days. Immigration was chiefly "family immigration," and Wakefield's system assured "the disproportion on the whole was very slight compared to that in other colonies." The consequences of this, the unmarried journalist argued, was that women were not as scarce as to be "spoiled" or so abundant as to be "neglected." She went on to explain that "every girl knew if she was tolerably pleasant, she could be married" and that a "good temper" was the chief prerequisite for a wife. Marriages were a source of "comfort" and "help" and were carried out simply and respectably, with little extravagance. In such a land of plenty and opportunity (premised on the dispossession of Indigenous populations), a fall in social status was chiefly dependent on matters of "character"—not income or wealth. Spence concluded by asserting that the "good old natural fashion" of young people taking a liking for each other, partaking in a happy courtship, and then being "bound together for life" was followed with "boldness" and "success" in South Australia. "What better beginning can there be all the world over?" she asked, referring seemingly to both the lives of those hopeful youths and the fledging colony itself. An interesting position, considering that Spence herself decided—unusually for the time—not to marry. But it seemed all founders agreed: South Australia, for reasons economic and political, was intended as a romantic "Utopia" for family flourishing.

So central was the idea of marriage to South Australia's systems and self-conception that during its first decades tremendous legislative effort was expended encouraging marriage, preventing marital discord and disintegration, and repairing damage incurred from family breakdown. English common law and its strictures of coverture applied in South Australia as early as 1837, when the civil courts were established. But ecclesiastical courts—which traditionally applied to procedures of marriage such as annulments and procedures for judicial separation, restitution, and adultery—did not migrate. In addition, few processes for formally marrying or recording marriages existed in the early colony, a problem addressed in 1842 with the passage of the Marriage Act and the Registration of Births, Deaths, and Marriages Act. The first of these acts deemed marriages made within religious ceremonies—Uniting, Church of England, Quaker, and Jewish—valid and mandated their registration within seven days. The latter act established the Registry Office in the province of South Australia and provided for its management. In 1844, the Catholic Marriages Act was similarly passed, formally recognizing those unions. Further legislation regulating marriages was passed in 1852, and in 1858-60, the South Australian parliament clarified that men were indeed allowed to marry the sister of their deceased wife.[6]

Marriage also formed the basis of Aboriginal land grants in South Australia. Mandy Paul and Robert Foster have documented land grants to Aboriginal women in South Australia and their relationship with changing colonial discourses of race, gender, and "civilisation."[7] In 1848, the first section of Aboriginal reserve land was granted to an Aboriginal person, Kudnarto (also known as Mary Ann Adams), in consequence of her marriage to English shepherd Thomas Adams. This was the first instance of a new policy encouraging interracial marriage. To prevent exploitation of the policy by European men, however, the Protector of Aborigines held such land in trust for Aboriginal women and their children during their lifetime. This policy was a doubly raced and gendered form of paternalist protection.[8]

Despite the visions of founders, families, of course, could just as easily end in misery as marital bliss, and thus the law also played a significant role in regulating family ties and their discontents. Therese McCarthy and Paul Sendziuk document the plight of deserted women and children in the colonial period, and the disjuncture between progressive legislative reform and its incapacity for enforcement.[9] During the 1840s and 50s, numerous acts were passed ameliorating the poverty caused to families by abandonment of their husbands and fathers, such as the Maintenance Act of 1843. McCarthy and Sendziuk argue that such laws were less about morally punishing desertion and more about relieving the financial burden placed on the government by destitute wives and children. The South Australian government was a paternalistic but reluctant custodian, preferring to prescribe and enforce the responsibilities of family members to each other rather than step into their shoes and replace them. The Maintenance Act stipulated that it was the legal obligation of "fathers, husbands and other near relatives" to provide "means of support" to their "wives and families" left destitute as a result of death, sickness, desertion, or neglect. Further, any husband or father who "unlawfully" deserted his wife or children could be arrested on warrant and summoned before the court to face a fine, a term of imprisonment, a maintenance order, and/or have his property seized. The act explicitly included illegitimate children in its purview, deeming them covered so long as there was evidence of paternity beyond the mere "oath of the mother."

Women were largely "protected" and restricted as dependents by legislatures and the courts, not enabled or encouraged as economic equals. In 1858, South Australia passed crucial divorce and judicial separation reforms, largely modeled on an English act, allowing men to divorce if their wife committed adultery, and women the same right—though only if the husband's adultery were combined with aggravating circumstances (incest, bigamy, and/or cruelty). One member of the South Australian parliament, Thomas Reynolds, sought to remove such aggravating circumstances, to "place a female on the same footing as a man," believing adultery to be morally equivalent for both husbands and wives.[10] But he did not succeed. There was generally far less social and judicial tolerance for women who breached feminine expectations of chastity, loyalty, or obedience.

However, the same Act also heralded a step towards economic independence for women, allowing a deserted woman the ability to seek a protection order over property she earned or acquired during her husband's absence. South Australia demonstrated an ambivalent and oscillating attitude between containing women within the dependence of matrimony and allowing them some legal and economic autonomy. The government envisioned itself as simultaneously progressive and paternalistic. In 1845,

South Australia was also on the front foot in allowing married women the ability to sell and will their property under the terms of the Married Women Conveyances Act. This was further bolstered by the Married Women's Property Act in 1883.

South Australia's sexual slander cases brought by women, and the subsequent slander of women reforms passed in 1863 and 1865, must be read in the context of the social, political, and legal institutions' unique emphasis upon regulating and managing marriage and the family. Accusations of adultery or unchastity threatened the formation of marital unions and thus South Australia's prosperity and population growth. Sexual slander was an infliction upon the exceptional reputation of and projected plans for the colony—as a uniquely romantic, moral, and patrician society—as much as upon the characters and circumstances of the individual women involved. Sexual slander threatened the formation of marriages, but it could also be cured via matrimony. In court cases where women lost due to the burdens and trials of proving special damage, the loyalty and actions of husbands or fiancés in confirming the unions became a crucial mechanism for removing aspersions on women's reputations and recuperating their status. It took a failed case involving a single professional woman, "defenceless" and bereft of a "natural guardian," for reform arguments to gain traction. Marriage was the preferred answer to the problem of slandered women, as it was for so many questions in South Australia. But the law would step in if necessary—demonstrating South Australia's distinctive approach of romantic paternalism combined with progressive reforms.

As Carol Bacchi has argued, South Australia's status as one of the first places in the world to give women the vote (1894) does not clash with, so much as result from, its emphasis and embrace of domestic ideology and a belief that women were purer, morally superior, and more reliable. Between 1840 and 1870, women married at lower ages and higher rates than in other Australian colonies, produced more children, and were less likely to engage in paid work. Bacchi writes that waves of reform legislation that affected women in nineteenth-century South Australia were less influenced by a burgeoning women's movement than by establishing and defending the essential family unit—mother and child—from deviant or irresponsible men.[11] In fact, these two strands were linked. Progressivism enshrined middle-class conservative values. Women's votes and voices would represent "The Home."

Slander of women cases were high-profile affairs in South Australia and were covered in great detail by the press. The first such case was brought in 1856: the same year the colony became self-governing and manhood suffrage was introduced. It was brought by Lucy Inskip, a young and unmarried migrant from Hertfordshire, England, who lived with her brother Thomas (a butcher) in the suburb of Unley.[12] Inskip sued Mary Swailes (the wife of an innkeeper) in the Supreme Court of South Australia.[13] According to court reports, the dispute originated with a paragraph published in the *Adelaide Observer* in January 1856, titled "An Ugly Rumour," written by reporter Patrick Parkinson:

> During the last week we heard from various parties that the inhabitants of a suburban village were in a great state of excitement in consequence of the strange birth and still stranger disappearance of a child in that locality. What causes the affair to have an interest almost horrible is the fact that the parties who reside in the house where the circumstance is said to have occurred are brother and sister. The police cannot be ignorant of the rumours that are afloat. We hope, therefore, that the matter will shortly be set to rest by a rigid enquiry in the proper quarter.[14]

The plaintiff alleged that the defendant, Swailes, bandied about the newspaper report to others in the community, naming the Inskips as the incestuous parties. She apparently stated: "Miss Inskip has a baby. Dr. Francis is now with her. It is a young butcher and her brother is the father."[15] Many others were also implicated in the transmission of the gossip, such as Mathew Cranston (a surveyor), John Gray (a horse dealer), William Crossman (a butcher), and a man named simply Angel. The slander spread thick and fast.

It seemed suspicion had fallen on Inskip due to her confinement in bed and attendance by a physician while recovering from "inflammation of the chest."[16] Represented by the advocate-general, Richard Hanson, Inskip sought compensation for the "double slander" of "unchastity" and "incest," stating that the rumors "greatly affected her prospects and wellbeing" and caused her "great distress and anguish of mind." Hanson, a British-trained lawyer and soon to be the fourth premier of South Australia, was well aware of English law on the subject and the burden of proving not only the utterance of the words by the defendant and their falsity, but also "some damage resulting from them." He confessed that he had always thought such English laws were "needlessly refined" in this way.[17] Nonetheless he stated that he could prove such damage in these circumstances. Hanson summoned John Hearn, "a respectable man," a gardener and widower, to testify that he became engaged to Inskip in December 1855 and was due to marry her three weeks later in January. Hearn stated that he then became privy to the rumors circulating about her and chose to visit Inskip several times seeking the truth. However, Inskip refused to see him (apparently on account of her sickness), which heightened his suspicions. Hearn questioned an attending nurse about what kind of child had been born, to which she oddly replied: "One that would not want feeding," alluding perhaps to a stillborn. Hearn broke off their engagement and subsequently received a letter from Inskip's lawyer threatening him with breach of promise to marry. Nonetheless, he stated to the court: "law or no law, he would have no more to do with the woman."[18]

Hanson explained to the jury some of the many difficulties facing this case, including the defendant's decision to plead "not guilty" on the basis of special damage, as opposed to trying to prove the truth of the rumors. Only if Swailes pleaded "justification"—that is, truth—could Inskip then bring "forward evidence of a medical man and a nurse who could completely disprove the slander." He reasserted her "innocence"—though he was stopped from proving it—and pressed the all-male jury in the slander case to do their paternal duty, asking them to consider how they "as men and brothers," would feel if their own unmarried sisters were charged in that manner with having had a child and that they were the father. By regarding the matter in that "proper light," Hanson argued, they would have no difficulty in fixing a fair measure of damages for slander "so baseless and malignant."[19]

Represented by James Hurtle Fisher, the defendant constructed her case upon two grounds. First, that although such slander was a "great evil," the plaintiff must show special damage—that her broken engagement was a direct result of the defendant's words, and this she could not do.[20] Fisher questioned Hearn's credibility, remarking that he demonstrated "extraordinary apathy" and "indifference" when confronted with such vicious rumors about his fiancée and Inskip's refusal to see him the very week they were supposed to be married.[21] But if the jury were to find the broken engagement was caused by the rumors, he submitted, there was no evidence connecting those rumors with Swailes, for she had merely repeated "rumours in the village alehouse." Hearn confessed that he had in fact first heard the slander from a man named Angel.

In summing up to the jury, English-appointed Justice Benjamin Boothby—soon to spark controversy by insisting on his appointment as chief justice and his actions usurping the role of jury in a criminal trial—did not hold back in sharing his opinions on the matter. It was clear the words were spoken, he stated, and the defendant had no right to promulgate them even if they were already circulating. He advised the jury to consider the damage occasioned by loss of marriage, but also the "annoyance and pain" that such a report would occasion to a young woman. "It was their duty as jurors, and as men," he declared, "to protect as far as possible the chastity of women."[22] Women, he pressed, "should know that virtue would be upheld" by the courts, especially as "[w]omen could not sit as Jurors." Expressing ample sympathy with Inskip, he also asked the jury to consider the terrible choices confronting her. In order to clear her name, she had been forced to "publish to the whole world that she was the young woman who had been accused of the unnatural crime of incest," and a person of whom "horrible things were said." Boothby explained that "he could not help expressing those opinions, relating as they did to the true interests of society."[23] Boothby's affective appeal to the jury's sense of social duty worked. They returned a sizable verdict of 300 pounds for Lucy Inskip.

However, Swailes appealed and won a new trial. Fisher, her lawyer, argued that no evidence during the trial established that Hearn's decision to break off his engagement to Inskip was the direct result of the defendant's actions. English law—as set out in the 1830 decision of *Ward v Weeks*—required that the plaintiff must show the special damage was caused by the defendant's words (not by another person simply repeating the slander).[24] This Inskip could not do because evidence in the first trial demonstrated no link between Swailes's tongue and Hearn's decision. Fisher also petitioned the court on a second point. He argued that Boothby had mistakenly advised the first jury to consider the myriad of terrible choices and circumstances facing Inskip when they decided her fate and awarded her compensation. In other words, Boothby erred in expressing too much sympathy for the plaintiff. Instead, Fisher submitted, the judge should have told the jury to merely calculate the material losses Inskip incurred from the broken engagement, that is, her special damage only. Chief

Justice Cooper shot back: "Well, a marriage cannot be broken off from such a cause without, as the learned judge has stated, great distress of mind, anxiety and a sense of unmerited degradation. All those circumstances... might be put to the jury."[25] A new trial was granted, but only upon the first ground—the ambiguous nexus of causation between the special damage and the defendant's words.

The *South Australian Register*, reporting on the new trial in June 1856, stated: "In that case, as in others, the requirements of the law were different from the requirements of common sense."[26] It is important to note that legal points about the relationship between damage sustained and the words uttered was only necessary to slander cases involving spiritual imputations, such as unchastity. If Inskip had been accused of being a thief, the slander itself would have been actionable, and the technicalities of loss (its type and issues of causation) would have been irrelevant. The technicalities of special damage were almost fatal to Inskip's second trial, but Justice Boothby, perceiving her legal vulnerability, intervened again and declared that the parties should simply settle and find a compromise that prioritized "vindication of character."[27] This they did, Inskip and Swailes agreeing that the latter would state her conviction that the report about incest was false and unfounded, and express her regret at having circulated it. During the second trial, the reporter Parkinson also came forth, swearing that his "Ugly Rumour" article in the *Adelaide Observer* neither pertained to the suburb of Unley, nor the plaintiff and her brother.

Inskip received no compensation from Swailes or others over the vicious gossip that made her notorious, not only within the community but within the wider province by virtue of her two drawn out and highly publicized trials in the Supreme Court of South Australia. She was also forced to pay her own legal costs, which would have been significant. However, by virtue of Justice Boothby's paternalistic overreach and her fiancé's loyalty, she did manage to re-establish her respectability and recover from—in Chief Justice Cooper's words—her "unmerited degradation." On November 5, 1856, Lucy Inskip and John Hearn married.[28]

In 1862, another similar sexual slander case in South Australia attracted substantial attention. Elizabeth Bell, a young housemaid at the Adelaide Hotel on Hindley Street, brought a case against Joseph Allen, son of the hotel's proprietor Mary Ann Richards, for making comments impugning her chastity.[29] During the trial, Bell pleaded that on numerous occasions while she was working as a maid, Allen attempted to "take liberties with her, which she resisted," and as a consequence for her "discouraging him," he forcefully threatened to take revenge.[30] This he did by seeking out her fiancé, Frederick William Deighton, and other acquaintances, and—with "gross and obscene words"—making allegations about Bell's sexual behavior.[31] Evidence was also given that sometime before Allen spread the rumors, Bell left her employment and lodgings at the hotel and moved in with another woman nearby, Mrs. Crosby. This was likely a result of the sexual harassment or assaults she endured at the hands of the defendant. According to Bell, the aspersions cast by Allen reportedly induced Deighton to break off their engagement. Deighton and Bell's solicitors confronted Allen numerous times and asked him to retract his scandalous and abusive comments. Allen refused.

In court, Allen and his mother both emphatically denied that he had ever uttered slanderous words about the plaintiff. Instead, Richards suggested that Deighton and Bell had simply initiated the court case due to "ill feeling" occasioned by Richards' refusing to lend Deighton a carriage. Richards stated that she had annoyed Deighton on one instance when she told him she would not lend him her "cart" to "drive the Diamond about," referring to the plaintiff.[32] Allen's lawyers, William Wigley and Attorney General Randolph Stow, submitted the defense's case on two grounds: first, that Allen had not said the words alleged; second, even if he had, no special damage resulted as Deighton was still enamored with and committed to marrying Bell.

This second argument emanated from the evidence given by Deighton, wherein he testified that he didn't believe a word of what Allen had said and would marry Bell as soon as the jury removed the "stain" from her character. This testimony—proffered by Deighton naïvely in the hope of defending and supporting Bell, as well as evidence that they had been seen picnicking together at the Botanic Gardens and that he had funded her court action—were problematic for Bell's case. His continuing affections and disbelief of the rumors put her necessary proof of economic loss in question. As Wigley and Stow plainly put it, there should be a nonsuit as the agreement to marry was still subsisting.

The special damage argument was a sizable impediment to Bell's suc-

CHAPTER FIVE

cess. So, like Justice Boothby in Inskip's case, Bell's lawyer—George Hartley Giles—attempted to distract the jurors by appealing to their sense of justice and responsibility as "men of the colony." He argued that

> the defendant had been guilty of a gross slander, and called upon the jury, in justice to the plaintiff, as well as their duty to the country, to give verdict for the plaintiff, which he hoped would act as a salutary check upon a vice too common in the colony, practised by evil disposed men in slandering the character of modest and virtuous young women.[33]

Giles was not a lawyer of considerable reputation or ability. Son of William Giles—a prominent politician and manager of the South Australian Company—George Giles was only admitted to the Supreme Court in 1862 and soon became entangled in charges of misappropriation of funds, before being struck off the legal roll.

It took only ten minutes for the jury to return a verdict for the defendant. On September 5, 1862, Elizabeth Bell lost her case and was forced to pay both her and Allen's costs, a large sum she could not afford. A couple of months later, Bell appeared in the Insolvency Court, seeking relief. The record cites her debts as 35 pounds and her assets as nil. It states:

> The insolvent is a domestic servant. The debts she comes to this court to be relieved from are the defendants' costs in two actions brought by her against Joseph Allen and Mary Ann Richards for slander, and in the first of which the verdict went against her, and the second was not taken to trial.[34]

Bell was partially relieved by the court from paying Allen and Richards. Importantly, however, as suspected by the defense's legal team, Bell's loss did not cost her relationship with Deighton. Despite being unable to clear her name, they married and went on to have one son. Bell suffered financial hardship as a result of the slander, but her status and respectability were recuperated via marriage.

During the Bell trial, political interest in the issue of the slander of women and inadequacy of current laws—inherited from England—gathered force in South Australia. In fact, on Tuesday, September 30, 1862, only five years after the formation of the South Australian parliament, thirty-one-year-old James Boucaut (a member of the General Assembly who would go on to become the youngest ever premier of South Australia) introduced the first bill to amend the law of slander.[35] However, the bill was withdrawn when Boucaut was defeated in a general election.

Salacious gossip and slurs on women's chastity put romantic unions—the cultural and legal bedrock of respectable society in South Australia—at risk. The "good old natural fashion" of young people taking a liking for each other, partaking in courtship, and being "bound together for life"—as articulated by Catherine Spence—was disrupted and derailed by casual accusations of sexual immorality, especially when the law provided insufficient remedy. The only option—if the courts could not rescue a woman's name due to "overly refined" laws—was the confirmation of her status via marriage. Both Inskip and Bell lost their court actions but managed to recover their respectability via marriage, to Hearn and Deighton, respectively. The special damage rules that plagued the English law of slander and made it harder for women to vindicate their reputations pushed them further towards dependency on matrimony and paternalism. Claims to status and respectability could only be validated and proved by a fiancé or husband's loyalty. Women could not, independently, seek to restrain others' verbal abuse using the courts. The inadequacy of this situation—its limits and losses—would become more apparent and pronounced when the next high-profile case was brought by a woman occupying different social and economic circumstances.

In 1863, a high-profile case garnered substantial public interest and pushed South Australia to reform the English common law of slander. Lauded public vocalist ("encored at every song"), singing teacher, and young widow Suzanna Wishart brought an action against rival performer Catherine Peryman for the latter's comments that she was a "bad woman" who spent her nights with many men.[36] During one alleged instance of slander, Peryman stated to a mutual contact and booking agent, Mr Crossman: "Mr. Schmitt and Mr. Linly Norman both passed the night in the same bedroom as Mrs. Wishart ... and she is such an infamous character that I have refused to sing with her at concerts and none of the lady singers will sing with her."[37] Peryman also told various others that Wishart was not, in fact, a widow but her husband had left due to her "immoral conduct." Other serious allegations of sexual immorality were made by Mrs. Peryman but were not reported by the newspapers as they were deemed "unfit for publication."[38] Wishart claimed that as a result of Peryman's malicious slander and attacks, she lost all business, "had no other means of obtaining a livelihood," and was left penniless. She claimed 100 pounds in damages.

Wishart was represented by Richard Bullock Andrews, an esteemed lawyer, who would become attorney general just a month later in July 1863. He was described as "amiable and kind-hearted," a naturally "diffident" man who became an advocate for those who "really needed help."[39] Andrews argued that Wishart was the victim of "wicked jealousy" incited in Peryman during a particular concert in Gawler Town wherein Wishart's every song was applauded and encored and yet Peryman's performance was "not so well received."[40] The ruinous slurs, he submitted, "crept very quietly into circulation," until the defendant passed them on one night to Mrs. Hill, a friend of Wishart's aunt, who then confronted Peryman about the matter. Andrews expressed deep sympathy for the plaintiff, describing her tragically and notably as being "deprived of her natural guardian," her husband, and so now seeking the support and intervention of the courts.[41]

Andrews knew about the strict special damage burden of such slanders and so attempted to wrangle a hybrid legal argument from the facts before him. It was only important, he stated, to inquire whether the words spoken interfered in preventing the plaintiff from exercising her "profession as a singer." He characterized the case as one involving slander affecting one's trade or profession—a traditional masculine category of English slander without the requirement of proving special damage. However, Andrews also hedged his bets by setting out that if special damage was required, evidence furnished at the trial demonstrated Wishart had been "deprived of other engagements at concerts" in Adelaide.

But the defense, led by Attorney General Randolph Stow, would have none of these novel and creative arguments. Cases involving imputations of sexual immorality were classed as spiritual transgressions at English common law, he asserted, and thus required special damage of a particular type for women: a broken engagement. Clearly Wishart could not prove such a loss. He therefore moved to nonsuit her, submitting that as she was injured in a private capacity relating to her sexual morality, and not a professional capacity (that is, concerning her skills as a singer), there was no action at common law.

In response, the plaintiff's counsel argued that imputations of bad conduct and bad character also inferred "unfitness for her profession."[42] However, Magistrate MacDonald agreed reluctantly with the defense, declaring that "the words complained of did not attack Mrs. Wishart in the way of her profession":

> If it had been said that Mrs. Wishart had no voice; that her conduct was so disagreeable that the other singers could not associate with her, or that her habits were so intemperate that she was incapable of performing her part, then these words would come within the rule established by the decided cases, and would be malicious slander.[43]

Wishart's action was quashed, with a costs order against her.[44]

The case, coming just after Elizabeth Bell's publicized defeat and involving two high-profile singers in Adelaide, attracted attention, and the outcome induced community outrage. A letter to the editor of the *South Australian Advertiser*, signed anonymously as A Defender of the Defenceless, on June 6, 1863, read:

> On the trial for slander, *Wishart v Peryman*, the plaintiff was nonsuited owing to the want of sufficient proof of "special damage." I wish to know whether we are to conclude from this that however much a woman's reputation is assailed she cannot get redress unless she can prove pecuniary loss? If so, then, indeed, may slanderers go with added zest to their foul work, knowing their victims are utterly helpless.[45]

And on June 27, 1863, in a column titled "Legal Anomalies," commentators in the *Adelaide Observer* took aim at the case and the English common law regarding slander and the special damage upon which it rested:

> We have no hesitation in saying such a law is unjust, irrational and cruel.... A person may say of a public singer that her conduct is such as to exclude her from the society of the pure and virtuous, and she had no redress; but if it be said that she croaks like a raven instead of singing like a nightingale, an action for damage will lie.[46]

They went on to comment that "such a law ... is a monstrous anomaly" as to a "virtuous and pure-minded man or woman a charge of professional incapacity, however detrimental that may be, is as nothing compared to one against character." The authors concluded by declaring that "there is something egregiously wrong either about the laws by which we are governed, or about the manner in which those laws are administered."[47]

Like Bell, Wishart had problems paying the costs order against her for

11 pounds. On July 1, her father came before the court seeking the return of his property that Peryman had acquired to satisfy Wishart's debts. On July 15, Wishart was summoned to court to account for failure to pay Peryman's costs. She testified that she was destitute, living in her father's house, and entirely dependent upon him for necessities since her name had been ruined. She stated that previously she had earned an annual income of 100 pounds but now "had no pupils and no professional engagements at concerts."[48] The court, confronted by the consequences of its own unjust laws, forgave Wishart her debts and declined to grant Peryman a new costs order against her.

Outrage over the *Wishart* decision captured the attention of the legislature, and a couple of months later, on October 1, 1863, member of the South Australian Legislative Assembly, William Bakewell, introduced a bill to "remedy a defect in the law of slander" because, he stated, "[a] virtuous woman's reputation for chastity might be assailed and she would have no remedy for the slander unless she was a governess."[49] Despite his legal training, this was a misunderstanding of the law by Bakewell: being a governess would not make the slander actionable (as the New South Wales case of Harriet Spencer attested). Nonetheless, his point was sound. Gossip or abuse that undermined a woman's good name could have far-reaching consequences for her social status, marriageability, and economic prospects within the colony. And without legal recourse, she could only rely on her "natural guardian"—a husband or husband to be—to vouch for her respectability through his loyalty, as Hearn and Deighton had done for Inskip and Bell. Women without matrimonial ties risked becoming destitute, despite their virtues, talents, and hard work, as illustrated by Wishart's predicament. Bakewell's bill would potentially untie a woman's reputation from the necessities of matrimony. The courts would effectively stand in and become the defenders of the "defenceless," as the author of the letter to the editor had proposed.

Some members of the House queried whether Bakewell's bill would unwisely increase litigation in the colony. Charles Bagot—mining investor and fierce temperance advocate—feared that the bill would mean "every trivial quarrel," "hasty words," or "verbal abuse" would become the basis for a civil action to recover damages. He asserted that a "high-principled lady would not take an action into Court for a few words that were said about her character."[50] But Bakewell urged that "The case of Wishart v Peryman proved the necessity for the Bill."[51] In that instance, he went on, "the character of a lady, against whom a word had never been said, was traduced by a professional rival, and although it had been proved that defamatory and slanderous words were used, yet by the law the magistrates were bound to say the plaintiff had no ground of action." Bakewell also referred to Lord Campbell's Select Committee recommendations in 1843, which he stated were "unfortunately" not passed by the House of Commons. Due to concerns about vexatious litigation, the attorney general suggested it be amended to include provision for an apology, to prevent a "malicious person taking advantage of a hasty expression." This was, however, rejected, as "an apology was not always a sufficient remedy for the mischief done." Reporting on this proposed "important" amendment to the law, the *South Australian Register* set out the clauses in full and commented that it was "evidently intended to meet that deficiency in the law relating to slander which was lately made apparent in the Adelaide local court."[52] Wishart's decision to go to court was the impetus for reform.

The Defamatory Words Bill passed the Assembly and went to the Legislative Council for consideration, where liberal merchant, thirty-nine-year-old George Marsden Waterhouse commended it, criticized the common law of slander for not punishing those who called a woman a prostitute, and declared that "such a state of law was not tolerated in any other country, and should not be in this."[53] It is likely that Waterhouse was referring to the United States, in which the slander of women reforms originated and were rapidly spreading. Waterhouse was familiar with the United States, having traveled there extensively during 1855 to discuss customs reciprocity between the British colonies and America.[54] At a dinner in Waterhouse's honor in Adelaide, just prior to his departure overseas, the host, Dr. Ward, addressed him:

> You are still a young man and have time and activity at your command to enable you to search into the records for by-gone ages, as well as for studying recent legislation. We trust you will be spared to traverse the old as well as the new world, and after having contrasted the effects of despotism with liberal legislation, that you will return to your adopted land imbued with practical wisdom, a still wiser, a still better, and a still more useful man.[55]

On his return, Waterhouse championed the slander reforms as progressive legislation appropriate to the new world.

However, as in the assembly, various objections were raised in the Legislative Council to the bill's potential to increase frivolous litigation in the colony. John Baker, pastoralist and second premier of the state in 1857, countered that adding a provision for the defendant to make an apology at any time to settle the matter would suffice. He supported the bill, considering it a "just measure," "especially to protect the reputation of females."[56] He referred to Wishart's case as a strong example of its necessity, "where a professional female had been slandered with impunity through the present defective state of the law."[57] The bill was passed. Clause 1 read: "Any person who shall, without just cause, speak and publish any defamatory words, tending to injure the reputation of another shall be liable to an action for defamation."[58] There was no need to prove any special damage.

The 1863 act was gender neutral. Soon, two cases—both brought by men—would challenge its legitimacy and question its purpose. Dr. Carle Muecke, a clergyman in the Lutheran Church in Tanunda, accused Carl Roundfeldt, a local farmer and member of Muecke's congregation, of slander.[59] According to court testimony, a discussion arose connected to a lawsuit concerning church deeds, wherein Roundfeldt told witnesses that Muecke had induced Roundfeldt to commit perjury. Subsequently, Roundfeldt also called Muecke "a liar" repeatedly in front of the congregation. According to court documents, the slanders caused the plaintiff to be "greatly injured and brought into disgrace, discredit and disrespect."

However, those feelings or consequences alone would not have previously sufficed as the basis for a slander action in South Australia. Muecke's lawyer, Randolph Stow, knew this and introduced the court and jury to the Defamatory Words Act of 1863, which

> he considered . . . was a very proper amendment of the law, because through the state of the law previous to the passing of that Act a person might slander a woman and declare and publish that she was not chaste, and would not be actionable, and many gross cases had gone unpunished in this colony in consequence of the defective state of the law.[60]

Here, however, as Stow contended, it was not the reputation of a chaste woman at stake, but "a man who lived for many years amongst neighbours by whom he was honored and respected" and who was "respected throughout the colony." Previously, in such circumstances, Muecke would have been required to prove special damage, but now, seemingly, he did not.

Stow believed he was presenting an unbeatable case. But Justice Boothby was not convinced. To him, the act of 1863 did not repeal the whole common law of defamation but merely amended it with regards to the specific issue of special damage. Therefore, Roundfeldt's words were protected by the doctrine of qualified privilege (a defense where someone believed themselves under a duty to communicate) unless Stow could show Roundfeldt was actuated by malice. Unable to substantiate malice, Muecke lost his case at first instance. A couple of months later, Stow filed for and won a retrial on the grounds that malice need not be proved, and even if it must, the circumstances of Roundfeldt repeatedly shouting that Muecke was a liar within the congregation were sufficient. The defendant pressed, alternatively, that Roundfeldt was simply moved by excitement. Much discussion in the retrial concerned conflicting and confused interpretations of the 1863 act—its intention and effect. The three justices retired to consider the verdict and then confirmed the initial decision for the defendant.

On November 8, 1864, the *South Australian Register* published a prominent opinion piece titled "The Law of Defamation," criticizing the Supreme Court's handling of the *Muecke* matter and pointing to the legal uncertainty around slander law in South Australia occasioned by the 1863 Bakewell Act.[61] The author described the present lack of legal clarity as a "grave moment" for the colony and declared that to "all right-minded persons reputation is far more important than any other consideration." But this was more than an issue of personal harm. Preserving the reputations of individuals from "false impeachment" was a "duty imperatively demanded of the guardians of public morality and conservators of the peace, order and good governance of the state." Calumniators should receive substantial punishment unless "very special circumstances" could be shown. They pushed for "further legislative action" to ensure that the "safeguard against slander that the Parliament intended to provide should be rendered effectual."

In the same month, another slander case was brought by a man in the Supreme Court. Unusually, it concerned sexual allegations. The plaintiff complained that the defendant had told others that he had committed adultery with his stepdaughter, injuring his otherwise "good character" and bringing him into "scandal and disgrace."[62] The defendant tried to have the case thrown out on the basis of the *Muecke* decision, arguing that the 1863 Bakewell Act had not effectively changed the law and so the plaintiff would need to prove special damage in order to succeed. Another long debate ensued concerning the meaning and implications of the Act. Mr. Way, acting for the defendant, submitted strongly that the legislature had clearly not meant to bring the law of slander into line with libel, or they would have explicitly said so. Drawing upon numerous examples of men slandered—a teetotaler accused of drinking wine, a man "who personally had an abhorrence of the Theatre" then being seen there—Mr. Way argued that the 1863 act should be regarded as changing little. However, Justice Gwynne determined that the present case was "correlative of imputing adultery to a married woman and want of chastity to a female" and that such words not being actionable "has always been a blot upon the law."[63] Mr. Way's demurral failed, and the plaintiff succeeded.

The following year, Stephens brought yet another slander case against Verner.[64] This time it concerned slanderous accusations by Verner that Stephens was the father of his stepdaughter's child. By this time, it seems his wife's daughter had given birth. Stephens's legal team clearly thought the case would proceed in line with the stepdaughter case (above) and thus return a favorable verdict. They did not take into account Justice Boothby's own "very strong views on the matter."[65] Absent from the first trial, but interventionist and strong-willed, Boothby took the opportunity to slap down Stephens's case on the basis that he did not show the words "were calculate[d] to injure" him, as required by the 1863 act; and—importantly—that the act had not altered English law with regards to sexual misconduct slander.

Justice Gwynne stated that "his opinion was that both by the law of England and the law of this colony if a man was accused of committing adultery it was not actionable without special damage."[66] Seeming to contradict his previous interpretation of the law, Justice Gwynne's position can only be understood as deeming it inappropriate that men should be protected via such legislation. Boothby's interpretation was more rigid and critical. Removing the burden of proving special damage when bringing a case for sexual misconduct slander was ill-advised, he said, and "if the Legislature intended bringing about such a state of law as was suggested, they were in reality bringing about the dissolution of society."[67] In supporting the nonsuit, Boothby declared:

If such words spoken by men were to be made the grounds of actions, the chastity of women and all other circumstances would be made the subject of discussion in the Supreme Court, and it would introduce a state of society which every right-thinking person would be shocked at.[68]

Boothby cleared favored the private resolution of such matters, via agreement or the act of marriage.

In May 1865, James Boucaut, newly elected to the South Australian House of Assembly as the member for West Adelaide, and with a "sound knowledge of the common law," introduced another bill attempting to reform the law of slander.[69] He explained that whereas Bakewell had attempted to do too much and had thus done nothing but cause confusion, his bill concerned itself with the primary and particular problem at hand: "protecting a woman accused of a want of chastity." Referring to the case brought by Inskip, he reminded the House that "cases had occurred in this colony where women accused of incest had been unable to bring the accuser to justice."[70] Boucaut did not think a gender-neutral bill like Bakewell's was desirable as it would increase litigation without any corresponding social justification. Men did not need recourse to the courts for sexual slurs cast on them. In a recent case, he explained, referring to *Stephens*, two justices of the Supreme Court had held that Bakewell's act was useless and granted no more rights than the common law. Surely, he opined, "the House would agree with him that a woman charged with unchastity should have a remedy."[71] He quoted Lord Campbell's words, after the failure of his own bill in England, that the "existing state of law" was "cruel and disgraceful to a civilised community."[72]

During debate in the Legislative Council, seventy-six-year-old George Fife Angas raised several concerns about the bill. Angas—prominent in founding South Australia, puritanical, and conservative—was an elitist who opposed manhood suffrage and was openly hostile to the migration of Roman Catholics, especially "pauper girls." His views on sexual slander reflected his other political and cultural positions.[73] "Women of unchaste character, as well as virtuous women, could take advantage of this Bill," he warned.[74] Charles Bonney responded that he did not think it right that protection should be withheld from "chaste women" because "unvirtuous women" might use its provisions. Angas, unimpressed, also questioned (to a resounding response—"Hear, Hear") why the bill had only one purpose and "why male chastity should not be protected as well as female virtue."[75] Seventy-seven-year-old Charles Bagot had similar worries. On the one hand, "he was very anxious to give protection to every person," not just women, but was also concerned that, "under this Bill, the commonest streetwalker if called a whore might bring an action."[76] Edward McEllister, who failed to be elected to the Legislative Assembly because of his support for compulsory Bible studies in state schools, was similarly disposed. The bill, if passed, would "put a dangerous power into the hands of a certain class of females."[77] William Peacock, businessman, replied that "it had been clearly shown that a certain class of individuals required protection and he should afford that protection by supporting the Bill." Forty-year-old Thomas Magarey agreed, remembering the case brought by "a lady professor of music" slandered about two years ago who could recover no remedy.[78] The ages of the members of parliament seem to have shaped their views. The older generation opposed the bill; the younger members supported it as a necessary and progressive reform.

South Australia's Slander of Women Act passed. Clause 1 repealed Bakewell's act in full. Clause 2 stated: "Words spoken and published of any woman imputing to her a want of chastity, shall be and shall be deemed to be slander, and an action shall be sustainable for such words in the same manner and to the same extent as for words charging an indictable offence."[79] It was the first gender-specific defamation legislation passed in the Australian colonies.

SIX

STAINED WHITENESS AND
THE CULT OF TRUE WOMANHOOD

New York

In 1863, George Waterhouse supported South Australia's slander reforms after being inspired by his visit to the new world of the United States. By that time, over a dozen states in the republic had changed their laws of sexual slander for women.[1] But, despite advocacy efforts, New York was not one of them. In May 1825, John Whitefield Hulbert, a Harvard lawyer and member of the New York Assembly, gave a rousing speech titled "The Slander of Females" that was published in newspapers and commended across the United States.[2] "Nothing is more delicate than the female character," he declared. "Once stain that character, and sooner shall the Ethiopian change his skin, or the leopard change his spots, yes, sooner shall wool dyed with the scarlet become white again, than that stain shall be washed away."[3] Metaphors and imagery of women's innocence and purity being sullied and stained by the scourge of slander pervaded his address. Frail and delicate, "females" without better protection would "wither and die" when subject to the "envenomed shafts of calumny." He called upon "all gallant and honourable men" to think of the wives of their bosom and the daughters they love by passing legislation to make it easier for women to sue for sexual slander. In many ways, rhetoric for reforming slander law in New York—enjoining white men to protect the unsullied innocence of their wives and daughters—aligned with that used in early North Carolina. However, whereas North Carolina was the very first state to enact a

Slander of Women Act (in 1808), New York would be one of the last in the United States, steadfastly sticking to English common law until 1871. This legislative lag led to slander reform in New York becoming entwined with the nineteenth-century cult of domesticity.

Hulbert's highly emotive and popular speech evoked ideals of true womanhood—piety, purity, submission, and domesticity—and connected the slander of women cause to their necessary protection and cultivation. As Barbara Welter described in her landmark article, the true woman emerged as a trope within magazines and other literature during the first half of the nineteenth century in the United States to become a pervasive figure of reverence and refrain.[4] To Hulbert and other nineteenth-century commentators, the "cold blooded slanderer" with his "assassin tongue"—conjured as a ghastly and malicious male monster—posed an existential threat to the true woman.[5] With her purity destroyed, domestic duties disrupted, and facing destitution, woman was injured by slander that placed these ideas of "civilized" femininity at risk. American women and girls, positioned as innocent and dependent, with characters "as pure as driven snow," were being unjustly "stained" by allegations of adultery, unchastity, and prostitution. Vivid imagery aligned idealized feminine virtues and sexual purity with whiteness, and social disgrace with discoloring and contamination, demonstrating the extent to which racial purity and sexual morality were discursively intertwined and mutually formative for white womanhood in this period.

As historians have noted since Welter's publication, the true woman mythologized a particular type of femininity and excluded or demeaned the experiences of women of other backgrounds—Black, poor, and/or those engaged in paid work.[6] This chapter demonstrates how jurists, legislators, and commentators in the northern United States invoked the figure of the true woman to argue for slander reform. Removing the burden of proving special damage, enshrined within English law, would indeed make it easier for women to defend their reputations for piety, purity, and chastity. It would also enable them to bleach unwarranted stains from their characters. Thus by evoking the idea of the true woman, slander of women reforms in New York not only constructed sexual morality as white women's primary purpose—but also as their exclusive possession and privilege. Unlike Georgia, which enacted slander of women laws referring explicitly to race, New York's alignment of whiteness and purity was implied, though no less important.

Hulbert's speech was spurred by his outrage over two cases heard before the Supreme Court of New York. The first, in 1807, concerned "words spoken" by a man, Mr. Gillespie, charging a married woman, Mrs. Buys, with adultery.[7] Mrs. Buys brought a slander suit jointly with her husband, as was legally required at the time. But Gillespie's attorneys immediately pushed to have her case dismissed. Adultery was not a crime in New York, they argued, but merely a spiritual matter. Therefore, in order to bring an action over such words at common law, they argued, Mrs. Buys had to prove special damage, which she had not done. The laws of England, they reminded the court, "were in force in this state."

In response, the plaintiffs' attorneys submitted that due to divorce laws, an accusation of adultery against Mrs. Buys put her at risk of serious financial peril if her good name was not vindicated. In 1787, New York had reformed its divorce laws, making adultery the sole ground for seeking a legal separation.[8] The attorneys for the Buyses argued:

> By this act, the marriage contract may be dissolved for adultery, and the adulteress not only loses her dower, but may be deprived of all support out of the estate of her husband, and is for ever disabled from marrying a second time. The consequence, therefore, of the act is a punishment and loss of property.[9]

However, despite Gillespie admitting to "the evil nature and injurious consequences" of the words he had spoken, his lawyers stood firm.[10] "No action lies in the common law courts for calling a woman a *whore* or *adulteress*," they stated.[11] Chief Justice Kent reluctantly agreed with Gillespie's attorneys, citing a British ruling that "such words are a great scandal, and for which, if we could, we would encourage an action, but the law has ordained otherwise."[12] Mrs. Buys's case was dismissed.

The *Buys* case highlights the connections and tensions between different legal doctrines governing women's lives in New York during the early nineteenth century. The common law doctrine of coverture determined that upon marriage a woman's legal personhood would be subsumed by that of her husband, disabling her from owning property, entering contracts, suing or being sued in her own name. From a legal standpoint, married women were "civilly dead."[13] This is why Mrs. Buys could not bring the slander suit in her own name, but also why being divorced on the basis of adultery would be so ruinous. Upon marriage, all property had vested in Mr. Buys via coverture, leaving Mrs. Buys only a legal right to dower, being the right to inherit a third of his assets upon his demise.[14] If Mr. Buys divorced her because of adultery, she would not be entitled to any maintenance from him, would be stopped from ever remarrying, and would lose her right to dower. Restrictive divorce laws in New York, which only allowed divorce on the ground of adultery, were the most onerous in the United States (except for South Carolina). They effectively locked spouses into marriages and by doing so reinforced married women's legal and economic incapacity and dependency.

In turn, the common law of slander bolstered these divorce laws, dramatically raising the stakes of an allegation of adultery against a woman. If she could not sue for slander imputing adultery, as Chief Justice Kent had effectively just declared, she could not redeem her reputation in the community, and her prospects dimmed considerably. In addition, it is not evident whether Mr. and Mrs. Buys had children, but if so, and Mr. Buys filed for divorce, he would almost certainly have been granted sole custody due to rules of paternal sovereignty, which were also tied to coverture.[15] At the beginning of the nineteenth century in the state of New York, laws of coverture knitted their way through interconnected doctrines of property, divorce, custody, and slander to create a perilous situation for married women. All it took was a slur of infidelity—made in earnest, annoyance, or vengeance—for one law to set off the next like a series of legal dominoes leading to destitution. The legacy of English common law made it almost impossible for married women to clear their besmirched names and placed them at considerable social and financial risk.

Just two years later, in 1809, another case came before the New York Supreme Court. Nancy Brooker, an unmarried young woman, brought a claim against Mr. Coffin after he uttered the "false, scandalous, and defamatory words" that she was "a common prostitute." He also pleaded that Brooker had been "hired to swear the child on him" (identify him under oath as the father of her unborn child); had given birth to "a child before this when she went to Canada" (meaning she had another child before the one she identified as the defendant's child); and "would come damn'd nigh going to the state prison" (meaning she was guilty of such "'enormous and wicked" crimes that she should be imprisoned).[16] The backstory to these allegations is unclear, but Brooker and Coffin were clearly known to each other. However, interestingly Coffin did not attempt to prove the allegations true. Rather, he objected to her slander suit on the basis that no special damage was shown, and no indictable crime had been imputed. This was an easier legal argument to advance than amassing evidence proving Brooker was, in fact, a prostitute.

At that time in New York, prostitutes were liable for punishment on the same basis as in England—for being "disorderly persons"—but that did not amount to committing an indictable or serious offense. Under the relevant statute, disorderly persons included "vagrants, beggars, jugglers, pretenders to physiognomy, palmistry, or such crafty sciences, fortune-tellers, discoverers of lost goods, persons running away from their wives and children, vagabonds and wanderers, and all idle persons not having visible means of livelihood."[17] It could not possibly be contended, Coffin's attorneys scoffed, that a person would be guilty of slander upon merely calling someone a juggler, fortune teller, or physiognomist. In addition, they argued that the other words allegedly spoken by Coffin about Brooker having had a child in Canada, accusing him falsely under oath of being the father of a child, and her being worthy of state prison were "too vague" to be considered legal slander.

The court agreed. Justice Spencer highlighted the legal quagmire facing them: "There is not, perhaps, so much uncertainty in the law upon any subject, as when words shall be in themselves actionable" for slander.[18] Faced with such uncertainty, the court stepped a cautious path, adopting the rules set out in English cases and approved in *Buys v Gillespie*. Only imputing an indictable offense to a person would be slanderous *per se*, they declared. The court was convinced by the defendant's argument that to hold otherwise would mean alleging a person engaged in physiognomy would be actionable, and that was too trivial. Judgment was given for the defendant, and Nancy Brooker lost her suit. But her case very quickly became highly respected authority across the United States for what constituted actionable slander.[19] For example, it was cited in the 1846 Georgia decision of *Pledger v Hathcock*, described in Chapter 4.

It is difficult to see why the imputation of prostitution was placed on an equal footing by the court with an accusation of someone being a juggler, a physiognomer, or merely an idler. For an unmarried woman to be labeled a prostitute meant much more than being reprimanded under the disorderly persons statute. It meant severely diminished prospects of respectable employment and—most important—marriageability. The year following *Brooker v Coffin*, a poem published in the local press titled "Blue-Ey'd Mary" again highlighted the stigma attached to allegations of unchastity for white women.[20] It told the story of a "meek" maid, forced into prostitution and a life of destitution after being seduced by a young man and becoming the subject of community gossip:

> But the fleece, when once stained, can know whiteness no more
> The aged folks whisper, the maidens look shy . . .
> Still of beauty possessed and not yet void of shame
> With a heart that recoils at a prostitute's name;
> She tries a service—her character's gone;
> And for skill at her needle, alas! 'Tis unknown!
> Pale Want now approaches—the pawn broker's near,
> And her trinkets and clothes, one-by-one disappear
> 'Till at length, sorely pinch'd, and quite desperate grown,
> The poor blue-ey'd Mary is forced on the town . . .

"Blue-Ey'd Mary" could "know whiteness no more." Not only were accusations of unchastity ruinous to the respectability and financial security of white women, but also to their racial purity. To lose one's character via allegations of sexual immorality or prostitution meant becoming stained and losing the status of white womanhood.

References to whiteness being stained by allegations or rumors of sexual immorality were pervasive in commentary about the slander of women in the United States in the nineteenth century. As historians Ibram Kendi and Nell Painter have demonstrated, this was a crucial period for establishing "whiteness" as a category, in both the US legal system and cultural imagination.[21] In his book *The Excellency of the Female Character Vindicated*, published in Philadelphia in 1808, Thomas Branagan warned his imagined women readers: "You should compare your character to a clean sheet of white paper, which, if once stained, will be always visibly unclean and unfit for use, unless for the most common purposes."[22] Such metaphors offered a vivid sense of what was at stake in slander actions brought by white women during the early nineteenth century in America. The imagery of stained white fleece or visibly unclean white paper conjured up sullied racial purity. The interlinking of racial and sexual purity is also evident in laws taxing interracial marriage in New York during this period and laws deeming "mulatto" children Black for the purpose of denying citizenship. As Leslie Harris has argued, these provisions also signified the linkage between the racial category of Black and lower-class social status and reinforced the cultural and monetary value of "whiteness."[23]

In New York, the "glacial" and "protracted" emancipation of enslaved people between 1790 and 1827 led to an intensification of the demonization of Blacks and determined segregation efforts by many whites in power.[24] Emancipation from slavery arguably strengthened consciousness of color and deepened racial discrimination. The language of staining was prevalent. Shane White cites Englishman William Strickland who, upon arriving in New York, remarked upon "the greater number of blacks particularly of women and children in the streets who may be seen of all shades until the *stain* is entirely worn out."[25] Similarly, publications such as *Godey's Lady's Book* (later known as *Godey's Magazine*)—cited by Welter as reflecting and reinforcing the ideals of true womanhood—drew heavily on imagery connecting purity with whiteness and staining with disgrace. A poem titled "Female Charms" mused "I would have her as pure as the snow on the mount." Another called "The Portrait" included the lines: "The brow whose snow is pure and white / As that of ocean foam / For grief has thrown no shadow there / And worldliness no stain."[26] In the northern states, where direct references to race were often omitted, literature and law both implicitly connected sexual morality with whiteness and a lack of chastity with color and contamination.

Among courts and commentators in New York and other US jurisdictions in the early to mid-nineteenth century, debate persisted regarding the validity of slander charges brought by women and whether it was fair to insist that they show economic loss, or special damage, in order to succeed. Many judges and writers recognized that no greater misfortune could befall a woman, who relied upon marriage for economic and social survival, than to be labeled unchaste or a whore, but while the New York judiciary agreed, they often felt constrained to follow English common law. Precedent trumped principle. This is why Chief Justice Kinsey's decision in the New Jersey Supreme Court in *Smith v Minor* was notable.[27]

It was the earliest example of the judiciary changing or reinterpreting the common law to give women a remedy. Other states, such as Ohio and Iowa, took a similar approach.[28]

Of course, many state legislatures had already begun to address the issue, particularly in the plantation South, where anxieties about the sexual reputations of white women ran deep. As discussed in Chapter 2, in 1808, North Carolina became the first common law jurisdiction in the world to introduce legislation enabling women to bring actions for sexual slander without needing to prove economic loss. As in New York, the language of North Carolina's Slander of Women Act—"unsullied purity"—revealed legislative intentions to align a reputation for chastity with whiteness. But in that state, such attempts were arguably unsuccessful, with Black and Cherokee women using the act to push for their rights to reputational recourse. In Black Belt Georgia, the racial alignment was more explicit and extreme, with the legislature passing laws in 1857 making imputations that a white woman had sex with a Black man slanderous *per se*.

In 1825, John Hulbert launched the first determined effort to change the law in New York with his bill "authorising any female to maintain an action of slander against any person who may charge her with incontinency or prostitution." Hulbert's address was roundly praised, including by the *Evening Post*, which described it as "one of the most able and eloquent speeches . . . ever heard."[29] Hulbert was personally commended as "a gallant champion of the fair" and "defender of the helpless and innocent."[30] He stated that the bill was of the "highest importance as regard[ing] the character of the female sex and the honor of the state" and argued it was absurd that if a woman was labeled a thief she can sue, "but if she [was] charged with prostitution, which is of the deepest dye . . . and ruins her prospects in life forever," she currently had no remedy at law.[31] He also alluded to a story—"no fictitious case," he assured the state assembly—of a slandered orphan girl and her widowed mother. The girl, he stated, with "tears, so pure, mild and meek they wouldn't *stain* an angel's cheek," had been admired and loved by all who knew her before the slanderer came, and then "that character and that happiness were blasted forever."[32] "Oh, where should she fly for protection?" he asked with a rhetorical flourish. "To the laws of her country, to the temple of justice?" "No!" Hulbert answered forcefully. "Those laws afford her no redress—the doors of that temple were barred against her."[33] The racial discourse of purity and staining gave power to his argument about the precious commodity that was female chastity.

The challenge of proving special damage that plagued cases of sexual slander in the United States pushed judges, legislators, and legal commentators to confront the fact that the common law was formed to address *men's* experiences and to protect *their* interests, an idea that would later become central to feminist legal theory in the twentieth century.[34] Newspapers described how Hulbert, in his speech, convincingly demonstrated how inadequate the law of slander was in addressing American women's interests, as distinct from those of men. The "reputation of men was guarded much better than that of women," he said. "The strong sex had taken care of themselves, and paid but little attention to the weaker."[35] A Vermont journal put it in slightly different terms: "He proceeded to show that while women are thus shamefully neglected, our own dear sex are treated with great kindness."[36] Hulbert had cited several cases in which it had been held actionable at law to say of an attorney "he is a dunce"; of a physician "he is no scholar"; of a tradesman "he is a sorry fellow and a rogue"; or of a Justice of the Peace "he is a debauched man." He continued in a reportedly sarcastic tone:

> You must not calumniate his honor or his worship. . . . No, he is a Justice of the Peace, and a gentleman; you must not call him a debauched man, for it will ruin his character. But you may slander, to your heart's content his honor or his worship's wife; it will not injure her reputation; and who cares if it does, she is no Justice of the Peace—she is nothing but a woman![37]

The unequal treatment of men and women within the common law of slander was "a stain," Hulbert stated, on "our character as gallant and honorable men."[38] Manliness too was liable to be stained if American men failed to step up and protect white women's sexual "innocence."[39] Hulbert's speech attracted praise from fellow assembly members but was also attacked. Unfortunately, critics' remarks were not reported, but their voices must have been persuasive because Hulbert's bill was referred to the House Judiciary Committee, where it languished and did not pass.

Perhaps, however, because of the publicity attracted by the bill, the

New York courts became more receptive thereafter to sexual slander cases brought by women. In 1828, Mary Miller, an unmarried woman, brought a case against Joseph Olmsted for telling people in the community that

> she was a bad woman, a very bad woman; that Phineas Barrett, Seth Palmer and others, were in the habit of visiting her frequently at her house; that even Robert, a black man, had been so much in the habit of going to the plaintiff's that the neighbours laughed at him about it.[40]

The slurs dug deep into sexual and racial anxieties. Not only was Miller's reputation, as a white woman, stained simply by an allegation of sexual immorality, but the allegation involved a relationship with a Black man. Miller claimed damages: that in consequence of such words being spoken, she was refused service at a public house. At trial, the jury of white men were sympathetic and found for the plaintiff, awarding her $500 in damages.

However, Olmsted appealed on two grounds: first, that Miller had not sufficiently proven the defendant had spoken the words pleaded, and second, that she had not suffered any special damage. Miller lost her case based on the first ground. But in relation to the second ground—that of special damage—the Supreme Court of Judicature of New York took a far more flexible approach than they had previously. Chief Justice Savage stated: "The special damage shewn, is probably sufficient. The plaintiff was refused civil treatment at a public house, in consequence of the words spoken by the defendant."[41] While not holding that allegations of incontinence or unchastity were actionable *per se*, as desired by Hulbert, the court nevertheless lowered the bar for white women seeking redress for sexual slurs in that state.[42]

Over subsequent years, numerous cases of sexual slander were brought by women in the New York courts, which were nearly all dismissed, often reluctantly by judges, for lacking proof of special damage. These cases all concerned the slander of married women and turned on whether her emotional loss—due to her status as a wife—could be considered as the husband's economic loss. In 1842, for example, Mrs. Beach brought a slander claim for imputations against her of sexual "incontinence."[43] She stated that the defendant's words caused her to suffer "pain of mind and body," to be abandoned by her husband, shunned by neighbors, refused assistance with "fuel, clothing and provisions," excluded from the Moral Reform Society, and subjected to children throwing "dirt, clubs, stones and other missiles" at her.⁴⁴ At trial, the defendants, like all those before them, argued that Beach had proved no special damage, and the court should throw her case out. The trial judge, Justice Gridley, did so, but the plaintiff appealed. The Supreme Court of New York gave her no relief, however, agreeing that she had not demonstrated recognizable loss. They also noted in passing that even if she did suffer pecuniary loss, it would be deemed "the loss of the husband," not hers.

This last point seemed to underline the logic in a case in 1855, when Olmsted (no apparent relation to Joseph Olmsted) sued Brown for making allegations that his wife was unchaste and guilty of infidelity.⁴⁵ The husband brought the case alone, without joining his wife, likely to strategically characterize any pecuniary loss as his, as the court in *Beach v Ranney* had required. He argued that as a consequence of the slanderous words spoken by the defendant, his wife became "depressed in her mind, weakened in her body, and injured in her health" and thus could not do her housework.⁴⁶ A witness testified that after hearing the rumors about her, Mrs. Olmsted "appeared considerably excited . . . acted almost as if she was crazy, and was not able to do her work."⁴⁷ Such distress and illness, if pleaded by the wife, would not sustain a slander claim as it did not constitute economic loss. However, the husband argued that as a result of her sickness, he lost her services in the home and was forced to employ other people. This type of harm the Supreme Court did recognize, holding: "A husband having by law a right to the services of his wife, whether he requires them or not, and being bound to maintain her, in sickness and in health, anything that diminishes the value of the right, or increases the burden of the duty, necessarily occasions a pecuniary loss to the husband."⁴⁸ The New York Supreme Court thus rendered *her* illness and suffering as *his* economic burden.

While the courts were willing to recognize pecuniary harms occurring to a husband as a result of his wife's depressive illness, they were not willing to recognize a man's own emotional and physical illness caused by sexual slander. In 1852, John Terwilliger, a farmer, heard from various sources that another man, Thomas Wands, had told others in the community that Terwilliger was having "a carnal connection" with Mrs. Jane Fuller, that Fuller was a "lewd and unchaste woman," and Terwilliger had said he was doing all he could to keep Mr. Fuller in the penitentiary so he could have "free access" to his wife.⁴⁹ At trial, Terwilliger's friend, adult children, and physician all testified that as a consequence of the slander against him,

Terwilliger had become severely ill and been unable to work. John Neipier (the friend) testified that when he told Terwilliger about the allegations against him, Terwilliger "threw down his hoe and left the field" and afterwards appeared "melancholy and looked bad, pale and sick."[50] Nancy Harpbun (the plaintiff's daughter) swore that as a result of the rumor, she saw "a great difference" in her father's appearance, and he was "not resting at night" and "did not pursue his work."[51] George Terwilliger (the plaintiff's son) testified that his father's health declined after the slanderous words until he was "entirely prostrated," could not attend the farmwork, and that "crops were neglected," "fences down," and "his corn suffered for want of hoeing."[52]

The defendant Wands argued a number of grounds, including that there was no evidence that the damage suffered by Terwilliger was the "natural, immediate and legal consequence" of the slanderous speech. In other words, that—unlike women—it was not natural for a man to become so sick and enfeebled because of sexual slurs against him. The trial court agreed with the defendant and the plaintiff appealed. The Supreme Court of New York was unsympathetic, Justice Allen declaring that while we know words "imputing incontinence to a chaste and sensitive female" might well affect "her spirits and her bodily comfort and health," the same words would only affect a minority of men in a similar manner.[53] "Other men," he chastised the plaintiff, were "differently constituted" and would not be remotely disturbed in body or mind by such charges. Where some people (women) might take to their beds following an attack upon their reputation, others (men) would be "more likely to commit an assault and battery."

The court clearly thought Terwilliger was being unmanly in his reaction to the allegations of his affair with Mrs. Fuller. While Wands's words led to an economic injury, including the costs of maintaining the farm and crops while Terwilliger was unable to work, the courts did not see this as a *natural* consequence but rather a symptom of Terwilliger's overly sensitive constitution and temperament. Terwilliger appealed further to the Court of Appeals of New York but was no more successful. Giving judgment for the court, the aptly named Justice Strong held that not all language that hurt people's feelings should be actionable. Otherwise, the doctrine would depend on the "sensibilities" of each person slandered, their "strength of mind" or "physical strength and ability" to bear or disregard abusive, insulting remarks concerning them.⁵⁴ Words that would make hardly an impression on most persons might be exceedingly painful to some, occasioning sickness and an interruption of their ability to engage in ordinary avocations. Justice Strong could barely contain his annoyance: "There must be some limit to liability." The appeals court regarded Terwilliger's emotional response as too sensitive and unnatural. They dismissed his appeal.

The *Terwilliger* decision—motivated by prescribing gender norms but expressed in gender-neutral terms—created difficulties when a similar case occurred a few years later concerning a woman. In 1855, John Wilson brought an action for slander against James Goit for words he spoke imputing adultery by his wife Lucy Wilson.⁵⁵ The Wilsons and Goits were farming families, living next to each other in Onondaga County. According to the complaint, the plaintiff's son, John Wilson Jr., was having an argument with James Goit when James stated, in front of various members of the community, that Norm Goit (the defendant's son) had "screwed his mother" (meaning Lucy Wilson) and that James Goit had seen them doing it "under the cherry tree below the barn."⁵⁶ As a consequence of the words being spoken by James Goit, the plaintiff alleged that Lucy was "greatly injured in her good name, fame and credit," brought "into public scandal and infamy," and became "sick, pained and diseased in mind and body" so she could no longer "attend to her ordinary business as the wife of said John Wilson."⁵⁷ The case went to trial where the plaintiff brought an array of witnesses testifying to Lucy Wilson's emotional and physical deterioration as a result of the slander. John Wilson Jr. testified that his mother was "crying most of the time," was always "in bed," and "neglected her work" so that he and his father were forced to make their own meals and do the washing until they could employ "a girl" to come and help.⁵⁸ Lucy Wilson's sister-in-law, Ann Wilson, testified to Lucy becoming "disconsolate, dejected and cast down" and that "she wept a good deal."⁵⁹

However, the defendants brought forth other witnesses to testify that Lucy Wilson had always been "a feeble woman," who "complained a good deal as to her health," and they argued that she was simply "a complaining, feeble, sickly, dyspeptic, dropsical, slatternly, dirty woman who allowed her sons and husband to do the housework."⁶⁰ They did not contend that the allegations of fornication and adultery were true, but rather that no legally recognized damage resulted. If Lucy had brought the case herself, it would have almost certainly failed. No amount of weeping could satisfy the economic basis of the special damage requirement. It is likely the case was instigated by her husband as he could at least try to argue that her incapacity to do housework due to emotional distress incurred him economic losses, as he was forced to employ a girl to help. This case again highlights how women's personal suffering and social humiliation could be translated in the courts as men's financial burden. Whether the jury of men felt sympathy for Lucy Wilson's plight or John Wilson's inconvenience, they found for the plaintiffs and awarded a large sum of $525.

But the defendants then appealed and won. The New York Court of Appeals stated that the "loss of a wife's services from illness, the consequence of mental depression resulting from defamatory words," was not actionable.[61] They went on to criticize the present state of the law: "In a moral point of view, there is no doubt but that one who will so far violate the proprieties and decencies of life as to make unfounded imputations of this nature, as to any one, and especially in respect to an *innocent female*, should be severely punished."[62] But they were wary of presuming to change the law and called upon the New York legislature to do so: 'Should the legislature be of opinion that such words ought to be made actionable of themselves, it will be easy for it to supply the existing defect. They can change the law, but we have not that power."[63] Unlike nearby New Jersey, the New York courts consistently took a conservative approach to the common law, seeing their role as one of declaration and application, not innovation.

The case of *Wilson v Goit* attracted wide media publicity and was the subject of fierce debate. One newspaper writer, called Vindex, argued that due to the strict requirement in sexual slander cases of economic loss, or special damage, the reputation of wives and daughters in the state of New York were unprotected and "at the mercy of every villain who seeks through malice or spleen their ruin."[64] In a series of articles he championed legal reform. Employing racially coded language, he characterized the wronged women as "cultivated" and "civilized," their "purity" and "injured female innocence" in need of legal protection. He also emphasized that the law unjustly privileged the "almighty dollar" over "humanity"—although he would in fact stress the economic value of women's housework.

Vindex's arguments reflected the nature of the New York slander cases, which were largely brought by white women engaged in domestic roles and defined via their relationships with men—as either wives or wives to be.[65] The law, he said, protected women engaged in "public occupations," as men were, but not those residing in the "domestic circle."⁶⁶ The writer explained that if a slandered woman was engaged as "a milliner, a seamstress, a teacher," she may be able to prove some economic loss and thus sustain the action, but those women who were not "forced" via "necessity" into paid labor and who constituted "the wives and daughters of the majority of people in the State" would continue to be left without justice.⁶⁷ Vindex was concerned with the disruptive effects of sexual slander upon the peace and sanctity of the domestic realm. Such allegations could cause a man to lose his wife's services—washing, meal preparation, sewing, farmwork—due to her depression or distress. As in *Wilson v Goit*, a man in such circumstances might be forced to employ "a girl" to fulfill such duties, or even worse, waste his time undertaking such feminine tasks himself. Without proper legal regulation, sexual slander posed a threat to "domestic peace," the stability of "separate spheres," and thus the economic productivity of the state.

Vindex also argued that sexual slander was a threat to American men's honor. He tied the cause of defending slandered women to the reputation of the state and the nation, and to the character of male citizens. He distinguished the United States and the "gallantry" of its men from the situation in England where such unmanly laws originated: "We claim to be a gallant nation; and so much we are distinguished for our consideration and attention to females tha[t] an Englishman proposes to discover an American by his gallantry. Let it not then be said that our superior refinement consists of mere etiquette."⁶⁸ In order to prove their distinctive gallantry, Vindex called upon the New York legislature to finally step in and rectify the humiliation of American women caused by English laws. He also appealed to their identities as "civilized" and progressive northerners at a time when tensions between the northern and southern states were increasing: "The Northern States have always claimed a higher civilisation, by their comparative freedom from the bowie knife and the pistol. . . . It is now for the Legislature to say whether it shall protect the citizens of the state or whether they shall protect themselves."⁶⁹ White American men in the northern states could prove their superior manliness by protecting white women from the stain of sexual slurs, and such protection was best achieved via law reform rather than vigilante justice. In his final article on the subject, Vindex chose to link sexual slander reforms to gains made in another area of women's rights:

Let us do this tardy justice, to the injured, the unprotected! Let it no longer be said, in the light of the nineteenth Century, that there is not a state in Christendom where the character of a woman is respected and protected! New York led the way in protecting the property of "married women," let us . . . protect her more sacred right, her more inestimable treasure—her character.[70]

In 1869, a new Slander of Women Act was introduced to the New York legislature, championed this time by Mr. Nathan Button Smith of Oswego.[71] Studious and bookish, Smith had graduated from Middlebury College top of his class in 1863 and went on to study law. In 1868, at age twenty-six, he was admitted to practice at the Supreme Court of New York, elected as the youngest member of the Assembly, and he sat on both the Judiciary Committee and the Committee on Privileges and Elections. He would soon be promoted to district attorney. Many newspapers supported Smith's bill, with the *Buffalo Commercial* commenting that such reforms would "have a tendency to restrain wagging tongues which find amusement in assailing female virtue."[72] The *New York Times* also reported upon the bill, stating: "Accompanying the bill is a communication, setting forth the injury that may arise through a slander imputing want of chastity to a female. . . . Legal opinions are quoted on the subject, and the imperfection of our present laws on the point is shown."[73]

During this period, there was strong interest by jurists on this topic. The October 1870 edition of the *Albany Law Journal* reported that it had been contacted concerning whether there was a law now allowing women to bring actions for slanderous words alleging unchastity or prostitution. The journal replied:

> We regret to say that there is not; that while the law has hedged about a man's reputation for honesty and integrity, it has left the reputation of a woman . . . entirely at the mercy of a villain who may seek to assail it . . . such a condition of the law is barbarous.[74]

Barbarous laws needed to be civilized in the new world. As in 1825, Smith's bill went to the Judiciary Committee for review. However, this time, on March 29, 1871, it became law. Chapter 219 of the New York sessional laws provided: "An action may be maintained by a female, whether married or single, to recover damages for words hereafter spoken imputing unchastity to her, and it shall not be necessary to allege or prove special damages in order to maintain such action."[75] In addition, the law stated: "In such actions, a married woman may sue alone, and any recovery therein shall be her sole and separate property."

New York was one of the last jurisdictions in the United States to give women the right to bring actions vindicating their reputations for sexual morality without needing to prove economic loss known as special damage. These changes afforded women greater reputational rights that in fact still exist today.[76] They could now clean the ruinous stains of sexual immorality from their characters, obtain compensation for their distress and destitution, and silence their attackers. But to achieve such change, legislators and commentators in the early to mid-nineteenth century sought to defend true womanhood, to protect and reinforce women's roles as wives and homemakers, to implicitly and discursively align whiteness with chastity. In many ways, the 1871 act echoed Hulbert's 1825 bill, but as the conclusion of Vindex's last article highlights, by the 1860s, the language surrounding the slander of women reforms had begun to shift to arguments for respecting women's legal "rights," as well as protecting their virtue. This shift was particularly evident once the Australian colony of Victoria took up the cause in the 1870s and 80s.

SEVEN

"THERE IS A TOTAL DISREGARD FOR THE RIGHTS OF WOMEN"

Victoria

In 1874, Rebecca Redman was working in the busy grocery store she had owned and run for thirteen years in the inner-city Melbourne suburb of Hotham, when her neighbor and the local publican, George Clayton, entered the store, abused her, called her "offensive names," and verbally "assailed her chastity."[1] Hotham, renamed North Melbourne in 1887, was the home of the most important fresh food market at the time and one of the most densely populated municipalities in the colony of Victoria. According to court documents, Clayton's slander of Redman caused customers to cease frequenting her store, and she suffered a sizable loss of trade. So Redman sued him for slander in the Victorian County Court. In reply, Clayton's lawyers argued that her action must be dismissed as she had not proven any special damage. Redman's business losses were legally irrelevant, they submitted. All that mattered in the eyes of English common law was whether she had suffered a canceled marriage proposal as a result of the words.

However, during the trial, Francis Quinlan—a lawyer who would soon become a prominent judge on the County Court and the Supreme Court in Victoria—intervened in the case as an *amicus curie* (a friend of the court) and presented Judge John Warrington Rogers with a report from the Victorian legal periodical *The Australian Jurist* pertaining to the Slander of Women Act of New York.[2] Published three years earlier in August 1871, the article titled "Women Slanderers" stated: "'we have to call the attention of our Legislators" to an act passed into law in the State of New York, which has "for its object the punishment of persons using words imputing unchastity to females" and is certainly "a desirable measure anywhere."[3] The short act was then reproduced in full within the article. Within the courtroom, Quinlan held aloft this report from the common law republic of the United States and argued that the *Redman* case, amongst many others, showed that New York's Slander of Women Act must be urgently adopted in the colony of Victoria.[4] Judge Rodgers agreed decisively with Quinlan, stating that he had adjudicated similar cases in the past, and "it always appeared strange to him that no provision had been made in our laws for women who were slandered in such manner." However, he confessed that as a single judge in a low-level court, he had no power to change the law, and so, reluctantly, he dismissed the case.[5] Judge Rogers stated in conclusion that "owing to the defect in the law, the words used were not slanderous, and damages could only be obtained by a single woman in a few cases, such as if she had lost an offer of marriage."[6]

Soon after, a fierce editorial in Melbourne's the *Age* newspaper referred to the *Redman* case, quoted New York's 1871 act, and took up the cause of slandered women in Victoria. Opining that a "defect" in the law of slander had recently been brought to light in the County Court, the newspaper explained to its readers that to call "a man a thief" without proof is a legal slander, but there is no redress for an "unmarried woman" when her "character is assailed." The writer was indignant that Clayton had abused Redman—a respectable "single woman who keeps a store"—with "coarse language" and yet, incongruously, the only damages she was technically allowed to claim were that she had "lost the chance of being married." Marriage, for Redman, was beside the point. This "legal defect," he wrote, was "remedied in America in 1871" when an act of one clause became law in the state of New York. "This short act might, with great advantage, be passed by our own Legislature," he pressed. It would extend "a very necessary protection to the softer sex, whose fair fame can now be assailed with impunity, by any rascal mean enough to do so." The *Age* pleaded with the public: "Will some honorable member be gallant enough to come to the rescue!"[7]

Victorian lawyers, judges, and commentators were more familiar with New York's recent slander of women reforms than with those in neighboring Australian colonies. No mention was made of the fact that South Australia had debated and passed almost identical legislation in 1865, six years earlier than New York; or that New South Wales had changed its defamation laws for similar reasons in 1847. Victoria and many of its educated and prominent legal and political minds looked to the "great republic" for progressive and worldly inspiration at this time, rather than to Britain or other Australian colonies. It is notable that *The Australian Jurist and Notes of Cases*, the first legal periodical and law reports compiled in Victoria (published between 1870 and 1873) frequently included articles, extracts, and case summaries from New York State, particularly from the *Albany Law Journal*. It aspired to be on an equal footing with the US publication and took a keen interest in the ways in which Victorian common law jurisprudence was being received and shaped abroad.

In December 1871, *The Australian Jurist* referred to the *Albany Law Journal* as its "spirited contemporary" and proudly shared that one of Victoria's local cases had been cited by the New York journal as authority. They were "also pleased to notice" that an original article penned by *The Australian Jurist* had been republished in full by the *Albany Law Journal*. Their reciprocal relationship was infused with curiosity and comparison, particularly when it came to issues of law and gender. In July 1872, *The Australian Jurist* published an article titled "What Is Thought of Us in America," with an extract from the *Albany Law Journal*: "The Australian antipodes, the dwellers in the land of spicy breezes, wool and gold have enacted that all offences against the chastity of women shall be punished by flogging." "While we agree," they went on, "that perfect protection should be afforded to women's virtue . . . we must dissent from the mode of punishment" as "inappropriate" to an "advanced civilisation" and unworthy of the "name and prospects of the people of Australia."[8] The journal was referring to details of an 1871 Victorian act that had amended the Criminal Law and Practice Statute of 1864, making whipping a sentencing option for all sexual offenses, in addition to a term of imprisonment. As discussed in the previous chapter, New York jurists frequently commented that female sexual virtue should be protected as far as possible, but only via "civilised" means. The slander of women acts, by granting women compensation for verbal abuse in the "civil" courts, were thus regarded as a progressive reform.

The Australian Jurist, which first brought the attention of Victorian minds to the slander of women movement, was the brainchild of James Purves and William McKinley (a Victorian barrister). It was an industry newsletter and periodical covering both political and practice issues that, though focused on Victoria, sought a national and international audience. Purves was born in Melbourne in 1843 and studied law in England before returning and being admitted to the Victorian Bar in 1866. Described as possessing "a quick intelligence" and a "fluent and often brilliant tongue," he was a theatrical and high-profile Queen's Counsel who had a "keen sense of humour" and "a penchant for the vigorous promotion of a cause."[9] Purves and McKinley edited the *The Australian Jurist* for its first two years, during which time its tone was aspirational, playful, and looked to America for legal direction and comparison. In 1872, Purves entered the Legislative Assembly as a Free Trader and Constitutionalist. The same year he also joined the Australian Natives' Association and became an ardent campaigner for federation. It was under Purves's editorship that *The Australian Jurist* published the "Women Slanderers" article about New York's reforms. He would become a crucial figure within the slander of women movement in Victoria.

In October 1876, Purves introduced a bill to the Victorian Legislative Assembly titled Females Protection Bill, to provide "redress for words imputing unchastity to a female."[10] In December, the bill was read a second time. Purves submitted that the object of the bill was a "right and proper one." He explained that a similar law had been passed in New York and in other countries and had "worked well." He opined, echoing *The Age* article, that currently when a woman was called a thief she had a legal remedy, but if called a prostitute, she had "no remedy whatsoever." This "strange anomaly," Purves argued, must be corrected, so that a slanderer could be rightly sued by the "person slandered."

However, lawyer and politician David Gaunson opposed the Purves bill on the basis that it was absurd and that the change should apply equally to men and women. What if "the Premier were accused of unchastity?" he asked, provocatively. Surely that would be "as serious an accusation" against "a man in his position" as against "any female." Gaunson was known as an obstructionist and unruly member of parliament—often drunk and with a violent temper. Purves replied by explaining the facts on the ground:

[E]very day lawyers in this colony and the home country... had cases brought to them in which some unfortunate woman was labouring under an imputation upon her virtue which was absolute ruin to her, and yet she could obtain no redress; she could not bring an action to put herself right before the world, apart from any damages, because such an action would not lie.

To compare that to the situation of men was "sheer nonsense." James Patterson, member for Castlemaine, agreed with Purves, calling the bill "laudable." Gaunson replied that the measure was "offensive to the public," and the country had thus far got on very well without it. The bill did not pass.

While many of the early arguments deployed in the colony of Victoria on the issue of the sexual slander against women were similar to those used in New York—calling upon "gallant" men to protect the "fair fame" of females—there were also marked differences. Whereas American calls for change often used a racialized discourse of stained whiteness and emphasized the barbarity of traditional English laws, arguments for change to the common law of slander in Victoria focused more upon protecting the respectability of women engaged in occupations and trades. Though a racialized discourse around sexual slander was absent from the Victorian cases, it is highly likely that—as in New York State—all the plaintiffs identified or presented to court as white. The status of Aboriginal people as British subjects was, at the time, ambiguous; local legislation and policy deprived them of civil law rights and refused to recognize them as full legal persons.[11] For example, in 1869, Victoria had passed the Aboriginal Protection Act, which exerted total control over Aboriginal people's living arrangements, employment, education, social and family relationships, marriages, and more.[12] Historian Leigh Boucher has described this act as "one of the most far-reaching intrusions into the lives and liberties of Indigenous peoples" in the nineteenth century.[13] It was therefore highly unlikely, if not impossible, for an Aboriginal woman to bring a slander case in colonial Victoria.

Though Victoria was inspired by New York's legislation and initially borrowed its arguments and form, there were stark differences between the types of cases brought in these jurisdictions that ultimately influenced the object and framing of the gendered legislation. Whereas most appeal cases in New York were instigated by women residing in rural communities and primarily engaged in domestic roles as wives and daughters (or by their husbands), the cases brought by women in Victoria nearly all concerned harm to single women's paid occupations and employment in urban settings. Their losses occurred not just in relation to familial bonds, but to their standing as proprietors and employees—grocery store owners, barmaids, and publicans. The types of occupations illustrated, as Diane Kirkby and Clare Wright have shown, the significance of pub and hotel work for women in the Australian colonies.[14] They also point to the nature of the economic and social landscape. During the second half of the nineteenth century, because of the gold rushes, Victoria's population exploded, and by 1880, Melbourne had grown into a "fully fledged metropolis" of a quarter of a million inhabitants.[15] It was also a very urban population. Approximately 31 percent of Victorians lived in Melbourne, whereas by comparison, only 23 percent of New York residents lived in New York City. The sexual slander cases that attracted attention and helped change the law in Victoria were predominantly brought by white women engaged in paid work within a bustling, industrialized society.

After Redman, the next woman to bring a high-profile slander case in Victoria was Maria White, in 1880.[16] White, an unmarried woman who worked as a barmaid and professional pianist at the Woolpack Hotel in Williamstown and lived in Carlton with her father ("a paperhanger"), sued John Jordan, chief officer of the ship *North American,* for slander. The circumstances of plaintiff and defendant reflected Melbourne's economic and social milieu. Williamstown was, at the time, the major seaport for Victoria and an expanding urban center. To meet the constant demands of travelers, sailors, workmen, and immigrants flooding its shores each day, accommodation and hospitality businesses had sprung up rapidly. By 1864 there were twenty-seven hotels operating in Williamstown, and by the 1880s it was a hub of engineering and rapid industrialization, promising to become the "Birmingham of Victoria."[17]

White and Jordan had apparently known each other for eight years, and according to the evidence of Jordan had been on "very intimate terms," seeing each other and going dancing each time he returned to the colony.[18] On the evening of January 18, 1880, the defendant had entered the hotel, approached the bar where the plaintiff was serving customers, and engaged her in conversation.[19] Then, according to the affidavit of Maria White, the defendant said loudly in front of others: "What did you do with the child you had?"[20] She warily asked him what he meant and warned him that he should be careful with his words, to which he replied: "Oh yes, you had a child, and one of its arms was crippled." White again told him to be careful and warned that her fiancé, Charles Macartney, was nearby in the parlor and listening to their conversation. According to White, Jordan then stated that there was no use in her getting in a "temper" about it and "I suppose you will serve him the same way you used the others."[21]

Macartney, an engineer, gave evidence at trial that as a result of hearing the defendant's aspersions on White's character, he immediately broke off the engagement and refused to marry her unless her name was cleared by the court.[22] Maria White also testified that she had been shunned by numerous friends, acquaintances, and customers.[23] Prior to instigating an action, White asked the defendant to apologize publicly to her, which he refused, replying he would only do so in private. He then attempted to leave the colony on his ship, when he was arrested and required to pay 100 pounds as security. Jordan gave evidence at trial that he had heard the rumor about White having a deformed child from someone else, perhaps another ship captain, and decided to tell it as a "joke." However, it is likely Jordan's slander was motivated by possessive jealousy, having just become aware of White's relationship with Macartney. A jury of six men returned a verdict for White of 30 pounds.[24]

But Jordan appealed, represented by James Purves, who perhaps sought to use the case to prove the necessity for the legislation he proposed four years earlier. First, Purves sought to question White's claim of special damage—or "temporal loss"—relating to loss of marriage. He argued that no date had been set for the wedding between her and Macartney and so there was insufficient evidence it had been canceled or delayed due to the words of Jordan. Second, he argued that the damages were excessive. The case went to the Supreme Court of Victoria. Chief Justice Stawell (with Justices Barry and Stephen concurring) dismissed the appeal and held that there was enough evidence of special damages for the jury to make a determination and award damages, as they had already done. The chief justice stated: "Proof of special damage such as loss of a marriage is necessary to lay the foundation for an action; but once it goes to the jury they have to say what damages they will award. . . . I think 30 pounds is a very small amount of damages for saying an unmarried woman has had a child."[25]

In 1886, another case again brought sexual slander to the forefront of public attention and highlighted the unjust burden placed on women required to prove special damage. It would culminate in a change of Victorian law. Elizabeth Albrecht, an unmarried woman and former publican at the Harp of Erin Hotel in the inner-city suburb of Collingwood, sued Annie Marks Patterson for slander.[26] Albrecht's father, Heinrich Albrecht, had once worked for George Patterson as a butcher, and it seemed Albrecht had known him her whole life. After her father's death, in 1885, Elizabeth Albrecht was apparently helped extensively by Patterson with business and legal affairs associated with running the hotel, and they had maintained a close relationship. As she testified, she was the eldest living child and had to provide financially for her siblings.

According to the statement of claim, Annie Patterson had made comments in front of others about Albrecht having an affair and "misbehaving" with her husband George.[27] According to the court documents, she stated: "You are the one that has been away to have a child to my husband; you have been a kept woman in that hotel; if you try for another hotel I will oppose your character."[28] The plaintiff forcefully denied the allegations at the time and subsequently, testifying at trial: "From first to last, there was no impropriety of conduct between us."[29] Albrecht claimed that as a result of the slander she was injured in her "credit and reputation" as a "licensed victualler" and lost the "assistance in business" of Henry Bell, another old friend of her father's.[30] She was afraid to apply for a new licence as Patterson had allegedly stated: "No matter what kind of business Miss Albrecht tries to go into, I will try to keep her out of it." Albrecht was represented by John Madden and Norman Bayles. Patterson was defended by James Purves and John Burnett Box. It was heard by Justice George Kerferd. These legal figures were all connected. Madden and Purves were keen professional rivals, and Box and Kerferd had published a legal treatise together in 1871.[31] The trial was covered extensively by the press, with journalists delighting in the "Extraordinary Slander Case" playing out before them.[32]

Upon its conclusion, a jury of six men awarded Albrecht 250 pounds for damage to her business and loss of the assistance of Mr. Bell. However, Justice Kerferd, uncertain about the technical rules of slander, reserved various issues to the Full Court (three or more judges) for consideration, such as whether the words uttered actually touched her in her "trade and business" and whether there was evidence of any special damage as a result of Henry Bell refusing her hospitality and advice.[33] Quoting Thomas Starkie, Madden and Bayles argued courageously that slanderous words were actionable if they prejudiced a plaintiff "in his office, profession or employment" and that under section 37 of the Licensing Act 1876 (Victoria), a woman was not able to hold a hotel licence if she was of "bad fame or character." Purves and Bayles replied that the words must relate "to the business or trade carried on," which aspersions of unchastity did not.

Justice Edward Holroyd gave judgment for the Full Court, agreeing with the defendant's counsel and holding that as Patterson's words did not relate to Albrecht's management of the hotel, they could not be considered as harming her trade or business for "chastity was not part of the plaintiff's duty as a publican."[34] He went on to say: "To have imputed to the plaintiff that she kept a disorderly house would have been very different from charging her with adulterous intercourse. Such an imputation would have reflected directly on her behaviour in conducting her business."[35] However, he did find that Albrecht's loss of friendship with Bell was enough to sustain some special damage: "that the loss of hospitality is sufficient special damage to sustain an action for slander, and is a natural and probable consequence of imputing unchastity to a woman."[36] The court thus refused to recognize the economic damage caused to working women by imputations of sexual immorality. Following English common law and American precedent, they were only willing to quantify loss in terms of relational harms. Albrecht could keep the damages relating to Bell, but her occupational losses were denied.

Working women like Redman, White, and Albrecht found themselves in a bind. Sexual slurs harmed them economically in their occupations and trades, but these were deemed not actionable by the courts as the imputations themselves did not relate to their actual employment or business activities—as allegations of incompetence, dishonesty, or corruption would have. Sexual slanders were insults of a private or spiritual nature, and according to English precedent, could only be measured in terms of privately incurred economic losses, such as loss of a marriage proposal, even if individuals such as Redman or Albrecht did not seek or require marriage for their financial security. Such a situation reflected defamation law's understanding that a man's reputation for sexual morality would rarely, if ever, affect him in his profession or occupation as it was considered largely irrelevant to his abilities as a proprietor, publican, or politician. However, for women, being sexually chaste was a precondition for social respect, in both the workplace and wider society. Sexual slander actions were as essential to establishing women's livelihoods through paid work as through marriage. This remained the case even as women entered the paid workforce in increasing numbers during the late nineteenth century. This predicament had also been faced by vocalist and performer Suzanna Wishart earlier in Adelaide, though in that context her difficulties were framed as lacking a "natural guardian"—a husband—and thus being "defenceless" without parliament's paternalist intervention. In Victoria, marriage was irrelevant to the political issue. It became a fight for equal rights to reputation for women in paid work.

In September, Purves and Bayles brought a motion seeking a new trial in the Albrecht matter on the basis that the damages of 200 pounds, awarded for her loss of hospitality from Bell, were excessive. Their case rested, in part, on the verdict and reasoning in *White v Jordan*. In reply, Albrecht's lawyers cited the New York case of *Olmstead v Miller*. Justices Williams and Webb gave judgment for the court, agreeing reluctantly with the defendant that Judge Kerferd was in error: "In our opinion . . . the jury are, we think, in awarding damages, limited to the special damage laid in the statement of claim, and proved at the trial."[37] Such a rule, they said, was unfortunate and undesirable, but they could not change it, stating in terms that echoed the New York Court of Appeals in *Wilson v Goit*: "That this should be the state of the law as regards this particular species of slander is deeply to be regretted, but the remedy lies with the Legislature, not with us."[38]

Chief Justice George Higinbotham, an early and fierce champion of women's suffrage and property rights and former member of parliament, agreed with their sentiments about the regrettable state of slander law for women in Victoria and the inability of the judiciary to alter it. He declared: "The law which withholds from a woman legal protection from an imputation of all others the most injurious, except where it has actually produced special temporal damage to her, is a law which, however unjust it may seem to us to be, must be upheld and applied until it is altered by the Legislature."[39] But he dissented with Williams's and Webb's conclusion, wishing instead to ameliorate—as far as possible—the harsh effects of the existing English law and improve women's reputational rights. He stated: "we are under no obligation, in my opinion, to extend the injurious effects that flow from the operation of such a law." Higinbotham proposed that if a plaintiff showed any special damage whatsoever, that would satisfy the unjust common law as it currently stood, and a jury should then be able to award damages for all losses occurred, including occupational or professional loss. He thought the appeal should therefore be dismissed and Albrecht awarded full damages of 250 pounds. But Williams's and Webb's majority opinion prevailed, and a new trial was ordered, one that attracted even greater interest on the part of lawyers, journalists, and the public.

While the appeal was being heard by the Full Court, the legislature was also moving on the issue. John Quick, a former *Age* journalist turned lawyer and strong advocate of federation, introduced a bill, Amend Libel and Slander, primarily aimed at greater press freedom but that included a clause to scrap the burden of special damage for women. In September 1886, *Table Talk* magazine reported on the amendment in an article titled "Slandering a Woman" and declared Quick's bill of "special interest to women" readers. The magazine went on to explain: "Every respectable woman should be grateful to Dr. Quick for inserting the clause which will protect them from foul slander without having to prove special damages."[40]

In parliament, Quick described that clause 10, the final clause, was "a very important clause in the interest of females."[41] He stated that it was "extraordinary" that under English law, which was "supposed to be one of the most liberal systems of jurisprudence the world has ever seen," words imputing unchastity or adultery to a woman, married or unmarried, however gross or injurious, were not actionable unless she could prove that they directly caused her special damage. Such a state of law, he claimed, was "utterly barbarous." There was much debate regarding the increased protections proposed for the press (additional libel defenses of absolute and qualified privilege), but on the protections for women there was greater agreement within parliament. Ephraim Zox, a conservative, submitted that he thoroughly endorsed the measure: "Why, when a woman's character is assailed, and her reputation is undermined, should she not have the same opportunity of vindicating herself that other persons have?" Ferguson Tuthill, member for Ovens, stated: "I am sure that every member of the Chamber must approve of clause 10—the last clause. In these civilized days we ought to allow a woman every species of fair protection." But Quick's bill proved controversial for its advocacy of press freedoms. It was referred to a parliamentary committee and then lapsed.

In February 1887, the matter of *Albrecht v Patterson* began again, garnering much excitement and attention. This time it was heard by Justice Hartley Williams.[42] No new evidence was furnished, but the plaintiff did have to quantify and detail the exact damages occasioned to her by the loss of friendship and hospitality of Henry Bell. How many meals had she been refused by the Bell household? How many social invitations had been withdrawn? Her loss of trade and prospects as a hotel proprietor had already been quashed. Williams made it clear what he thought of the law he was administering:

> The plaintiff [is] obliged to prove special damages, and this must be measured in pounds, shillings and pence. A man [is] not hampered by such a condition. It [is] outrageous that in our present state of civilisation such a barbarous law should exist. It [is] a relic of the old feudal times, when every woman on an estate was regarded by the baron as his serf, and might be used by him as he pleased, being treated as a mere chattel. There [is] a total disregard to the rights of women, and I trust that some member of the Legislature [will] make it his duty to frame a law to amend such a monstrous state of things.[43]

The Argus observed that it was the judiciary who were most actively pushing for these gendered reforms: "still another plaintive appeal comes from a judge of the Supreme Court to the public in general, and to any member of Parliament in particular who has the time to introduce a bill to amend the law relating to the slander of women."[44] Williams was "not alone," they submitted, in calling for this "radical change" in defamation law, the most recent plea coming from Chief Justice Higinbotham. The newspaper noted that lawyers were "proverbially conservative," and it was rare for them to argue—repeatedly—for the English common law to be altered. The judges of the Victorian Supreme Court were much "deserving of the thanks of the community" for advocating on this necessary and important issue of justice for women.

The jury in the second Albrecht trial returned with damages of 40 pounds (split between 5 pounds for loss of meals and 35 pounds for loss of access to the Bell house). But Justice Williams reluctantly queried the legality of the damages compensating for loss of access to the house (given the social visit involved no pecuniary value) and wished to remit the matter, once again, to the Full Court. Feeling exhausted, frustrated, and aware of her mounting legal costs, Elizabeth Albrecht simply agreed to abandon the 35 pounds. As a result of winning her case against Annie Patterson after two years of complicated litigation, she was awarded a paltry 5 pounds in damages.[45]

There was much critical commentary and many calls for reform. The *Geelong Advertiser* wrote that it was a "monstrous anomaly" that a woman such as Albrecht was "virtually left without remedy for slander upon her character," however "gross and unjustifiable."[46] The *Albrecht* outcome, they argued, was "a greater insult to the woman than the original offence." The law was complicit in furthering injuring women who had been verbally abused. In not recognizing the numerous dimensions of loss that a woman suffered from such slander, it placed her "upon the footing of a mere animal," devoid of "greater sensibilities." Slander law for women was a "disgrace" and "opposed to every consideration of propriety and justice." *Table Talk*, a popular magazine in Melbourne, ran an article titled "A Woman's Reputation" that linked the oppression of the law to the backwardness of the British empire: "That a systematic attempt to blast a woman's reputation should be paid for at the rate of the value of a certain number of meals which she might otherwise have eaten, is a legal joke, which finds no parallel outside of the British Empire."[47] It was outrageous, they argued, that "[i]f a man's character is assailed, however worthless it may be, the law provides him with a substantial remedy," but if a woman's reputation is "besmirched" with the "foulest calumnies," the courts are largely powerless. The article looked towards Williams Shiels, a leading liberal and "promising young member" of parliament, for a workable solution, commenting that he had already shown his gallantry on such issues upon the floor of the Assembly.

William Shiels took the hint. In 1887, spurred by community outrage over the outcome of *Albrecht v Patterson*, he acted to advance "the rights of women" by scrapping the necessity for women to prove special damage when bringing cases to silence insults and allegations of sexual immorality against them. The 1887 bill enjoyed greater success than Purves's earlier bill, perhaps because the rhetoric used in its advocacy was responsive to new interest in Victoria in advancing the rights of women. Instead of arguing that "females" should be better "protected"—echoing New York's paternalistic language as Purves had in 1876—Shiels fashioned it as an issue of "equality": "That was to say that an accusation calculated to affect a woman more deeply than any other words that could be uttered would be placed in the same category with the accusations which, if used against a man would render the person using them liable."⁴⁸ The bill attracted the support of Jonas Levian, member for Barwon, who stated that he was a great admirer of Shiels because of the way in which he "upheld the rights of women."⁴⁹ There was some discussion over the exact form and wording of the bill, and it was reintroduced for a second reading a month later. During that debate, the language of equality gathered force. Frederick Sargood, member for South Yarra, declared: "There was no good reason why a female should be placed in a very much worse position than a man."⁵⁰ He stated that many Victorian judges, including Chief Justice Higinbotham, had expressed hope that the legislature would "place women on the same legal footing as men."⁵¹ Henry Cuthbert (member for Wellington) concurred, declaring that the present state of British common law was "barbarous" and a "disgrace to the English nation."⁵² *Table Talk* magazine also supported Shiels's measure, stating they were glad it had received the "hearty approval of Parliament."⁵³ On December 17, 1887, the bill became law.

The Slander Act of 1887 was drafted and debated as the women's movement gained ascendancy in Victoria.⁵⁴ In 1880, women had won the right to attend the University of Melbourne, and in 1883 Bella Guerin became the first woman to graduate. In 1884, the Victorian Women's Suffrage Society had been formed "to obtain the same political privileges for woman as are now possessed by male voters . . . [and] equal privileges in marriage and divorce."⁵⁵ The following year, the Woman Christian Temperance Union established its first branch in Melbourne, and the campaign for women's suffrage was well underway. Levian was right about Shiels being a proponent of women's rights. Shiels sponsored an act granting mothers custody rights to their children upon divorce in 1883, as well as amendments to the Married Women's Property Act in 1884 and crucial divorce reforms in 1889.⁵⁶ Four years after the Slander Act, young suffragist and social reformer Vida Goldstein and others petitioned for and secured major changes to the Crimes Act that raised the age of consent from twelve to sixteen years.⁵⁷ And in 1902, Victorian women joined all other (white) Australian women in winning federal voting rights. American women, however, after repeated defeats, would not see suffrage until 1919.⁵⁸ Reforms granting women greater rights to sue for sexual slander in the colony of Victoria occurred within this broader movement for women's rights and, as such, were framed by and understood within a political discourse of gender equality.

EIGHT

BARBAROUS COMMON LAW AND DOUBLE STANDARDS OF MORALITY

England

In February 1832, a Royal Commission into the procedures and operations of the ecclesiastical courts of England released its final report.[1] It included a recommendation for the abolition of the courts' defamation jurisdiction, which primarily dealt with imputations of incontinency against women. A *Law Magazine* commentary on the proposal noted that "considering how freely words of the sort are bandied about by the lower classes, nothing but great prudence on the part of the Ecclesiastical Judges [has] prevented the nuisance from becoming long ago intolerable."[2] Sexual slander suits, they argued, had been clogging the canon courts of England for centuries. As a substitute remedy, the commissioners recommended the establishment of a new criminal offense of sexual slander, punishable by magistrates in the courts of petty sessions by fines and terms of imprisonment. A criminal offense would have the benefit, they argued, of only being prosecuted at the discretion of the state (not by individual women). It would stop the "lower classes" from burdening the courts with their petty private disputes and grievances.

However, the *Law Magazine* noted that as "no action lies for words imputing incontinency without special damage, the proposed substitute [was] either unnecessary or not extensive enough."[3] In other words, depending upon your position regarding the burden on women to prove special damage for sexual slander, a new criminal offense would either go too far and burden the speech of men without sufficient justification, or not go far enough in giving women effective legal recourse. In the end, no new criminal offense was enacted. The enlargement of the criminal law always has costs, and those costs were perceived as too high. Criminal law was regarded too heavy a mechanism for curbing men's abusive speech against women.

Soon after the Royal Commission recommended the abolition of the defamation jurisdiction of the ecclesiastical courts, Lord Campbell pushed for a Select Committee of the House of Lords to investigate the issue of defamation reform within the common law, telling their lordships that "on this important subject the law of England is more defective than that of any other civilised country in the world."[4] The Select Committee's report, released in 1843, highlighted that one of the most pressing issues at play was the slander of women: whereas any words in writing that injured a person's reputation, even if read by only one other individual, could form the basis of an action in libel, there was no remedy for words "publicly spoken" that imputed—in the coarsest terms and on the most public occasion—"a Want of Chastity to a Woman."[5] They noted contemptuously that, in contrast, an "action may be maintained for saying that a Cobbler is not skilful in mending Shoes." It was outrageous to the Select Committee that a cobber's trade was protected by English defamation law but a lady of "high station" or a "gentleman" could not bring an action because they could not prove special damage. The committee concluded that "these Distinctions, which are quite peculiar to the Law of England, do not rest on any solid foundation." However, a bill incorporating the Select Committee's recommendations failed. The attorney general, Sir Frederick Pollock, worried about too much litigation—every "offensive" conversation becoming a ground of action—and thus wanted to tighten libel law in line with slander, not the converse.[6] And so, the distinction between slander and libel remained. Women subject to slurs of unchastity, prostitution, or adultery in England continued to be barred from bringing claims in common law courts by the almost impossible burden of proving special damage.

Debates about slander reform in England were dominated by concerns about opening the floodgates to vexatious and vindictive women. For decades, starting in the 1840s, many senior judges in the Australian colonies and US states, faced with the plight and concrete circumstances of individual women seeking justice, decried the common law as barbarous, defective, and cruel. But English commentators and politicians, like Pollock, persistently argued in reply that there must be limits on the ability of women to sue men for sexual slander. Otherwise, the court system would struggle under the weight of seemingly trivial suits brought by women over words expressed by men rashly or in a moment of temper. Englishmen displayed a unique anxiety about women suing them for slander and burdening their free speech. Such concerns were not—as demonstrated in the preceding chapters—echoed in the United States or Australian colonies. It would take Victoria's 1887 Slander of Women Act and a high-profile case brought by a leading temperance campaigner and suffrage supporter for the issue to receive national press attention in England and for politicians to take the issue seriously. However, by then the change pushed in other jurisdictions—gender specific legislation—was moving out of fashion, as suffragists sought equal rights and to abolish the double standard in morality.

The abolition of the ecclesiastical courts of England was a major disappointment for slandered women. The church courts were not perfect—they offered penance not compensation—but they were the primary mechanism for women seeking public vindication and reputational rehabilitation. Such matters were seldom mentioned in discussions about ecclesiastical reform and abolition in the 1850s. One legal periodical reflected a growing hostility towards the canon courts and anticipated their "speedy extinction."[7] They wrote that while the courts "declare their willingness to submit to any reform that may be desired," they "protest against their abolition." But abolition was the only feasible solution, the authors concluded:

> [I]t is not a case for reform: the objection to them is not merely that they abound in monopolies and abuse, but that their foundation and structure are unsound, unfitted for the time, an insult to one half of the community, and an injustice to the other. It is as Ecclesiastical Courts that they are condemned.... But then they say, you must have tribunals for these questions. Why not the regular Courts of Law and Equity?[8]

In February 1854, while debating the future of the ecclesiastical jurisdiction, Lord Campbell remarked that actions for "slander and defamation ought to be brought in the courts of common law, where they would be tried by a jury, rather than in the ecclesiastical courts, the imposition of a penance by which was not so effectual a punishment as the levying of damages."[9]

But strangely—given his interest in the issue of the slander of women a decade earlier—Lord Campbell did not mention the difficulties faced by women in the common law courts: tasked with proving special damage in cases of sexual imputations and thus unable to obtain any remedy for slander. Moving slander to the exclusive determination of the common law would leave thousands of women without reputational recourse. Such matters were not raised or debated by parliamentarians or jurists. In February 1855, the Bill for Abolishing the Jurisdiction of the Ecclesiastical Courts of England and Wales in Suits for Defamation was introduced. It stated that the ecclesiastical court's determination of spiritual defamation had become "grievous and oppressive to the Subjects of this Realm" and thus it would no longer be lawful for any canon court to entertain or adjudicate such a suit. At this point in time, the ecclesiastical courts, as Stephen Waddams documents, were still providing hundreds of women in England with an accessible and practical way of addressing sexual slurs and verbal abuse hurled at them by men in their communities.[10] Therefore, the "Subjects of this Realm" imagined by the bill as oppressed and aggrieved by such suits were clearly men. The bill passed, and from 1855 onwards, women's options for bringing defamation claims in England were severely curtailed.

It was not long before the gender injustice of abolishing the ecclesiastical courts while not simultaneously reforming the common law became apparent. In April 1860, the Court of Exchequer heard a case brought by farmers William and Hannah Allsop, thirty-seven and thirty-four years old, respectively, of Brassington, Derbyshire, against their relative, Thomas Allsop. According to newspaper reports, Thomas had spoken "some most beastly and disgusting words reflecting upon the chastity of all the fair ladies residing within the vicinity within which he himself resided, as well as upon the wife of the plaintiff."[11] The words specifically imputed that he, Thomas, had had a "carnal connection" with Hannah while she was married to William. According to the pleadings, in consequence of Thomas's words, Hannah lost the company of her friends and neighbors and sank into a protracted illness whereby she was unable to attend to her "necessary affairs and business." William incurred great expense trying to cure his wife of her illness and "lost the society and association of his wife for a long time in his domestic affairs." The couple claimed damages for their combined losses. But the defendant demurred, arguing that "the declaration was bad" because no special damage was proved. Loss of association of friends and neighbors had never been held to be sufficient special damage, he said. Further, Hannah's illness and attendant expenses were not "the natural result of the slander but arose from a peculiarity of temperament." The plaintiff's lawyers submitted in reply that the natural consequence of "such an imputation"—being a gross sexual slur aimed at Hannah—was to "undermine and affect her health." Slanderers should have to pay damages when their words caused others illness.

The Court of Exchequer, by now an exclusively common law court, unanimously upheld the defendant's demurrer and dismissed Hannah and William's slander claim. Chief Baron Pollock held that there was no precedent for the kind of special damage alleged in the pleadings. Here, the "particular damage" suffered depended on the "temperament of the party affected," and "it may be laid down that illness arising from the excitement which the slanderous language may produce is not that sort of damage that forms a ground of action."[12] Part of Pollock's reasoning involved a keen interest in limiting slander litigation. He worried about expanding the definition of special damage to include illness, given "what a large class of actions" it would apply to and "what a dangerous use might be made of it."

Debates and discussion about special damage in England during the nineteenth century frequently voiced fears that women would bring slander cases against men too often, and for malicious purposes, if its scope and remit were not restricted. Unlike in the United States, where the primary social and legal problem identified was the slander of (white) women, in England the issue was often framed as women's spurious or vexatious complaints against men, which needed to be controlled and discouraged. The other three barons—Wilde, Martin, and Bramwell—agreed with Pollock (chief baron). Only Bramwell expressed any uncertainty over the decision, noting that the decision posed "some difficulty" because "a wrong is done to the female plaintiff," and she had indeed suffered damage.[13] However, he quickly dismissed his feelings of sympathy, agreeing that "there is certainly no precedent for such an action."

Allsop v Allsop was quickly followed by the similar case of *Lynch v Knight*, which originated in the Court of Queen's Bench in Ireland. William and Jane Knight, married and living in Dublin, claimed that in July 1858, James Lynch said to William:

Jane is a notorious liar, and she will do her best to annoy you, as she takes delight in creating disturbances wherever she goes, and I advise you not to introduce her into society. Any singularity of conduct which you may have observed in your wife must be attributed to a Dr. Casserly of Roscommon, as she was all but seduced by him; and I advise you, if Casserly comes to Dublin, not to permit him to enter your place, as he is a libertine and a blackguard. . . . I have no other object in view in telling you about her conduct, and in speaking to you as I have done, but your own welfare. She is an infamous wretch, and I am sorry that you had the misfortune to marry her; and if you had asked my advice on the subject, I would have advised you not to marry her.[14]

Lynch further stated that Jane was "a horrid young villain," "a notorious liar," and "a dangerous character." There seems to have been some history of familiarity between the parties.

The plaintiffs argued that as a result of hearing and believing Lynch's words, William "was induced to refuse and in fact refused to live any longer with the plaintiff Jane as his wife." He contacted Jane's father in the countryside and demanded that he take back his daughter—which he did—and Jane thus left Dublin and resided with her father for a considerable time. Jane argued that William abandoning her was entirely and solely caused by Lynch's words and claimed 1,000 pounds in damages. The jury found for Jane, awarding her 150 pounds. Lynch appealed the Queen's Bench decision to the Court of Exchequer Chamber in Ireland, which affirmed the lower court's judgment. He then appealed to the House of Lords in England, arguing that "the words complained of not being actionable in themselves, the special damage assigned was too remote, also that the damage, if taken to be the damage to the wife alone, was not such a temporal loss as a Court of Common Law could take cognisance of."[15] In other words, William choosing to throw Jane out of the house after the slander was not sufficient special damage.

Lynch's lawyers argued that there was no precedent for finding that marital separation constituted special damage and cited *Allsop v Allsop* as authority. Special damage meant pecuniary loss, they submitted—"feelings alone will not sustain the action"—and no such damage had been sustained by Jane Knight.[16] In reply, the Knights' lawyers argued that Jane had suffered "a substantial injury" in losing the consortium of her husband. Further, such damage or injury was the "natural result of the words" as the defendant "must have foreseen and intended the mischief he caused." They submitted: "The wife is entitled to be clothed and fed at the expense of the husband [and] here she was deprived of those advantages."[17]

Lord Campbell, who had once championed defamation reform on this very issue to no avail, presided over the case but died before judgment was handed down. Lord Brougham read out Campbell's penned decision. A wife could maintain an action for slander against a third party for words resulting in loss of consortium, he declared. Loss of consortium was sufficient special damage. However, there needed to be a close nexus between the loss or damage suffered and the acts of the defendant. In this case, Jane Knight's action was "not maintainable, because, looking to the frame of the declaration, the loss or special damage relied upon [was] not the natural or probable consequence of the injury of, viz, the slanderous words."[18] To Lord Campbell, if William Knight had been informed by Lynch that Jane had committed adultery and this caused him to throw her out, then an action for slander would be maintainable. Such a response would be the "natural and probable consequence" of an allegation of adultery leveled at a wife.

Unfortunately for Jane, the case hinged on what the House of Lords considered a "reasonable," not "idiosyncratic," husband would do in such circumstances. In the present case, faced with allegations by Lynch that Jane simply suffered a "levity of manners," that she required "vigilance," and that she "would bring disgrace on him" at social occasions, it was unreasonable and excessive for William to evict her from the marital home. Therefore, the special damage suffered by Jane—being loss of conjugal society—was not a natural and probable effect of the slander against her.

Jane's slander action against Lynch was unsuccessful. Her husband, it was decided, had overreacted. Lord Brougham largely agreed with Lord Campbell, stating that the words spoken by Lynch—alleging Jane had "all but been seduced" before marriage —"in an ordinary case, and with ordinary men, would not have led to the consequence of the wife being turned out of the house, and sent home to her father."[19] William Knight was, according to Brougham, not an "ordinary" man, nor a "reasonable" husband. Lord Cranworth agreed with Lord Campbell and Lord Brougham, stating that the "natural result" of the imputations leveled against Jane would surely be for the husband to "watch his wife more carefully"—not to send her away to live with her parents.[20]

In dismissing Jane's case, Lord Campbell lamented upon the "unsatisfactory state" of slander law for women in England, "according to which the imputation by words, however gross, on an occasion, however public, upon the chastity of a modest matron or a pure virgin, is not actionable without proof that it has actually produced special temporal damage to her."[21] However, having attempted to change the law via legislation years earlier, he noted regretfully in conclusion: "But I am only here to declare the law." Lord Brougham also affirmed Lord Campbell's general remarks about English slander law for women, but he went further, stating: "I think that such a state of things can only be described as barbarous."[22]

Lord Wensleydale also found for Lynch, but for different reasons. He stated that loss of consortium was not sufficient special damage for a wife to maintain a slander action, but it was for a husband. This was because "the benefit which the husband has in the consortium of the wife, is of a different character from that which the wife has in the consortium of the husband."[23] He compared the relationship of husband and wife to master and servant, stating that the wife's duties—resembling the roles of "hired domestic, tutor or governess"—were of "material value" and "capable of being estimated in money." Therefore, when a husband lost the consortium of his wife, he lost a material benefit, but when a wife lost consortium, she merely suffered "mental pain" and "anxiety," as he was still legally obliged to maintain her financially. Lord Wensleydale surmised that the common law of defamation and rules about special damage were primarily about money: "It is to the protection of such material interests that the law chiefly attends."[24]

The decisions of *Allsop v Allsop* and *Lynch v Knight* rested upon normative assumptions about marriage roles and prescribed the limits of reasonable relations and behaviors. Hannah Allsop's protracted illness, occurring after gross public slander alleging adultery against her, was deemed not sufficient special damage because it was too "remote." That is, it was not a foreseeable consequence but resulted due to her "peculiarity of temperament." Similarly, Jane's loss of consortium, occurring after Lynch slandered her, was not special damage as it was not the "natural and probable result" of Lynch's words. William Knight's decision to throw her out and send her back to her parents was not the reasonable reaction of an ordinary husband, but excessive and idiosyncratic. Both Hannah and Jane lost their sexual slander actions—against Thomas Allsop and James Lynch, respectively—not because the words were not proven or because no harm was done, but because either they or their husbands were framed as peculiar and acting beyond the bounds of marital normality.

Further cases concerning the slander of married women soon came before the appeal courts in England. Robert Roberts and his wife Margaret, farmers in their forties, sued the defendant (who also had the surname Roberts) after he spoke the following words: "You have got for a wife as great a whore as any in the town of Liverpool. I had connection with her several times, the last night or two before she left for Liverpool."[25] Margaret was a proud member of a sect of Protestant Dissenters—Calvinist Methodists—and belonged to a society and congregation in Denbigh, North Wales. The sect was subject to rules and regulations, and members could not join these societies or congregations before being certified by leaders and elders as "morally fit and proper." The defendant publicly spoke the slanderous words about Margaret, causing her to be ejected from the society and congregation in North Denbigh and unable to join the same in Liverpool. She was thus prevented from attending religious worship, became "greatly injured in her good name and reputation," and grew "sick and ill and greatly distressed in body and mind." Her husband Robert incurred "great expense in and about nursing the plaintiff Margaret and endeavouring to get her cured from her sickness, illness and distress of mind." They claimed 500 pounds in damages.

But the defendant demurred. Citing *Lynch v Knight*, he argued that the words were not actionable without special damage. Citing *Allsop v Allsop*, he submitted that sickness and ill health suffered by a wife as a result of slander were not regarded as special damage. The fact Margaret had been excluded from the society and congregation of Calvinist Methodists and prevented from worship was "not temporal or pecuniary damage." In reply, the plaintiffs' attorney leaned on Lord Campbell's decision in *Lynch v Knight*. He had held that loss of consortium was a form of special damage, and so, the plaintiffs argued, loss of congregation should be recognized as well. They also put forth that if special damage was confined to purely pecuniary damage, an action for sexual slander by a wife could never be maintained as damage would be incurred to the husband, not her. Via the doctrine of coverture, a wife could not separately own property and thus could not suffer its loss.

Chief Justice Cockburn "reluctantly" dismissed Margaret's case and gave judgment for the defendant. He did not regard loss of membership of the society and congregation—constituted for religious and spiritual purposes—as special damage, as no real or material advantages attached to it. But, like Lords Campbell and Brougham in *Lynch*, he went on to give his opinion about the present state of the English common law for women: "I think that to prevent a woman whose character for chastity is assailed from bringing an action for the purpose of vindicating it is cruel."[26] Justice Crompton agreed with the chief justice. "Though I wish the law were different in the case of words affecting the chastity of a woman," he commented, "here there was no loss of a temporal nature."[27] And Justice Blackburn concurred, noting with disappointment: "The law upon the subject of disparaging words spoken of other persons is not in a satisfactory state."[28]

After a discouraging set of appeal cases for slandered wives, there was a brief victory in 1871. John and Isabella Davies sued the defendant, Solomon, after he said in the company of various people: "'I can prove John Davies' wife had connection with a man named Labrach two years ago, but I would rather have the tongue cut out of my mouth than separate man and wife."[29] As a result, John Davies separated from Isabella, and she was ostracized by friends and denied hospitality. Citing *Lynch v Knight*, particularly the judgment of Lord Wensleydale, the defendant argued the loss of consortium was not sufficient special damage. Solomon's lawyers also stated that there was no pecuniary loss to the wife as her husband was still legally obliged to supply her with necessities. Justice Blackburn disagreed. Putting the thorny issue of loss of consortium to one side, he declared that being deprived of the hospitality of friends was a natural and probable consequence of an allegation of adultery. He referred to the case of *Moore v Meagher* as authority for the proposition that loss of hospitality constituted special damage, for the word meant "simply that persons receive another into their houses, and give him meat and drink gratis."[30] Blackburn distinguished *Roberts v Roberts* by noting that there Margaret's exclusion did not incur temporal or pecuniary losses, whereas here Isabella did suffer temporal damage "small though it be." Blackburn was eager to bend slander law as far as he could to offer some justice to Isabella. He put coverture to one side, stating that to regard such pecuniary losses as the husband's (because he is the sole legal person) was "artificial" and that "the real damage in this case is to the wife herself."³¹ For he might be obliged to provide her with necessities, but from friends she might have enjoyed luxuries. Justices Mellor and Hannen concurred.

After that time, there was little agitation about the issue in England until Victoria passed its own slander of women legislation in 1887, inspired by New York's act of 1871 (see Chapter 7). This colonial development finally put the issue on the political agenda in England. On February 2, 1888, the London *Times*'s Melbourne correspondent reported upon various measures that had been passed in the far-flung colony in the last parliamentary session.³² He singled out the Slander and Libel Law Amendment Act 1887 (Victoria's Slander of Women Act) for detailed commentary and praise and noted that it offered a "distinct and substantial improvement" to defamation law, which "to lawyers and laymen alike" was regarded as "a disgrace to English law." That women were without effective slander remedies in England seemed a "strange anomaly in this our age of professed regard for even-handed justice to man and woman alike." Quoting Lord Brougham's words in the decision of *Lynch v Knight* that the English common law was "barbarous" for women, the correspondent declared that "our Parliament"—the Victorian parliament—had, in the last session, passed an act "which gives a right of action in such cases without the necessity of the plaintiff proving special damage." He concluded with pride: "We may, therefore, on Lord Brougham's authority, claim in this advance to be less barbarous than are the old folks at home."

It must have been galling for many in British Parliament to be regarded as barbarous by the colonies and lagging in "civilized" law reform. And so, only a few months later, on July 2, 1888, Edward Pickersgill, barrister and Liberal member of the UK House of Commons for the constituency of Bethnal Green South West, referred to Victoria's Slander of Women's Act 1887. On the floor of the House, he questioned the attorney general, Sir Richard Webster, as to whether his attention had been called to a recent act of the parliament of Victoria, which provided that words spoken and published of any woman imputing to her a want of chastity shall be slander and actionable without needing proof of special damage and asked whether he was prepared to take steps to amend the law of England in a similar sense.³³ Webster replied dismissively: "My attention has not been called to the Act in question. It is a matter for consideration whether it is desirable to amend the Law of England in a similar sense; but I am not prepared at present to introduce a Bill with that object."³⁴ Pickersgill was on the radical wing of the Liberal Party and an ardent campaigner for criminal law reform, including abolition of the death penalty. He was also a supporter of women's suffrage.

Later that same day, Pickersgill joined Thomas Milvain, a lawyer and member of the Conservative Party, and others to introduce a Slander of Women Bill to the UK Parliament.³⁵ It proposed that in an action brought for words spoken, which imputed unchastity or adultery to a woman, it would no longer be necessary to prove special damage. But damages for such actions would be limited to 100 pounds, unless special damages could be showed.³⁶ It sought to copy Victoria's bill but limit damages in order to better appeal to politicians worried about opening the floodgates to vexatious women. This was a bipartisan measure, also supported by Queen's Counsel John Addison (Conservative member for Ashton under Lyne), Henry Hartley Fowler (Liberal member for the borough of Wolverhampton), John Shiress Will (Liberal member for Montrose Burghs), and Thomas Burt, a trade unionist and one of the first working-class members of the House of Commons.³⁷

On July 5, 1888, the *Liverpool Mercury* published a commentary on the bill. "Libel Law has its sister," the article began insightfully, highlighting the gendered division engrained within defamation law. It went on to state that "most people [would be] surprised to learn [that] a woman slandered as to her virtue cannot punish her accuser without proving special damage." This "hiatus in the law" would be filled by Milvain's bill, the author noted. However, they doubted the necessity of the 100 pounds cap on damages, arguing that it would "be read as an invitation to slander on the part of those who can indulge in their amusement and pay the price." Nonetheless, they concluded that the restriction on damages would "help the bill to pass [and would be] an improvement upon a condition of the law which leaves women with no remedy at all."³⁸ The author intimated towards the class dynamics of this bill, with a damages limit of 100 pounds, which would function to punish the tongues of the lower classes and bear no real threat to professional and aristocratic men. Despite this built-in reassurance to members of Parliament, there was no further mention of Milvain's bill. It is likely, given the attorney general's opposition, that it was simply abandoned and not put to a vote.

But advocacy on the issue continued within newspapers. On January

10, 1890, the barrister C. H. M. Wharton published an article on slander in the Manchester *Stockport Advertiser* titled "Absurdities in English Law."³⁹ Opening with Shakespeare's lines from *Othello* about the unique value of a "good name," Wharton observed that this wisdom from "the great poet whose knowledge of human nature has no parallel" had clearly not been received by the great lawyers and lawmakers of England. He decried the current state of affairs where "to call a woman a 'strumpet' or a 'bawd'; or to say of a woman that 'she had a bastard' is not actionable without special damage." Noting that such reforms had occurred elsewhere in the British empire, the author asked: "Why in the name of common sense should not that privilege extend to England?" Citing and quoting the judgments of important preceding slander cases—*Allsop v Allsop, Lynch v Knight, Roberts v Roberts*—wherein the current state of slander law for women was labeled by senior judges as unsatisfactory and barbarous, the author noted it was "a remarkable fact [that] the Legislature has not thought fit to remove the injustice." He concluded: "we think we have said sufficient to show that the law on the subject requires revision, and we must leave some of our ambitious law reformers to do the rest."

A few months later, in April 1890, a slander case brought by leading British temperance campaigner Elizabeth Ann Lewis garnered extensive public attention and sympathy and offered law reformers an opportunity to put slander reform back on the political agenda.⁴⁰ At the time, Lewis was one of the most well-connected and effective temperance advocates in England. Born in Shropshire in 1843 to parents who were strict adherents to "total abstinence," Lewis had accompanied them to outdoor temperance meetings as a child and then took on their cause with fervor. In 1867, she married Thomas Lewis, who shared her views on the ills of alcohol, and they settled in Blackburn where he operated a coach-building business and she worked tirelessly: giving public talks across the country, seeking people to sign "the pledge," lobbying government to restrict liquor licenses, organizing temperance parades and concerts, helping women discharged from workhouses re-enter the community, accompanying the working poor to and from factories so they avoided entering the ubiquitous public houses. In the late nineteenth century, Blackburn was known as the drunkest town in England. The 1881 census records that more than 600 establishments were licensed to sell alcohol (for a population of around 129,000), the equivalent to one beer shop or pub to every 34 houses.⁴¹

Lewis believed alcohol abuse was the cause of most social ills, from poverty to family violence to child neglect. As well as her temperance work, she carried out other social programs for the poor, such as free breakfasts for children in Blackburn. Lewis was also a strong supporter of women's suffrage, declaring: "I object as a woman to be classed for voting purposes with lunatics and criminals. Women know what is best for their own sex, and I am positive that if they had the vote they would use it on the side of temperance."[42] Lewis allowed suffrage groups to meet in the hall of her temperance organization without charge. To fund her work expenses and the salary of her assistant—first Richard Kilshaw, and later Edward Moss—Lewis sought subscriptions and donations. Some were received from powerful supporters, including Catherine, the wife of Prime Minister William Gladstone. Lewis soon became known in England as the temperance queen and the drunkard's friend. She was a longstanding member of the British Women's Temperance Association and was vice president of the British Temperance League.

However, Lewis's indefatigable work earned her passionate enemies. In 1889, she learned that a Blackburn publican, John Shaw, had been spreading malicious rumors about her being sexually immoral. Lewis employed the services of Queen's Counsel William Gully (then also a Liberal member for Carlisle in the House of Commons) and sued Shaw for slander. She claimed that in October 1889, Shaw told several customers at his hotel that she and her assistant temperance missionary, Edward Moss, had been in Blackpool the previous day and "misconducted themselves."[43] Evidence was given at trial by various men who heard Shaw relay this story in his public house. They testified that Shaw told them he was with a group of men out hunting in Blackpool that day, two of whom were fellow publicans, and they were on St. Annes beach, when they saw Lewis and Moss disappear into the sand dunes together. According to Shaw, Lewis laid Moss's overcoat down on the sand, and Moss looked around furtively to see if anyone was watching them. They were there for almost an hour, and Shaw reported that during that time "improper intercourse took place twice."[44] To be accused of adultery with her professional assistant and having sex in public was horrifying to Lewis.

On the stand, she swore that no such events ever took place. She stated that she had traveled by train with Moss to Blackpool to meet people as part of her temperance work, and they had, at one point, walked along the beach as it was a fine day. They stopped for a moment to observe a jellyfish on the sand. But, she assured the jury, they had never ventured into the sand dunes together, let alone engaged in any immoral activity.[45] Moss also testified, stating that he did not know at the time that there was ill feeling directed at him by Shaw but that "if he were successful in his business, the defendant would be unsuccessful in his."[46] In other words, the issue of temperance was a major cause of enmity between the parties and the primary motive of Shaw for discrediting and ruining Lewis. In the reply to Lewis's case, the defendant's lawyers submitted that Shaw had never uttered the slander, but that in any case the imputations were true, and Lewis had proved no requisite special damage.

Gully was aware of the burden of proving special damage in such cases and explained the problem to the jury. In his opening remarks, he stated that Lewis was forced by the "unfortunate state" of the law of England to prove she had suffered pecuniary losses. He noted that a person might say a woman was bad in her business or had committed a minor offense and that would be slander, but for imputations affecting her "honor," a woman in England could not bring an action to clear her name "unless she could prove what the law called 'special damage.'"[47] Only if she could show she had "lost a penny" could a woman seek vindication. Gully said that "he regretted that state of the law" and apologized in advance to the jury for the evidence he was required to furnish—"evidence he would have gladly left out." He stated he would soon call evidence to prove Lewis had lost subscriptions to her temperance cause as a result of Shaw's slander: "But the jury would understand he did so only because the law compelled him to do it, and not because it was anything material to the reasons that really brought Mrs. Lewis into court that day." It was not money Lewis was after, but justice. Several witnesses were therefore called who testified that they ceased subscribing to Lewis's temperance mission after hearing Shaw's rumors. Shaw's lawyer, Queen's Counsel Bingham, argued in reply that the subscriptions had to have been canceled as a direct result of hearing the defendant's words and this was not shown.

Sensing his client was in danger of losing her case on the point of special damage, Gully agreed to settlement terms put forth by Bingham. If Lewis discontinued her case, Shaw would "unreservedly" accept their narrative of events, withdraw all imputations that he might have conveyed about Lewis, express his "deep regret" that he made such statements, offer damages of 40 shillings, and pay 50 pounds towards Lewis's court costs.

Upon her return to Blackburn semi-victorious, Lewis's friends, associates, and neighbors met her at the train station, and, according to newspapers, the crowd "cheered vociferously" with men waving their hats and women running up to kiss her. At a meeting later that night on a street in Blackburn, Lewis declared that "from the very first she did not want money; she wanted what she had now got—her character, her purity and her honour recognised by a judge and jury." She thanked "the working people of Blackburn for the sympathy they had shown her and the confidence they had in her from the beginning of the case."[48] However, Lewis was waist-deep in legal debt. The 50 pounds paid by Shaw only affrayed a small portion of her legal costs, and she was forced to call upon friends and organize temperance events for the rest of the year to pay the remainder of between 250 and 300 pounds.[49]

Newspaper coverage of the *Lewis v Shaw* case was extensive in England. Given Gully's emphasis upon the unjust burden of special damage facing women in such cases, many commentators also picked up and discussed the issue. Despite Lewis achieving vindication via settlement, journalists and jurists highlighted the injustice she faced in securing a proper verdict. The *Liverpool Mercury* published a long column, opening with the observation that "the law of this country prides itself on the axiom that for every wrong there is remedy," before highlighting how slander law for women in England exposed this axiom as false.[50] The author likened special damage to "'a lion" laying in Lewis's path to vindication. They concluded that although Lewis achieved some remedy via the terms of settlement, "owing to the cranky state of the English law, she has been obliged to do so at considerable charge to her pocket," and her traducer has escaped without penalty.

Riding on the publicity and outrage generated by Lewis's case, Gully swiftly took the matter back into Parliament. On May 15, 1890, he—joined by a bipartisan group of politicians (Reid, Addison, Dugdale, Caine, and Milvain)—introduced another Slander of Women Bill to the House of Commons.[51] Press reports on the new bill reminded readers that "such slanders are not actionable unless it can be proved that special damage has been sustained by the victims of the slanders," which was "a most unsatisfactory condition of the law."[52] The author went on to note:

[T]his was abundantly shown in the Blackburn slander case, the unsatisfactory ending of which in the absence of substantial reparation will in all probability lead to a much needed reform in legal procedure. This is one result of the action upon which all parties may congratulate themselves.

In July 1890, the bill was read a second time, and Gully explained its purpose and the longstanding view of the House of Lords that the law was barbarous and desperately in need of reform.[53] Sir Richard Webster objected to the bill, arguing that it would unjustly burden men's speech, especially that expressed in the heat of passion. He put forth that "it is well known that when temper gets the upper hand of a person," he might use "words that ought not to be used [and] there would be a number of cases in which hardships would be inflicted" on such men. He feared that "actions might be brought for words spoken rashly and hastily," and that would be a "dangerous thing." Mr. Kelly also expressed his concern about women using the law to bring "vexatious" or "frivolous" actions against men and that "there are no graver scandals in our Courts of Justice than the enormous number of trivial actions brought for libel and slander, especially slander." Captain Verney objected on the grounds that "woman" should be substituted with "person" as it was "a very dangerous thing" to grant women an action for sexual slander, but not men.

Gully replied to these criticisms, assuring Webster and Kelly that judges could dismiss trivial claims and explaining to Verney: "The fact is, that men do not suffer under the imputation to the same extent that women do. There is not the same practical hardship, or the same danger of an imputation against men being made maliciously." The sexual slander of men was not a social problem that required a remedy. Some minor amendments were made to Gully's bill, and it was reintroduced to the House of Commons in December 1890.[54] In March 1891, it was read a second time.[55]

In 1891, newspaper commentary and debate about the Slander of Women Bill and its reform of English law gathered momentum, in part due to another failed case brought by a woman over slurs of unchastity.[56] The *Liverpool Mercury* declared that on this issue "the common law presents a grotesque-appearance" and "a satire on the age of civilisation."[57] The author opined: "we do not expect that English law in every case to accord with national sentiment, but we do expect that the one shall not hit the other directly in the face." He concluded by analogizing the reform of slander law to other pressing legal issues of equality:

> The Radical member who has championed the rights of the sex by attempting to make divorce accessible to women ... has only taken a narrow survey of his duties. Let him bring in a Bill to make the slander of a woman's chastity actionable without special damage; and by freeing the sex of their cowardly traducers he will earn a fame more imperishable, because more real, than that of any of the knight-errants of antiquity.

Women should be liberated from their slanderers, as they should be allowed to be freed from their husbands.

Debates about women's rights to reputational justice attracted the attention of the suffrage movement. In May 1891, the Women's Franchise League submitted a petition advocating for an amendment to the Slander of Women Bill on the grounds of equality. Ursula Bright and Harriet Stanton-Blatch wrote that they regarded "the moral character of men and their good reputation as of equal importance and concern to the community and to themselves as the reputation of women." Therefore, they argued, they objected to the "one-sided measure known as the Slander of Women Bill" as it would encourage "the present double standard of morality for the sexes." They pushed that "legislation regarded as necessary for the protection of women against slander may apply equally to men." The Women's Franchise League did not oppose the Slander of Women Bill but wanted it amended, as they were concerned the wording would reinforce feminine expectations of purity and modesty for women and encourage men's sexual license. They sought a gender-neutral reform to slander law, so that both women and men could bring cases for sexual slander without the archaic burden of special damage. In other words, they wanted what New Jersey had implemented a hundred years earlier.

The distinction made within the common law of slander between married and single women—in terms of how they could prove special damage—would also have been deeply troubling to the Women's Franchise League. Founded in 1889 by Emmeline Pankhurst (political activist and suffragette) and her husband Richard Pankhurst (English barrister and socialist), the WFL was a radical suffrage organization with international links to American suffragists that distinguished itself from other suffrage groups in the UK by advocating for the right of married women, as well as single women, to vote. As historian Sandra Holton has noted: "The platform of the Women's Suffrage League was an expansive one from the beginning and radical by the standards of the existing suffrage societies."[58]

The inaugural meetings of the WFL were held at the Pankhurst home in Russell Square, London. Its objects included "to extend to women, whether unmarried, married, or widowed, the right to vote at Parliamentary, municipal, local and other elections on the same conditions that qualify men." Second, they wished "to establish for women equal civil and political rights with men." Early members included Josephine Butler (leader of the Ladies' National Association for the Repeal of the Contagious Diseases Acts), Ursula Mellor Bright (founding member of the Manchester Society for Women's Suffrage in 1867), and Harriot Eaton Stanton Blatch, daughter of US suffragist Elizabeth Cady Stanton (Cady Stanton herself was also closely aligned with the WFL). Harriet McIlquham was the first president of the WFL. The Pankhursts and Bright had been instrumental in drafting and advocating for the Married Women's Property Act 1882 (UK). The WFL explained that "the practical work of the League is great; its province being to seek the removal of every disability imposed upon women by a privileged sex ascendancy, whether enforced by law or by social custom."[59]

The burden of special damage was, in the eyes of WFL petitioners Ursula Bright and Harriot Stanton Blatch, one such disability. But removing that longstanding legal disability and replacing it with a measure that only applied to women would not suffice. The WFL sought equal legal rights in areas of voting, divorce, child custody, property, contract, inheritance, as well as reputation. They feared, as they stated in their petition, that the Slander of Women Bill as presently drafted would encourage a "double standard of morality for the sexes." Men should also be able to sue for slander if they were accused of adultery, unchastity, or fornication. These ideas had been put forward, as noted earlier, by Sir Edmund Verney in the House of Commons when he said "woman" in the bill should be substituted with "person." Verney was likely influenced by his "Aunt Florence"—Florence Nightingale—who, among her other causes, had worked to reform prostitution laws that unfairly penalized women and ignored the behavior of soliciting men.

In late-nineteenth-century Britain, suffrage and equal rights for women were closely intertangled with hauling down the double standard of sexual morality. As historian Susan Kent has argued, British feminists challenged the double standard on two grounds: they attacked "laws that restricted or confined their scope of opportunity," and they protested against "laws that legitimised unequal standards of behaviour and imposed unequal penalities on the sexual transgressions of men and women."[60] The Slander of Women Bill sought to remove a legal restriction on women seeking reputational vindication, but it reinforced the different expectations of sexual behavior for men and women. Suffragists, such as those involved in the WFL, sought, as Kent explains, to "raise up the moral standard applicable to men to those pertaining to women." In essence, the WFL argued that all persons should be able to bring slander suits when accused of sexual misconduct.

The WFL was not, however, successful in amending the Slander of Women Bill. In May 1891, Gully's bill, spurred by Lewis's slander action, passed the House of Commons. The *Liverpool Mercury*, after its many columns championing the reform, was triumphant and seemingly ignorant of suffragist concerns about the bill: "The public, therefore, may regard the anomaly which the bill proposes to abolish as practically extinct, and we may congratulate the sex upon the attainment of a right often advocated in these columns."[61] The *Observer* noted that the bill was one that removed "a scandalous anomaly in the law."[62] The *Weekly Standard and Express* explained the bill would remedy "a grave injustice."[63]

In June 1891, the Slander of Women Bill reached the House of Lords for consideration.[64] Lord MacNaughten took carriage of the measure, stating that it removed "a reproach to the administration of justice in England." However, as in the House of Commons, the bill again faced opposition on the basis that it might open the floodgates to frivolous suits brought by vindictive women. The Lord Chancellor argued that English history had showed that "the power for bringing actions for words spoken has been the subject of the greatest possible abuse," and therefore lifting any current restrictions must be subject to deep scrutiny. He noted that "a serious danger" would result from "opening a new field of litigation upon this subject of words spoken" and allowing women to bring such claims against men. However, this time arguments about tidal waves of scorned women vexatiously pursuing suits of slander against men did not halt the bill's progress. The floodgates argument and fears of men's intemperate speech being unfairly restricted was overwhelmed by a desire to reform "barbarous" laws so that Britian appeared to be as "civilized" as the colonies of Australia and the former colonies of the United States. The Slander of Women Bill passed the upper house on July 30, 1891, and made sexual slander claims for women actionable *per se*.[65] It was one of the last jurisdictions in the common law world to enact this reform.

CONCLUSION

In 2005, Georgeann Walsh Ward sued Gene Simmons (of the 1970s rock band KISS) and Viacom International, in the New York Supreme Court, alleging they made a documentary that portrayed her as a "sex-addicted nymphomaniac."[1] In the documentary—*When KISS Ruled the World*—Simmons boasted of his sexual prowess: "There wasn't a girl that was off limits, and I enjoyed every one of them." The narrator stated: "Everywhere [Simmons] went, he found a woman, and it didn't matter who they were, what size, shape, or anything, he'd find a woman and disappear with her." These comments, part of a segment titled "24 Hour Whore," were intercut with numerous photographs of the plaintiff. According to Ward, this segment— bragging about Simmons's sexual conquests—was littered with demeaning falsehoods about her. Ward and Simmons had met in 1972, prior to the formation of KISS, and had been involved in an "exclusive, monogamous relationship." Ward brought proceedings against Simmons and Viacom on two grounds. First, she argued that the use of her photograph in the documentary breached her right to privacy. Second, she claimed that the documentary depicted her in a defamatory manner. The defendants sought to dismiss her lawsuit, submitting that Ward had proven no special damage.

Justice Rosalyn Richter presided over the case and was quick to knock down this argument: "To constitute a slander per se, plaintiff need only show that the defamatory words alleged impute unchastity or promiscuity to her." This was, since 1871, the law in New York. Looking at the facts before her, Richter surmised that the documentary had the potential to impugn Ward's reputation: "The repeated use of plaintiff's photographs during the documentary could lead a reasonable viewer to conclude that plaintiff was a woman who would regularly make herself available to Simmons, at his beck and call, for casual sexual encounters." The defendants argued that public standards and social attitudes had changed, and it was no longer defamatory to impute sexual immorality. But Richter was not convinced. She declared that while the court recognized that "changing social mores" affected how sexual conduct is viewed by the community, there was no "legal authority or social science data" to support the argument that allegations of sexual immorality were no longer defamatory.

Like New York, most US states and territories now deem slurs of sexual immorality as defamatory *per se*. Such imputations are regarded as inherently damaging to an individual's reputation, and therefore special damage does not need to be proved. The near uniformity of this position is recognized within the current *US Restatement of Torts, Second*, that declares: "One who publishes a slander that imputes serious sexual misconduct to another is subject to liability to the other without proof of special harm."[2] Note the gender-neutral language. Due to recent cases brought by men as well as arguments about the gender-specific slander of women laws violating the equal protection clause of the US Constitution, many state courts have since extended the common law to cover both men and women.[3] In 2008, the New York Supreme Court declared that in some circumstances imputations of sexual immorality against men can be slanderous *per se*.[4] In 2003, the Supreme Court of Alabama ruled that the state's "gender-based provision" was unconstitutional and would need legislative amendment in order to apply to both men and women.[5] In contrast, the Supreme Court of South Carolina has definitively held that their Slander of Women Act—still enshrined in its 1824 wording—is not unconstitutional.[6] The US Supreme Court is yet to rule on the issue. But in the meantime, the *US Restatement of Torts* reflects the settled common law position in the United States that sexual immorality represents a fourth category of imputations considered slanderous *per se*, alongside the traditional English law categories of criminality, being infected with a loathsome infectious disease, and imputations affecting one's business, trade, profession, or office.

The 1984 South Carolina case, *Wardlaw v Peck*, was brought by a female college student, Mary Jo Wardlaw, who was slandered at a public college event by a visiting guest speaker, author Robert Peck. He was angry Wardlaw had failed to pick him up from the airport the day before and continually insulted her in public, as well as making derogatory references to her "breeding" with a male student. In defending Wardlaw's slander suit, Peck argued that South Carolina's Slander of Women Act created an unconstitutional and "impermissible gender classification" because it gave only women a cause of action. Judge Bell turned to history to explain why the act was not, in fact, unconstitutional. He labeled South Carolina's 1824 Slander of Women Act "classic remedial legislation" that only "applied to women because the rule laid down in the cases applied to women." He explained that the act "simply removed a disability imposed by the common law on women." The cases showed women required this immediate remedy, he declared, and thus the law responded. He concluded that the act did not stop men from pressing that sexual slander should be deemed defamatory *per se* for them. They too could bring cases and seek to change the common law or advocate for legislative reform. The court stated that law always evolved. "Precedents," Bell noted, should be "stepping stones, and not halting places." The court would not freeze the law "in a sixteenth century English mold" just so Peck could escape liability. Judge Bell duly affirmed judgment for Mary Jo Wardlaw, ordering Peck to pay her $24,000 in damages.

It was women, not men, bringing slander claims across the English common law world during the late eighteenth and long nineteenth centuries that changed defamation law and led to sexual slurs being taken seriously. It was women's court cases that wrote a fourth category of defamation *per se* into the *US Restatement of Torts* that is still in use today.

In 2000, Mandeep Walia sued her former boss, Vivek Purmasir, and his company, alleging several claims of sexual harassment and defamation.[7] Walia had been hired as a secretary to Purmasir, but soon after she commenced, he started sexually harassing her physically and verbally. Due to the harassment, Walia quit her job, but when she went to pick up her final paycheck, Purmasir said he would only give it to her if she agreed not to sue him. She refused to release him of liability and left without her check. Purmasir also threatened Walia that he would publish things about her if she sued him. Walia later heard from various people that Purmasir had been telling people she was a whore and a slut and had come to work dressed in a blouse with all the buttons undone. Purmasir also made phone calls to her house, telling her family members she was a whore. Walia testified that she became withdrawn, stopped working, stayed in her room, and became physically and psychologically unwell. The US District Court held that Purmasir's statements amounted to slander *per se* under New York law and awarded Walia $20,000.

Similarly, in 2013, a Californian court heard a case brought by an employee, Deanna Rangel, who sued her employer, American Medical Response West, and her workplace supervisors on numerous grounds, including sexual harassment and defamation.[8] Rangel argued her supervisors defamed her, telling other employees she was "a bitch, whore, worthless, not a good employee and did not deserve to be working as an EMT." The court held that the word "bitch" was disparaging but not actionable because it was a mere insult: "a crude and vulgar expression." But "whore" was different, they stated, as it could, depending on the circumstances, impute a "want of chastity" and thus be slander *per se*.

Also in 2013, "Jane Doe" sued Tobi Simone, her estranged husband, on numerous grounds, including defamation, invasion of privacy, intentional infliction of emotional distress, assault and battery.[9] The plaintiff alleged a history of abuse and physical violence inflicted by Simone. She also stated that Simone had contacted a variety of people—her friends, neighbors, co-workers, family members, and acquaintances—both by phone and in person, accusing her of adultery and calling her a "slut," the "queen of sluts," and a "whore." The plaintiff suffered severe emotional distress, disruption to her relationships with others, humiliation, and fear for the safety of both herself and her children. The US District Court for New Jersey granted Jane Doe default judgment and damages for sexual slander.

In 2016 in Pennsylvania, Carole Mallory (supermodel, writer, and journalist) sued author J. Michael Lennon and publisher Simon & Schuster for defamation, false light, and commercial disparagement.[10] The case concerned Lennon's 2013 biography of novelist Norman Mailer, titled *Norman Mailer: A Double Life*. From 1983 to 1992, Mallory had been in a relationship with Mailer. Mallory alleged that the biography mischaracterized her partnership with Mailer as being "strictly sexual" when in fact the two were in a "long-time, loving relationship." Specifically, Mallory objected to Lennon's portrayal of her as a "venal harlot" who seduced celebrities to advance her career and who was only interested in Mailer for his wealth and professional assistance. The court held that the list of men that Mallory "picked up" and the references to her being a "star seducer" were reasonably capable of defamatory meaning.

These recent court cases demonstrate the diversity of circumstances in which sexual slander still occurs and is pleaded. Legal scholars have also proposed it as an effective way of combating deepfake pornography online.[11] Such cases were only made possible by changes in defamation law that removed the burden of special damage for sexual imputations, changes pioneered by Mary Smith in 1790.

Though driven by women's cases, changes to the law of sexual slander were not always gender specific. The politics as to whether changes to sexual slander law should apply only to women or be extended to men was a persistent point of tension and debate and remains so today (as seen with the US constitutional law arguments regarding the equal protection provision).[12] Men rarely brought sexual morality slander suits, and when they did—such as Terwilliger in New York or Stephens in South Australia—it was often regarded as inappropriate, and their masculinity was called into question. Those jurisdictions that did usher in gender-neutral changes to sexual slander law—New Jersey, New South Wales—did so while proactively imagining new societies and defining them against the past. "Calumny," Chief Justice Kinsey declared, as New Jersey rebuilt after the Revolutionary War, "struck at the peace of society" and must be discouraged. Defamation reform, Paul Windeyer advocated in New South Wales, was necessary to put down savage abuse and encourage an entrepreneurial community with "equal enjoyment" of social rights. In England, the Women's Franchise League suffragists petitioned for the Slander of Women Bill to apply to both men and women in order to haul down the "double standard of morality." Such politics sought formal equality within the law. Men might not bring sexual slander actions but enabling them to do so was symbolic. For what if, one day, "the Premier were accused of unchastity?" asked Victorian politician David Gaunson in 1876.

Laws pertaining only to women, by contrast, responded to the situation on the ground. As the court noted in the 1984 case of *Wardlaw v Peck*, it was "classic remedial legislation." It recognized that the problem was, in fact, gendered. For centuries, women had been verbally abused and slandered on the basis of their sexuality—usually by men. In communities, boarding schools, migrant ships, farms, grocery stores, streets, hotels, private residences, workplaces, and musical performances, women were attacked: "damned whore," he has "fucked" her, "big with child," "lewd and incontinent," "dirty, sluttish woman," "Negroes have been with your wife," "infamous character," "wicked prostitute," "very bad woman," "screwed his mother," "infamous wretch." Many of the words thrown at or about women were considered so gross or obscene that they were omitted from court documents and accounts in newspapers. The slander was usually meant to be punitive, occurring in circumstances of a grudge, enmity, or revenge. She had refused his sexual advances when she worked as a maid in his mother's hotel. She was Native American and living on land next door to his expanding slave plantation. She was a temperance campaigner interfering with his profits as a publican. She was part of a family feuding with their rural neighbors.

It is true, as Andrew King and Lisa Pruitt have separately argued, that the discourse surrounding slander of women cases and legislation often reinforced conceptions of feminine virtue and commodified women's sexual purity.[13] But what were these slandered women to do? They lived in societies where women were defined by their sexual value *and* were denigrated and abused on those terms. They sought to escape stigma and shame and silence their attackers. And to do so, they needed to show the courts that sexual slander was serious. It harmed their standing in their communities, their ability to marry or stay married, their custody of children, their professional and occupational prospects, their health and well-being, and their political status. Getting the court or legislature to recognize these harms meant convincing them that the existing burden of special damage within English common law was sexist and unjust.

This was largely achieved via case law, not speeches or treatises. To see and understand the problem at hand, men—as politicians, lawyers, and judges—had to be shown the injustice via concrete examples in front of them. Theory and rhetoric—the words of Thomas Starkie, Lord Campbell, or John Hulbert—were not sufficient. The sympathies of judges and legislators needed to be aroused by the dire circumstances facing the plaintiffs: young Mary Smith, governess Harriet Spencer, farming wife Lucy Wilson, singer Suzanna Wishart, publican Elizabeth Albrecht, temperance campaigner Elizabeth Lewis, and others. In courts, newspapers, and parliaments, advocacy for the reform of sexual slander law to remove the burden of special damage repeatedly cited and referred to the details of these cases and others. They were stories that captured the public imagination and proved the point. Women needed effective legal recourse for sexual slander immediately. "Everyday lawyers of this colony and the home country had cases brought to them in which some unfortunate woman was labouring under an imputation upon her virtue which was absolutely ruin to her and yet she could obtain no redress," declared Victorian lawyer and politician James Purves in 1876. William Gully, an English Queen's Counsel and member of the House of Commons, explained in 1890: "The fact is, that men do not suffer under the imputation to the same extent that women do. There is not the same practical hardship or the same danger of an imputation against men being made maliciously." It was precisely the ubiquity of sexual slander against women in society that caused many politicians, especially in England, to refuse to pass reforms. Doing so, they feared, would open the floodgates to vindictive and vexatious women.

But garnering sympathy from judges and politicians carried risks. What kind of women and what types of circumstances would attract the most sympathy and concern? Discourses on feminine virtue, that bastion of US republican civil and domestic morality, linked purity and chastity to an iconography of whiteness. A woman's reputation—"pure as driven snow," "a clean sheet of white paper," white as "fleece"—could be "stained," "colored," and "blackened" by slander. The existence of "innocent and unprotected women" rested upon the "unsullied purity" of their characters. Debates about the sexual slander of women in New York and North Carolina implicitly prescribed the racial parameters of the action. This was an area of law intended for the protection of white women. Discussion by jurists and commentators discursively linked white womanhood with chastity—lose one and risk losing the other. Black women—sexually violated and exploited via slavery and/or denigrated as naturally promiscuous—were not regarded as possessing sexual reputations worth defending. Nor were other women on the margins—poor, racially ambiguous, Native American, "lunatics." Nonetheless, a diverse collection of American women *did* bring sexual slander suits, especially in antebellum North Carolina. The 1808 Slander of Women Act enabled them to do so. Cherokee sisters Mary and Catherine Watts won their suits against a powerful plantation owner in the eyes of two all-white, male juries (only to have their victories overturned on technicalities by the state Supreme Court). A woman of color, Nancy Waters, successfully brought a slander action against her much older white neighbor. But cases that attracted most attention by judges were accusations of interracial sex against white women. In the Black Belt of antebellum Georgia, a society built on slavery and white supremacy, slurs against illiterate farming wife Martha Kelly—"Negroes have been with your wife and I can prove it"—led to the first and only racially specific slander of women laws in the common law world. Georgia made it defamatory *per se* to say that a white woman had sexual intercourse with a "slave, negro or free person of color."

Concerns about protecting white women's sexual purity from being "blackened" by slander did not sound as loudly in the Australian colonies or Britain in the nineteenth century. Rather, in Australian frontier colonies, beset by anxiety about their "civilized" status, discourses about savagery, civilization, and barbarism informed debates about the slander of women, constructing an argument that reforming the law and giving women greater reputational rights would be a step towards enlightened progress. Indigenous women in Australia were routinely dismissed as "gins" and "lubras" and not regarded as sufficiently civilized to enjoy a reputation for chastity. "To a *civilised* female, in any part of the globe, a fair reputation is an inestimable possession," declared Chief Justice Stephen of the NSW Supreme Court. "It is outrageous that in our present state of civilisation such a barbarous law should exist," thundered Justice Hartley Williams of the Victorian Supreme Court. "I think such a state of things can only be described as barbarous," declared Lord Brougham. Chastity was framed as a "civilized" virtue, slandering women was for "savages," refusing to provide legal redress was "barbarous." It was only when England was called out by Victoria for being backward on the issue of slander of women that they finally acted to change the common law.

If protecting white women in their communities and relationships was the preoccupation of US slander of women debates, enabling women's economic advancement was the focus of cases and commentary in the fluid and mobile Australian colonies. The cases that attracted the most publicity and legislative attention in Australia were brought by women in situations of paid work. New South Wales governess Harriet Spencer, South Australian singer and performer Suzanna Wishart, Victorian store owner Rebecca Redmond, and publican Elizabeth Albrecht found themselves in a bind under English common law. Sexual slurs harmed them financially in their occupations, trades, and professions, but these were deemed not "actionable" by the courts as the imputations themselves did not relate to their employment or business, as would have allegations of incompetency, dishonesty, or corruption. Such a situation—reflecting defamation law's understanding that a man's reputation for sexual morality was largely irrelevant to his standing and abilities as a proprietor, publican, or politician—seemed ridiculous to many lawyers and laypersons. "A person may say of a public singer that her conduct is such as to exclude her from the society . . . and she has no redress" a commentator remarked in the *Adelaide Observer*, "but if it be said that she croaks like a raven instead of singing like a nightingale, an action for damage will lie." Slander of women reforms enabled women to recuperate monetary losses sustained as employees and business owners and redeem their prospects for paid work. In this way, slander law reform functioned as a precursor to sexual harassment laws in the 1970s and 1980s, protecting women against gendered attacks on their earning capacity and economic activity.

In 2005, the Australian states repealed their slander of women acts. This was part of the uniform defamation acts passed across all the state and territories that abolished the distinction between slander and libel and thus made all claims for defamation actionable without proof of special damage.[14] The United Kingdom similarly repealed its Slander of Women Act in 2013. However, both the UK and Australia have, in recent years, introduced a new threshold burden on defamation plaintiffs, requiring them to show (possibly ahead of trial) that they have suffered "serious harm" as a result of the imputations published against them. In adjudicating upon the meaning of serious harm, the UK Supreme Court cited their Slander of Women Act and was keen to distinguish it from the longstanding burden of special damage that hampered women's claims.[15] Special damage in the past, they described, meant "damage representing pecuniary loss, not . . . harm to the reputation of the Claimant." In other words, this new burden of serious harm is broader, encompassing general damage to a person's reputation beyond pure financial loss. But this explanation obscures the complicated history of special damage. It was never defined as straightforward pecuniary loss. It was both vague and nonquantifiable (the loss of a marriage proposal) and did not extend to women's actual pecuniary losses (the loss of trade). It also assumes that "serious harm" will not suffer the same fate, over time, of qualifying and quantifying damage in a gendered manner. The requirement likely favors certain plaintiffs, for instance those who have privileged economic circumstances (jobs to lose) and a high profile (more likely to be the subject of widespread media reporting). Men are more likely to have assets, public status, and profiles to seriously harm due to persistent social and economic gender inequalities. Does this mean women's defamation cases will be less likely to meet the threshold and succeed?

The story of women's cases for sexual slander in the long nineteenth century and consequential law reforms is a transnational one, connecting people, arguments and ideas across parliaments, precedents, and the pages of periodicals. US judges cited and distanced themselves from their English common law ancestors. "The reason of the English cases is inapplicable here," declared Chief Justice Kinsey of the Supreme Court of Judicature of New Jersey. "They have in England no inferior race as slaves, as we have here, with whom it is disgraceful to be on terms of social intercourse. Who can say that there, a case of the sort before us would not be made an exception to this established rule," observed Justice MacDonald of the Supreme Court of Georgia. In New South Wales, Harriet Spencer lost her court case because of English precedent, and the colony took up the House of Lords failed reforms to slander and libel with gusto. In South Australia, George Waterhouse, a member of the Legislative Council, urged the colony to adopt the Slander of Women Act as "such a state of law was not tolerated in any other country," meaning the United States—a country he had visited for inspiration. New York held strong to English case law before departing in 1871, a move that was watched by the editors of *The Australian Jurist* and copied by the Victorian parliament in 1887. The following year, the House of Commons, shamed as more barbarous on this issue than their antipodean colonies, discussed Victoria's reforms and proposed their own Slander of Women Bill. The transatlantic suffrage organization, the Women's Franchise League, sought to make it gender neutral in line with a rejection of the "double standard of morality" advocated by international women's movements. An action brought by a woman over slurs of interracial sex in rural New York could directly influence the outcome of a case brought by a woman publican in urban Melbourne.

The jurisdictions chosen for this study played important roles in the transnational story of the slander of women movement. However, they were, of course, joined by other common law jurisdictions. After North Carolina's 1808 act, other US states followed this lead, either via judicial innovation or legislative amendment: Kentucky in 1811,[16] Indiana in 1813,[17] Illinois in 1823,[18] South Carolina in 1824,[19] Massachusetts in 1829,[20] Ohio in 1833,[21] Missouri in 1835,[22] Arkansas in 1837,[23] Maryland in 1838,[24]

Alabama in 1839,[25] Iowa in 1844,[26] and California in 1874,[27] to name a few. British India moved before England did, changing slander law for women via a High Court decision in 1884.[28] Canadian provinces and territories also reformed their laws towards the close of the century: Ontario in 1889, British Columbia in 1898, Nova Scotia in 1900, and Yukon Territory in 1902.[29] Other Australian colonies passed laws at a similar time: Tasmania in 1895 and Western Australia in 1900.[30] New Zealand introduced their Slander of Women Act in 1898.[31] And finally, Singapore reformed their laws in the mid-twentieth century. "Slander against the chastity of women or girls is now legally actionable without the persons defamed producing proof of actual financial damage," Singapore's *Straits Times* victoriously announced in May 1957.[32]

In many ways, the slander of women cases and reforms tracked changes in communication and media and the primary means by which a person's reputation was constructed and maintained. The plaintiffs often resided in small communities—the penal settlements of Botany Bay, rural Black Belt of Georgia, scattered plantations in western North Carolina, farming towns in upstate New York—places in which speech was the primary way by which information was conveyed, especially about residents and neighbors. Even in larger centers—Trenton (New Jersey), Adelaide (South Australia), Melbourne (Victoria)—defamation cases about women originated as slander, not libel, even if they were then covered in detail by the local press. The importance of oral culture was clear in the pervasive embodied references to speech and hearing in poems, political debates, and commentary: "envenomed tongue," "to wound of modesty the ear," "the breath of slander," "assassin tongue," "from ear to lip, from lip to ear." Oral culture was fundamental in societies where literacy rates were relatively low, and people gathered physically in groups to live, socialize, become educated, and work.

Slander was related to gossip—defined as "private talk" by Kathleen A. Feeley and Jennifer Frost—but was not synonymous with it.[33] Gossip was largely and derogatively defined as a feminine pursuit, the sharing of "unverified information about a person's private life that he or she might prefer to keep hidden."[34] Some sexual slander cases involved gossip—stories passed along within a community. But many, if not most, were more akin to verbal abuse than gossip. Such attacks, often in the presence of the woman herself, were motivated by a desire to shame, humiliate, and harm a woman via her sexuality. Most, but certainly not all, such attacks were carried out by men. Such cases defied defamation's attempt to cleanly circumscribe or separate mere abuse—never considered actionable—from damaging imputations. Calling a woman a whore or a dirty, sluttish woman was both an insult and a meaningful message. It was an attempt to wound her dignity and to lower her in the estimation of others.

During the nineteenth century, various social and technological shifts influenced the direction of defamation law. Rates of literacy and education increased in the Australian colonies, US states, and England. Populations became more urbanized, creating more modern, diverse, and anonymous cities. Methods of transportation and communication—railroads and printing—expanded, allowing newspapers and periodicals to proliferate and boom in circulation. Women entered professions and appeared in public in increasing numbers. In an age of yellow journalism and muckraking, libel cases rose in number and prominence. By the late 1800s, there was a noticeable uptick in the number of civil libel suits brought by public officials. The vast majority of plaintiffs in these suits were men.[35] However, such shifts towards urbanization and the increase in libel cases were also evident in the first newspaper cases brought by women over sexual imputations.

In 1898, Ida Gates sued the *New York Recorder,* a newspaper, for publishing an article, three days after her marriage, stating she was "a dashing blonde . . . said to have been a concert-hall singer and dancer in Coney Island."[36] In fact, Gates was a teacher, who moved recently from rural New York to Brooklyn—intending, as "a stranger in that city," to make her home there. The Court of Appeals of New York held the publication was libelous *per se* as—given the reputation of Coney Island—it held the plaintiff up to "the public gaze, not only as unchaste, but as belonging to one the lowest classes of the great army of fallen women." The same year, Nellie McFadden sued the *Morning Journal* regarding an article they published (intended to be comedic) about her competing in a boat race against another woman for a man's affections.[37] The article was entirely fabricated and McFadden claimed that she had subsequently received "hundreds of indecent or immoral missives, sent to her by degraded men" and that the article had "caused her to cry, and had kept her from sleeping and eating and going into society." The court held it was libelous *per se* as it "charges her with ridiculous, immodest, and forward behavior, such as no respectable girl could be guilty of without meeting the condemnation of every right-minded man and woman." The end of the nineteenth and early twentieth century also witnessed the emergence of a legal right to privacy, as women brought cases seeking to control their photographic and cinematic images, often where the images were used without their consent for reasons of objectification and voyeurism.

It is easy to suggest that the slander of women cases and laws were old-fashioned, based on outmoded ideas and expectations of femininity. Such a conclusion positions women's cases as quaint and misguided, capitulations to patriarchal standards. It shifts focus away from the men (and few women) who made such slanderous attacks and sought to abuse, denigrate, humiliate, and shame women via their sexuality. To see such cases as a relic of the nineteenth century ignores the scourge of gendered hate speech and nonconsensual pornography running rampant across the internet today. If women can no longer be shamed, humiliated, and denigrated via their sexuality, why does deepfake pornography involving women (accounting for 90 percent of all deepfakes produced) continue to be manufactured and ruin lives?[38] If women can no longer be silenced with abusive words, why are women journalists, politicians, actresses, and activists subject to onslaughts of vicious hate speech online? For most of the nineteenth century, speech was the primary medium available to ordinary individuals to attack and disempower women—as individuals and as a group. It was then joined by the invention of photography. In recent times, online platforms and tools have become the method of choice. We now seek to regulate internet content providers and criminalize the creation and distribution of intimate images and deepfake pornography. And defamation persists as a legal avenue to address hate speech and sexual slurs against women, both on- and offline. It is a resilient and evolving doctrine with an illuminating and important gendered history.

NOTES

Introduction
1. *Smith v Minor*, 1 NJL 16 (1790).
2. *Spencer v Jeffery* [1826] NSWSC 28.
3. *McBrayer v Hill*, 26 NC 136 (1843); *Brooker v Coffin*, 5 Johns. 188 (1809); *Bell v Allen* [1862] SASC reported in *South Australian Register* (Adelaide, SA), 9 September 1862, p. 3.
4. "Publican" is a commonly understood word in Australia and England. It means someone who owns or manages a public house (abbreviated to pub), an establishment open to the public that serves alcohol.
5. *Wilson v Goit*, 17 NY 442 (1858); "The Lewis-Shaw Case," *Weekly Standard and Express*, 5 April 1890, p. 6.
6. See Beth Ashley, *Sluts: The Truth About Slut Shaming and What We Can Do to Fight it* (Penguin, 2024).
7. Alyssa Goldberg, "Kamala Harris, Megyn Kelly and Why the Sexist Attacks Are So Dangerous," *USA Today*, 31 July 2024; Robert Tait, "Trump Takes Sexist Harris Attacks to 'Whole Other Level' on Truth Social," *The Guardian*, 30 August 2024; see also Clare Corbould, "Twice as Good for Half the Respect: Kamala Harris' Battle for the White House," *The Conversation*, 26 July 2024.
8. Madeleine Achenza, "Former Yarra Valley Grammar School Student Calls out Behaviour After 'Unrapeable' List Released," *News.com.au*, 8 May 2024.
9. Jessica Lake, *The Face That Launched a Thousand Lawsuits: The American Women Who Forged a Right to Privacy* (Yale University Press, 2016); Jessica Lake, "Privacy, Property or Propriety: The Case of 'Pretty Portraits' in Late Nineteenth-Century America," *Law, Culture and the Humanities* 10, no. 1 (2014): 111-29.
10. See Lin Farley, *Sexual Shakedown: The Sexual Harassment of Women on the Job* (McGraw-Hill, 1978); Catharine A. MacKinnon, *Sexual Harassment of Working Women: A Case of Sex Discrimination* (Yale University Press, 1979); Catherine A.

MacKinnon and Reva B. Seigel, eds., *Directions in Sexual Harassment Law* (Yale University Press, 2003).

11. Danielle Keats Citron and Mary Anne Franks, "Criminalizing Revenge Porn," *Wake Forest Law Review* 49 (2014): 345-91; see also Danielle Keats Citron, *Hate Crimes in Cyberspace* (Harvard University Press, 2014).

12. See Louise Richardson-Self, *Hate Speech Against Women Online: Concepts and Countermeasures* (Rowman & Littlefield, 2021); Anjalee de Silva, "Addressing the Vilification of Women: A Functional Theory of Harm and Implications for Law," *Melbourne University Law Review* 43, no. 3 (2020): 987-1032; Caterina Flick, 'The Legal Framework on Hate Speech and the Internet: Good Practices to Prevent and Counter the Spread of Illegal Hate Speech Online," *Language, Gender and Hate Speech: A Multidisciplinary Approach* 1 (December 2020); Tanya D'Souza et al., "Harming Women with Words: The Failure of Australian Law to Prohibit Gendered Hate Speech," *University of New South Wales Law Journal* 41, no. 3 (2018): 939-76; Anjalee de Silva, "'Words Can Harm Us': The Need for Gender Vilification Provisions in Victorian Law," *Law Institute Journal* 88, no. 8 (2014): 40-45; Kylie Weston-Scheuber, "Gender and the Prohibition of Hate Speech," *Queensland University of Technology Law and Justice Journal* 12, no. 2 (2012): 132-50.

13. Thomas Starkie, *A Treatise on the Law of Slander, Libel, Scandalum Magnatum and False Rumours* (W. Clarke and Sons, 1813), 33.

14. James Anthony Sharpe, *Defamation and Sexual Slander in Early Modern England* (Borthwick Papers, 1980), 4.

15. Laura Gowing, *Domestic Dangers* (Oxford University Press, 1996).

16. Stephen Waddams, *Sexual Slander in Nineteenth Century England* (University of Toronto Press, 2016).

17. Ibid., xii.

18. Re "women's court," see Richard Wunderli, *London Church Courts and Society Before the Reformation* (Medieval Academy of America, 1981), 76.

19. R. C. Donnelly, "History of Defamation," *Wisconsin Law Review* (1949): 121.

20. Starkie, *A Treatise*, 647 (my emphasis).

21. W. Blake Odgers, *A Digest of the Law of Libel and Slander* (Stevens & Sons, 1887), 298.

22. *Thorley v Kerry* (1812) 4 Taunt 355 (my emphasis).

23. Starkie, *A Treatise*, 187-88.

24. Ibid., 185.

25. Ibid.

26. See Mary Beth Norton, "Gender and Defamation in Seventeenth-Century Maryland," *William and Mary Quarterly* 44, no. 1 (1987): 4-39; Clara Ann Bowler, "Carted Whores and White Shrouded Apologies: Slander in the County Courts of Seventeenth-Century Virginia," *Virginia Magazine of History and Biography* 85 (1977): 411-26; Donna J. Spindel, "The Law of Words: Verbal Abuse in North Carolina to 1730," *American Journal of Legal History* 39 (1995): 25-42.

27. Roscoe Pound, *The Formative Era of American Law* (Peter Smith, 1950), 20.

28. See Michael Grossberg, *Governing the Hearth: Law and the Family in Nineteenth Century America* (University of North Carolina Press, 1985).

29. See Andrew J. King, "Constructing Gender: Sexual Slander in Nineteenth Century America," *Law and History Review* 13 (1995): 63-110; Andrew King, "The Law of Slander in Early Antebellum America," *American Journal of Legal History* 35, no. 1 (1991): 1-43.

30. Lisa R. Pruitt, "On the Chastity of Women All Property in the World Depends: Injury from Sexual Slander in the Nineteenth Century," *Indiana Law Journal* 78 (2003): 965-1018; Lisa R. Pruitt, "Her Own Good Name: Two Centuries of Talk About Chastity," *Maryland Law Review* 63, no. 3 (2003): 401-539.

31. Diane Borden, "Reputational Assault: A Critical and Historical Analysis of Gender and the Law of Defamation," *Journalism and Mass Communication Quarterly* 75, no. 1 (1998): 98-111; Diane Borden, "Pattwena of Harm: An Analysis of Gender and Defamation," *Communication Law and Policy* 2, no. 1 (1997): 105-41.

32. See, e.g., M. Lindsay Kaplan and Katherine Eggert, "'Good Queen, My Lord, Good Queen': Sexual Slander and the Trials of Female Authority in the *Winter's Tale*," *Renaissance Drama* 25 (1994): 89-118; Laura Gowing, "Gender and the Language of Insult in Early Modern London," *History Workshop*, no. 35 (1993): 1-21; Laura Gowing, *Domestic Dangers* (Oxford University Press, 1996); Sharpe, *Defamation and Sexual Slander*; K. Augustine-Adams, "Defamed Women: *Salve Deus Rex Judaeorum*," *Harvard Women's Law Journal* 22 (1999): 207-38; Norton, "Gender and Defamation"; Bowler, "Carted Whores"; Spindel, "The Law of Words"; Terri L. Snyder, *Brabbling Women: Disorderly Speech and the Law in Early Virginia* (Cornell University Press, 2003); Kristin A. Olbertson, *The Dreadful Word: Speech Crime and Polite Gentlemen in Massachusetts, 1690-1776* (Cambridge University Press, 2022).

33. King, "Constructing Gender"; King, "The Law of Slander"; Pruitt, "On the Chastity of Women"; Pruitt, "Her Own Good Name"; Borden, "Reputational Assault"; Borden, "Pattwena of Harm"; Daniel Stephens, "The Evolution and Confusion of the Sexual Misconduct Category of Slander Per Se," *Regent University Law Review* 31 (2018-2019): 277-308; Alice Krzanich, 'Virtue and Vindication: An Historical Analysis of Sexual Slander and a Woman's Good Name," *Auckland University Law Review* 17 (2011): 33-59; Lawrence Friedman, *Guarding Life's Dark Secrets: Legal and Social Controls over Reputation, Propriety, and Privacy* (Stanford University Press, 2007).

34. An exception to treating national jurisdictions as discrete, though not related specifically to gender, is Lyndsay M. Campbell, *Truth and Privilege: Libel Law in Massachusetts and Nova Scotia, 1820-1840* (Cambridge University Press, 2022).

35. Samuel Brenner, "Negro Blood in His Veins: The Development and Disappearance of the Doctrine of Defamation Per Se by Racial Misidentification in the American South," *Santa Clara Law Review* 50 (2010): 333-406; Ariel J. Gross, "Litigating Whiteness: Trials of Racial Determination in the Nineteenth-Century South," *Yale Law Journal* 108, no. 1 (1998): 109-88; Jonathan Kahn, "Controlling

Identity: Plessy, Privacy, and Racial Defamation," *DePaul Law Review* 54 (2004): 755-82; Mark M. Carroll, "'All for Keeping His Own Negro Wench': Birch v. Benton (1858) and the Politics of Slander and Free Speech in Antebellum Missouri," *Law and History Review* 29, no. 3 (2011): 835-97.

36. See, e.g., Robert C. Post, "The Social Foundations of Defamation Law: Reputation and the Constitution," *California Law Review* 74 (1986): 691-742; Paul Mitchell, "The Foundations of Australian Defamation Law," *Sydney Law Review* 28, no. 3 (2006): 477-504; David Rolph, *Defamation Law* (Thomson Reuters, 2024); David Rolph, ed., *Landmark Cases in Defamation Law* (Hart, 2019); Patrick George, *Defamation Law in Australia* (Lexis Nexis, 2023).

37. Nadia Khomami, "#Metoo: How a Hashtag Became a Rallying Cry Against Sexual Harassment," *The Guardian*, 21 October 2017.

38. See, *Rush v Nationwide News Pty Ltd (No 7)* [2019] FCA 496; Harriet Tatham and Heath Parkes-Hupton, "Craig McLachlan Drops Defamation Case Against ABC, Nine and Christie Whelan Browne," *ABC News Online*, 20 May 2022; *Porter v Australian Broadcasting Corporation (No 2)* [2021] FCA 1036; Michaela Whitbourne and Toby Crockford, "Nine Apologises to Andrew Laming in Settlement of Defamation Suit," *Sydney Morning Herald*, 14 September 2022; Christopher Knaus, "Bruce Lehrmann Files Defamation Proceedings Against the ABC," *The Guardian*, 5 April 2023.

39. Irene Khan, *Promotion and Protection of the Right to Freedom of Opinion and Expression*, United Nations General Assembly, Report, 20 July 2021, p. 8.

40. See, e.g., Pooja Bhaskar, "Milkovich, #MeToo, and 'Liars': Defamation Law and the Fact-Opinion Distinction," *Fordham Law Review* 88, no. 2 (2019): 691-732; Alyssa R. Leader, "A SLAPP in the Face of Free Speech: Protecting Survivors' Rights to Speak up in the Me Too Era," *First Amendment Law Review* 17, no. 3 (2019): 441-76; Mary Anne Franks, "Witch Hunts: Free Speech, #MeToo, and the Fear of Women's Words," *University of Chicago Legal Forum* (2019): 123-46; Deborah Tuerkheimer, "Unofficial Reporting in the #MeToo Era," *University of Chicago Legal Forum* (2019): 273-98; Shaina Weisbrot, "The Impact of the #MeToo Movement on Defamation Claims Against Survivors," *CUNY Law Review* 23, no. 2 (2020): 332-63; Nicole Ligon, "Protecting Women's Voices: Preventing Retaliatory Defamation Claims in the #MeToo Context," *St. John's Law Review* 94, no. 4 (2020): 961-70; Chelsey N. Whynot, "Retaliatory Defamation Suits: The Legal Silencing of the #MeToo Movement," *Tulane Law Review* 94, no. 1 (2020): 1-28; Juliet Dee, "Fighting Back: Is Defamation Law a Double-Edged Sword for #MeToo Victims?" *First Amendment Studies* 55, no. 2 (2021): 148-74; Aliosha Hurry, "Defamation as a Sword: The Weaponization of Civil Liability Against Sexual Assault Survivors in the Post-#MeToo Era," *Canadian Journal of Women and the Law* 34, no. 1 (2022): 82-108; Mandi Gray, *Suing for Silence* (UBC Press, 2024); Michelle Harradine, "Defamation Law and Epistemic Harm in the #MeToo Era," *Australian Feminist Law Journal* 48, no. 1 (2022): 31-55; Amanda Mason, "Defamation Law and the Me

Too Movement in Australia," *Media and Arts Law Review* 23 (2020): 325-46; Vanisha Babani, "Does Australia Have the Laws It Needs in the #MeToo Era?" *Canberra Law Review* 17, no. 2 (2020): 147-53. See also Sarah Ailwood, "'Collateral Damage': Consent, Subjectivity and Australia's #MeToo Moment," *Australian Feminist Law Journal* 46, no. 2 (2020): 285-303.

Chapter 1

1. *Smith v Minor*, 1 NJL 16 (1790).
2. Ibid.
3. *Smith v Minor*, original Supreme Court case file #36843 (1788-1790), held by the New Jersey State Archives, Trenton.
4. *Smith v Minor*, 1 NJL 16, 18 (1790).
5. The current record of the judgment cites the statute as Act of December 12, 1794 (Allinson's Laws of NJ 4). But this could not be correct as it was enacted after the case. The original case files in the New Jersey State Archives do not refer to the relevant statute by name or date.
6. *Smith v Minor*, 1 NJL 16, 20 (1790).
7. *Abigail Sharp v Abraham Shotwell*, original Supreme Court case file #38755 (1727), held by the New Jersey State Archives, Trenton.
8. *John Pittinger v Hugh Reid*, original Supreme Court case file #30709 (1716), held by the New Jersey State Archives, Trenton.
9. *Stephen Arnold v Samuel Walker*, original Supreme Court case file #1464 (1715), held by the New Jersey State Archives, Trenton.
10. *Daniel Hendrickson v James Allen*, original Supreme Court case file #15043 (1785), held by the New Jersey State Archives, Trenton.
11. *Adam Hay v John Dear*, original Supreme Court case file #15696 (1738), held by the New Jersey State Archives, Trenton.
12. *Robert Hoops (Esquire) v Peter Quick*, original Supreme Court case file #17421 (1778), held by the New Jersey State Archives, Trenton.
13. *William Livingston v Peter Hopkins*, original Supreme Court case file #22627 (1782), held by the New Jersey State Archives, Trenton.
14. See Graham Russell Gao Hodges, "New Jersey in the Early Republic," in *New Jersey: A History of the Garden State*, eds. Maxine Lurie and Peter Veit (Rutgers University Press, 2012), 91.
15. Ibid., 104; see also Graham Russell Gao Hodges, *Black New Jersey: 1664 to the Present Day* (Rutgers University Press, 2018).
16. Constitution of New Jersey, Article IV (1776).
17. Constitution of Maryland, Article V (1776).
18. Constitution of Pennsylvania, Article VII (1776); Constitution of North Carolina, Article VII (1776).
19. Constitution of Georgia, Article IX (1777).
20. Constitution of New York, Article VII (1777).

21. See, e.g., Constitution of Massachusetts, Article IX ("all inhabitants") (1780).

22. Mary Beth Norton, *Liberty's Daughters: The Revolutionary Experience of American Women, 1750-1800* (Cornell University Press,1980), 191.

23. Judith Apter Klinghoffer and Lois Elkis, "'The Petticoat Electors': Women's Suffrage in New Jersey, 1776-1807," *Journal of the Early Republic* 12, no. 2 (Summer 1992): 163.

24. Jan Ellen Lewis, "Rethinking Women's Suffrage in New Jersey, 1776-1807," *Rutgers Law Review* 63, no. 3 (Spring 2011): 1020.

25. See Klinghoffer and Elkis, "'The Petticoat Electors'"; Lewis, "Rethinking Women's Suffrage."

26. Edmund Raymond Turner, "Women's Suffrage in New Jersey: 1790-1807," in *Smith College Studies in History*, eds. John Spencer Bassett and Sidney Bradshaw Fay (Dept. of History of Smith College, 1916), 166.

27. *Smith v Minor*, original Supreme Court case file #36843 (1788-1790).

28. Ibid. (my emphasis).

29. *The Instructions from the Queen in Council to the Governor of the Province of New Jersey*, 16 November 1702, Article XV: ". . . And that no Freeholder shall be capable of Voting in the Election of such Representative, who shall not have One hundred Acres of Land of an estate of Freehold in *his* own right, within the Division for which *he* shall so vote . . ." (my emphasis); See Julian P. Boyd, ed., *Fundamental Laws and Constitutions of New Jersey, 1664-1964* (Van Nostrand Company, 1964), 131.

30. Klinghoffer and Elkis, "'The Petticoat Electors'"; Lewis, "Rethinking Women's Suffrage"; Irwin N. Gertzog, "Female Suffrage in New Jersey, 1790-1807," *Women & Politics* 10, no. 2 (1990): 47-58; Campbell Curry-Ledbetter, "Women's Suffrage in New Jersey 1776-1807: A Political Weapon," *Georgetown Journal of Gender & Law* 21 (2019): 705-24.

31. New Jersey Election Statute 1790: "[N]o person shall be entitled to vote in any Township or precinct, that that in which he or she does actually reside at the time of the election"; see also Gertzog, "Female Suffrage in New Jersey," 49; Acts of New Jersey (1790), 669.

32. New Jersey Voting Rights Act 1797, Section XI:

> And be it enacted, That every voter shall openly, and in full view deliver his or her ballot (which shall be a single written ticket, containing the names of the person or persons for whom he or she votes) to the said judge, or either of the inspectors, who, on receipt thereof, shall, with an audible voice, pronounce the name of such voter, and if no objection is made to the voter, put the ballot immediately into the election box, and the clerk of the election shall thereupon take down the name of such voter in a book or poll list, to be provided for the purpose.

See also Acts of New Jersey 1796, 49.

33. Gertzog, "Female Suffrage in New Jersey," 52.

34. William Griffith, *Eumenes: Being a Collection of Papers Written for the Purpose of Exhibiting Some of the More Prominent Errors and Omissions of the Constitution of New-Jersey* (Trenton, 1799), 30-31; Klinghoffer and Elkis, "'The Petticoat Electors,'" 178.

35. Turner, "Women's Suffrage in New Jersey," 174; *Centinel of Freedom* (Newark, NJ), 11 November 1800 (emphasis in original).

36. Votes of the Assembly (New Jersey), 29 November 1802.

37. Lewis, "Rethinking Women's Suffrage," 1022.

38. See Richard P. McCormick, *Experiment in Independence: New Jersey in the Critical Period, 1781-1789* (Rutgers University Press, 1950): "[Dropping the property qualification to £50] marked a fundamental departure from the concept that political rights were connected with landed property."

39. Gertzog, "Female Suffrage in New Jersey," 53.

40. Julian Ursyn Niemcewicz, *Under Their Vine and Fig Tree: Travels Through America in 1797-1799, 1805, with Some Further Account of Life in New Jersey (1797-1807)* (New Jersey Historical Society, 1965), 208.

41. Linda K. Kerber, *Women of the Republic: Intellect and Ideology in Revolutionary America* (University of North Carolina Press, 1980), 283: "In the years of the early Republic, a consensus developed around the idea that a mother, committed to the service of her family and to the state, might serve a political purpose.... The Republican mother was to encourage her son's interest and participation."

42. *Genius of Liberty*, 7 August 1800.

43. "Lines, Written by a Lady, Who Was Questioned Respecting Her Inclination to Marry," *Centinel of Freedom*, 21 October 1800; also quoted in Norton, *Liberty's Daughters*, 242.

44. Edwin B. Bronner, "The Disgrace of John Kinsey, Quaker Politician, 1739-1750," *Pennsylvania Magazine of History and Biography* 75, no. 4 (October 1951): 400-15.

45. John Whitehead, "The Supreme Court of New Jersey," *Green Bag* 3, no. 9 (September 1891): 406.

46. Jean R. Soderlund, "Women's Authority in Pennsylvania and New Jersey Quaker Meetings, 1680-1760," *William and Mary Quarterly* 44, no. 4 (1987): 722-49.

47. *Smith v Minor*, 1 NJL 16, 23 (1790).

48. Ibid., 24.

49. Roscoe Pound, *The Formative Era of American Law* (Peter Smith, 1950), 7.

50. Ibid., 25.

51. *Mary Smith v John Dye*, original Supreme Court case file #34779 (1788), held by the New Jersey State Archives, Trenton.

52. Andrew King has argued that *Smith v Minor* "illustrates how a judge's reaction to a case pressed him to interpret the law to avoid a result he believed unwise." See Andrew J. King, "Constructing Gender: Sexual Slander in Nineteenth-Century America," *Law and History Review* 13, no. 1 (Spring 1995): 82. He argues that the judge was not being judicially innovative but trying to use statutory interpreta-

tion to arrive at a preferred outcome. But the judgment does not support this view. Chief Justice Kinsey states that even if he were incorrect about Minor's words making Mary an "object of punishment," "yet" an action for spiritual defamation would still lie in New Jersey.

53. Demonstrating the gender-neutral effect of the judgment in *Smith v Minor*, in 1807 a man brought a case in New Jersey for slander regarding allegations of adultery, and the court stated in passing that the words were "in themselves actionable." See *Cook v Barkley*, 2 NJL 169 (1807).

54. *Mary Stockton v Thomas Hopkins*, original Supreme Court case file #35835 (1805-1806), held by the New Jersey State Archives, Trenton (my emphasis).

55. For general information about the family and estate, see, e.g., Alfred Hoyt Bill, *A House Called Morven: Its Role in American History, 1701-1954* (Princeton University Press, 1954); Linda Arntzenius, "Richard and Annis Stockton—An Epic Tale," *Princeton Magazine*, 2024, https://www.princetonmagazine.com/richard-and-annis-stockton/

56. See https://www.morven.org

57. These facts were not contested at trial. See Thomas Hopkins, *An Appeal to the Tribunal of Public Justice; Being a Concise Statement of the Facts Which Led to the Extraordinary Case of Stockton Versus Hopkins* (Philadelphia, printed for the author, 1808), 6. Copy held by the New York State Archives, Cultural Education Center, Albany.

58. Ibid., p. 7

59. This story and its circumstances were relayed at trial by two women servants of Elizabeth Hopkins: Mrs. Wilson and Alice MacNally. See "Testimony of Mrs. Wilson" and "The Evidence of Alice MacNally," in Hopkins, *An Appeal to the Tribunal of Public Justice*, 45-46.

60. Hopkins, *An Appeal to the Tribunal of Public Justice*, 7-8.

61. "The Evidence of Alice MacNally," 46.

62. Hopkins, *An Appeal to the Tribunal of Public Justice*, 9.

63. Ibid., 13.

64. Ibid., 17.

65. See "[T]he examination and deposition of Nicholas Odersook" (26 October 1805), in *Mary Stockton v Thomas Hopkins*.

66. *Mary Stockton v Thomas Hopkins*.

67. Hopkins, *An Appeal to the Tribunal of Public Justice*, 15:

> Mr Stockton, in the course of his testimony, declared that his daughter had sustained no injury whatever from any thing I had said; that, on the contrary, she ranked infinitely higher, not only in his estimation, but in the estimation of the whole circle of her friends than ever she did before. If that was the case ... for what injury then did the jury find a verdict of $5000, the whole amount of the damages laid in the action, and when by Mr Stockton's own confession, on oath, no injury was sustained.

68. Hopkins, *An Appeal to the Tribunal of Public Justice*, iii.

69. Ibid., i; "To Richard Stockton, Esq.," *Aurora General Advertiser*, 16 October 1807, p. 1.

70. Ibid.

71. Hopkins, *An Appeal to the Tribunal of Public Justice*, v.

72. Hopkins, *An Appeal to the Tribunal of Public Justice*.

73. Ibid., 18.

74. Ibid., 19.

75. See Maya Jasanoff, *Liberty's Exiles: The Loss of America and the Remaking of the British Empire* (HarperCollins UK, 2011); Maya Jasanoff, "The Other Side of Revolution: Loyalists in the British Empire," *William and Mary Quarterly* 65, no. 2 (2008): 205-32.

76. See Hodges, *Black New Jersey*.

77. "Twenty Dollar Reward," *The Federalist*, 29 September 1806.

78. "Princeton and Slavery" project, in particular: https://slavery.princeton.edu/stories/betsey-stockton

79. Ibid.; see also Gregory Nobles, *The Education of Betsey Stockton: An Odyssey of Slavery and Freedom* (University of Chicago Press, 2022), 1-14; Constance K. Escher, *She Calls Herself Betsey Stockton: The Illustrated Odyssey of a Princeton Slave* (Wipf and Stock Publishers, 2022); Eileen F. Moffatt, "Betsey Stockton: Pioneer American Missionary," *International Bulletin of Missionary Research* (April 1995): 71-76.

80. Despite Betsey Stockton's beginnings in slavery, she led a remarkable public and professional life, becoming a missionary to the Sandwich Islands (the second single woman in the United States—and first African American woman—to be sent overseas as a missionary), teaching in various schools for children of color and founding Princeton's First Presbyterian Church of Color in 1840. See Nobles, *The Education of Betsey Stockton*.

81. *Sally Stillwell v James Syme*, original Supreme Court case file #38310 (1808-1810), held by the New Jersey State Archives, Trenton.

82. *Sally Stillwell v James Syme*, pleading documents and Supreme Court Judgement Book E (1809-1812), 150-153, for case #38310, held by the New Jersey State Archives, Trenton (my emphasis).

83. Ibid.

84. *Centinel of Freedom*, 30 September 30 and 14 October 1806; *Genius of Liberty*, 31 July 1806, 7 August 1806, and 2 October 1806; See also Klinghoffer and Elkis, "'The Petticoat Electors,'" 187.

85. William H. Shaw, *History of Essex and Hudson Counties, New Jersey* (1884, p. 213):

> Men usually honest seemed lost to all sense of honor, so completely were they carried away by the heat of the strife. Women vied with the men, and in some instances surpassed them, in illegal voting. Only a few years ago there were

living in Newark two ladies, who, at the time of the election in their 'teens, voted six times each. Married women, too, indignant, perhaps, at being placed on the same political level as children and idiots, in defiance of the law, voted six times each. Governor Pennington is said to have escorted to the poles a "strapping negress." Men and boys disguised themselves in women's attire, and crowded about the polls to assist in winning the day for Newark.

Quoted in Lewis, "Rethinking Women's Suffrage in New Jersey," 1032; see also Curry-Ledbetter, "Women's Suffrage in New Jersey," 21.

86. An Act to Regulate the Election of Members of the Legislative-Council and General Assembly, Sheriffs and Coroners in This State, ch. II, 1807 NJL 14.

87. Jacob Katz Cogan, "The Look Within: Property, Capacity, and Suffrage in Nineteenth-Century America," *Yale Law Journal* 107 (1997): 473-98.

88. Lewis, "Rethinking Women's Suffrage," 1035.

Chapter 2

1. *Spencer v Jeffery* [1826] NSWSC 28 (Chief Justice Stephen).

2. See Alan Frost, *The Precarious Life of James Mario Matra: Voyager with Cook, American Loyalist, Servant of Empire* (Miegunyah Press, 1995); Maya Jasanoff, *Liberty's Exiles: The Loss of America and the Remaking of the British Empire* (HarperCollins UK, 2011).

3. Cassandra Pybus, *Epic Journeys of Freedom: Runaway Slaves of the American Revolution and Their Global Quest for Liberty* (Beacon Press, 2006); Cassandra Pybus, *Black Founders: The Unknown Story of Australia's First Black Settlers* (University of New South Wales Press, 2006).

4. Grace Karskens, *The Colony* (Allen & Unwin, 2010).

5. James Dunk, *Bedlam at Botany Bay* (New South, 2019), 8, 13.

6. Ibid.

7. Penny Russell, *Savage or Civilised? Manners in Colonial Australia* (New South, 2010), 29.

8. Joy Damousi, *Depraved and Disorderly: Female Convicts, Sexuality and Gender in Colonial Australia* (Cambridge University Press, 1997).

9. Richard Neville, *Mr JW Lewin, Painter & Naturalist* (New South, 2012), 42.

10. Ibid.

11. Grant quoted in Neville, *Mr JW Lewin*, 44.

12. Neville, *Mr J W Lewin*, 44.

13. A. T. Saunders, "HMS Buffalo: Facts Disclosed for the First Time," *The Register* (Adelaide, SA), 28 December 1925, p. 8.

14. George Barrington, *The History of New South Wales* (M. Jones, 1802), ch. 9.

15. Ibid.

16. *Lewin v Thompson* [1799] NSWSC 8. This case is also discussed briefly in Bruce Kercher, *Debt, Seduction and Other Disasters: The Birth of Civil Law in Convict New South Wales* (Federation Press, 1996), 100.

17. *Thompson v McCarthy* [1804] NSWSC 1.
18. "Civil Court Intelligence," *Sydney Gazette*, 12 February 1804, p. 2; "Civil Court Intelligence," *Sydney Gazette*, 24 June 1804, p. 2.
19. *Lewin v Thompson* [1799] NSWSC 8, testimony of Elizabeth Grono, court minutes held by New South Wales Archives.
20. *Lewin v Thompson* [1799] NSWSC 8, testimony of Thomas Hobby, court minutes held by New South Wales Archives.
21. Ibid.
22. *Lewin v Thompson* [1799] NSWSC 8, testimony of Hugh Michan, court minutes held by New South Wales Archives. Hugh Machin's name is incorrectly spelled as Michan in the minutes of the trial.
23. *Lewin v Thompson* [1799] NSWSC 8, testimony of Francis Wheeler, court minutes held by New South Wales Archives.
24. Damousi, *Depraved and Disorderly*, 12.
25. Amy J. Lloyd, "Education, Literacy and the Reading Public," in *British Library Newspapers* (Gale, 2007).
26. B. M. Penglase, "Literacy and the Settlers: New South Wales 1788-1881," *Education Research and Perspectives* 15, no. 1 (1988): 98-106.
27. Alan Atkinson, *The Europeans in Australia: A History*, vol. 1 (Oxford University Press, 1997), x.
28. Kercher, *Debt, Seduction and Other Disasters*.
29. Russell, *Savage or Civilised?*
30. *Lewin v Thompson* [1799] NSWSC 8, court minutes held by New South Wales Archives.
31. In 1812, Lord Mansfield confirmed this longstanding distinction, stating "for mere general abuse spoken, no action lies." See *Thorley v Kerry*, 4 Taunt 355 (1812).
32. *Atkins v Harris* [1799] NSWSC 4.
33. *Atkins v Harris* [1799] NSWSC 4, opening address by Richard Atkins.
34. Kercher, *Debt, Seduction and Other Disasters*, 9.
35. Ibid.
36. "Poetry," *Sydney Gazette*, 9 June 1825, p. 3.
37. *Spencer v Jeffery* [1826] NSWSC 28.
38. Stuart Macintyre, *A Concise History of Australia* (Cambridge University Press, 1999), 55.
39. *Campbell v Jeffery* [1826] NSWSC 27.
40. "Campbell v Jeffery," *The Australian*, 3 May 1826, p. 3.
41. M. Jeanne Peterson, "The Victorian Governess: Status Incongruence in Family and Society," in *Suffer and Be Still*, ed. Martha Vicinus (Indiana University Press, 1972), 8.
42. Peter Cunningham, *Two Years in New South Wales* (Henry Colburn, 1827), 20; Gwenda D. M. Jones, "A Lady in Every Sense of the Word: A Study of the Governess in Australian Colonial Society" (master's thesis, University of Melbourne, 1982), 53.

43. *Spencer v Jeffery* [1826] NSWSC 28, testimony of Margaret Campbell, court minutes held by New South Wales Archives.

44. *Sydney Gazette* (Sydney, NSW), 6 May 1826, p. 3

45. See Peterson, "The Victorian Governess"; M. Jeanne Peterson, "The Victorian Governess: Status Incongruence in Family and Society," *Victorian Studies* 14, no. 1 (1970): 7-26.

46. Elizabeth Rigby (Lady Eastlake), *"Vanity Fair, Jane Eyre,* and the Governesses' Benevolent Institution," *Quarterly Review* 84 (December 1848): 176.

47. *Spencer v Jeffery* [1826] NSWSC 28, testimony of Margaret Campbell, court minutes held by New South Wales Archives.

48. *Sydney Gazette* (Sydney, NSW), 6 May 1826, p. 3.

49. *Spencer v Jeffery* [1826] NSWSC 28, court minutes held by New South Wales Archives, state: "Enter steward with a countenance black and shining as the lacquered part of a tea tray."

50. *Spencer v Jeffery* [1826] NSWSC 28, testimony of William Simmons, court minutes held by New South Wales Archives.

51. *The Australian* (Sydney, NSW), 6 May 1826, p. 3.

52. *Spencer v Jeffery* [1826] NSWSC 28 (Chief Justice Stephen).

53. Kirsten McKenzie, *Scandal in the Colonies: Sydney and Cape Town 1820-1850* (Melbourne University Press, 2004), 86.

54. Liz Conor, "The 'Lubra' Type in Australian Imaginings of the Aboriginal Woman from 1836-1973," *Gender & History* 25, no. (2013): 230-51.

55. *Sydney Gazette* (Sydney, NSW), 6 May 1826, p. 3.

56. *The Australian* (Sydney, NSW), 6 May 1826, p. 3.

57. *Sydney Gazette* (Sydney, NSW), 6 May 1826, p. 3.

58. Ibid.

59. Ben Huf, "The Capitalist in Colonial History: Investment, Accumulation and Credit-Money in New South Wales," *Australian Historical Studies* 50, no. 4 (2019): 418-40.

60. See *Report of the Commissioner of Inquiry into the State of the Colony of New South Wales* (1822), 1st Report; *Report of the Commissioner of Inquiry on the Judicial Establishments of New South Wales and Van Diemen's Land* (1823), 2nd Report; *Report of the Commissioner of Inquiry on the State of Agriculture and Trade in the Colony of New South Wales* (1823), 3rd Report.

61. See Kirsten McKenzie, "Of Convicts and Capitalists: Honour and Colonial Commerce in 1830s—Cape Town and Sydney," *Australian Historical Studies* 33, no. 118 (2002): 199-222. See also McKenzie, *Scandal in the Colonies*.

62. Penny Russell and Nigel Worden, eds., *Honourable Intentions?* (Routledge, 2016), 10.

63. Kirsten McKenzie, "Defining and Defending Honour in Law," in *Honourable Intentions?*, 27 (note 1).

64. *Parliamentary Debates* (series 3), vol. 66, 13 February 1843, at col. 395.

65. Ibid.

66. *Sydney Morning Herald* (Sydney, NSW), 10 June 1847, p. 2.

67. Paul Mitchell, "The Foundations of Australian Defamation Law," *Sydney Law Review* 28, no. 3 (2006): 494.

68. Max Thompson, *The First Election: The New South Wales Legislative Council Election of 1843* (Max Thompson, 1996), 70.

69. Mitchell, "The Foundations of Australian Defamation Law."

70. *Sydney Morning Herald* (Sydney, NSW), 3 July 1847, p. 2.

71. *Libel Act* 1847 (NSW) s1.

72. See, e.g., "Canavan v Loder," *Sydney Morning Herald* (Sydney, NSW), 29 March 1851, p. 4; "Douglas v Foster," *Sydney Morning Herald* (Sydney, NSW), 25 November 1857, p. 4; "Amstrong v Johnson," *Sydney Morning Herald* (Sydney, NSW), 17 July 1858, p. 5; "Cavenagh v Erwin," *Sydney Morning Herald* (Sydney, NSW), 4 March 1859, p. 3; "Brown v Cohen," *Sydney Morning Herald* (Sydney, NSW), 13 July 1861, p. 6; "Moore v Downey," *Sydney Morning Herald* (Sydney, NSW), 22 May 1863, p. 2; "Markey v Turvey," *Sydney Morning Herald* (Sydney, NSW), 23 February 1864, p. 2; "Neily v Gee," *Sydney Morning Herald* (Sydney, NSW), 20 August 1867, p. 2; "Flynn v Wilson," *Sydney Morning Herald* (Sydney, NSW), 12 November 1868, p. 2.

73. "Canavan v Loder," *Sydney Morning Herald* (Sydney, NSW), 29 March 1851, p. 4.

Chapter 3

1. James Davis, *The Office and Authority of a Justice of Peace* (Newbern, 1774), 111.

2. Donna J. Spindel, "The Law of Words: Verbal Abuse in North Carolina to 1730," *American Journal of Legal History* 39, no. 1 (1995): 25-42.

3. See Donna J. Spindel, "Women's Civil Actions in the North Carolina Higher Courts, 1670-1730," *North Carolina Historical Review* 71, no. 2 (1994): 151-73; Mary Beth Norton, "Gender and Defamation in Seventeenth Century Maryland," *William and Mary Quarterly* 44, no. 1 (1987): 4-39.

4. Kirsten Fischer, "'False, Feigned, and Scandalous Words': Sexual Slander and Racial Ideology Among Whites in Colonial North Carolina," in *The Devil's Lane: Sex and Race in the Early South*, eds. Catherine Clinton and Michele Gillespie (Oxford University Press, 1997).

5. Adelphos, "On the Frequent Satire upon Women," *The Raleigh Minerva* (Raleigh, NC), 25 August 1806, p. 4.

6. *Edenton Gazette* (Edenton, NC), 23 December 1808, p. 3.

7. See, e.g., "Legislature of North Carolina," *The Raleigh Minerva* (Raleigh, NC), 6 December 1810, p. 3; "General Assembly," *Weekly Raleigh Register* (Raleigh, NC), 29 November 1811, p. 2.

8. US Census 1800, New Hanover County, North Carolina; held by the US National Archives and Records Administration (NARA).

9. William Jones, Will 1802, North Carolina Probate Records, 1735-1970, New Hanover, Wills 1732-1864, vol. 3, p. 201.

10. See, e.g., "A Narrative of That Extraordinary Case of Stockton Versus Hopkins," *Aurora General Advertiser* (Philadelphia, PA), 18 March 1808, p. 4.

11 1808 NC Laws, 33rd sess., ch. XIII.

12 See Linda K. Kerber, *Women of the Republic: Intellect and Ideology in Revolutionary America* (University of North Carolina Press, 1980); Jan Lewis, "The Republican Wife: Virtue and Seduction in the Early Republic," *William and Mary Quarterly* 44, no. 4 (1987): 689-721; Ruth H. Bloch, "The Gendered Meanings of Virtue in Revolutionary America," *Signs* 13, no. 1 (1987): 37-58.

13. Bloch, "The Gendered Meanings of Virtue," 46.

14. Deborah Gray White, *Ar'n't I a Woman? Female Slaves in the Plantation South*, rev. ed. (Norton, 1998).

15 Milton Ready, *The Tar Heel State: A New History of North Carolina* (University of South Carolina Press, 2020).

16. *Snow v Witcher*, 9 Ired 346 (1849). Justice Pearson at 348: "His testimony, if true, showed that the plaintiff was not one of those 'innocent' chaste women whose 'unsullied purity' the recital declares it was the intention of the Act to protect."

17. Spindel, "The Law of Words," 25, 31.

18. Victoria Bynum, *Unruly Women: The Politics of Social and Sexual Control in the Old South* (University of North Carolina Press, 1992).

19. See Ready, *The Tar Heel State*.

20. Martha Hodes, *White Women, Black Men: Illicit Sex in the Nineteenth-Century South* (Yale University Press, 1997), 65.

21. *State v Neese*, 4 NC 691 (1818).

22. Neese's note is reproduced as recorded in the documents.

23 US Census 1820, Orange County, North Carolina, source p. 282, held by the US National Archives and Records Administration (NARA); external ID: NC-M33_82-0161.

24. *Horton & wife v Reavis*, 6 NC 380 (1818).

25. *Horton & wife v Reavis*, 6 NC 380 (1818), original court file held by the North Carolina State Archives, Raleigh

26. Ibid.

27. *Horton & wife v Reavis*, 6 NC 380, 381 (1818).

28. New Jersey in 1790; Kentucky in 1811 with the Act of 1811 (4 W. Littell, the Statute Law of Kentucky 385); Indiana in 1813 with the 1813 Indiana Acts 110.

29. "Actions of Slander," *Hillsborough Recorder* (Hillsborough, NC), 7 November 1821, p. 3.

30. *King v Wood*, 10 SCL 184 (1818).

31. Ibid., 185 (Justice Nott).

32. Ibid; see also the decision of *Eden v Legare*, 1 SCL 171 (1791), where the Courts of Common Pleas and General Sessions of the Peace of South Carolina held that "calling a man a mulatto is actionable slander."

33. 1824 SC Acts, c. 4 s. 3.

34. *Watts v Greenlee*, 12 NC 210 (1827); *Watts v Greenlee*, 13 NC 115 (1829); see

also *Watts v Greenlee* (1827) original case file #986, held by the North Carolina State Archives, Raleigh, containing papers from the cases brought by Mary Watts and also her sister Catherine Watts.

35. *Watts v Greenlee* (1827), 3-4.
36. Ibid., 13-14.
37. Ibid., 4-5; see also *Watts v Greenlee*, 12 NC 210, 211 (1827).
38. *Watts v Greenlee*, 12 NC 210, 213 (1827)
39. *Watts v Greenlee*, 13 NC 115, 116-117 (1829); *Watts v Greenlee* (1827), 15-24.
40. *Watts v Greenlee*, 13 NC 115, 118 (1829).
41. Ibid., 119.
42. Robert J Conley, *The Cherokee Nation: A History* (University of New Mexico Press, 2005), 79.
43. Theda Purdue, "Race and Culture: Writing the Ethnohistory of the Early South," *Ethnohistory* 51, no. 4 (Fall 2004): 709.
44. Ibid., 704.
45. See also Theda Purdue, *"Mixed Blood" Indians: Racial Construction in the Early South* (University of Georgia Press, 2005).
46. Affidavit of Catherine Watts, State of Georgia, Rabun County, 18 November 1885, included in Cynthia A. Brought's Eastern Cherokee application.
47. Cynthia A. Brought, application #20233 (30 March 1907), Eastern Cherokee applications, Records of the US Court of Claims 1835-1984, National Archives identifier 56622935, https://catalog.archives.gov/id/56622935
48. Affidavit of M. L. Hood, Indian Territory, Muscogee, Creek Nation, 15 September1881, included in Cynthia A. Brought's Eastern Cherokee application.
49. See, e.g., the story of Elizabeth Watts: https://www.digitalhistory.uh.edu/active_learning/explorations/indian_removal/human_meaning.cfm
50. See Ralph Stebbins Greenlee and Robert Lemuel Greenlee, *Genealogy of the Greenlee Families in America, Scotland, Ireland and England* (Privately printed in Chicago, 1908).
51. See https://www.nclandgrants.com
52. The Greenlee brothers are mentioned at length in Edward W. Phifer, "Slavery in Microcosm: Burke County, North Carolina," *Journal of Southern History* 28, no. 2 (1962): 137-165; see also John C. Inscoe, "Mountain Masters: Slaveholding in Western North Carolina," *North Carolina Historical Review* 61, no. 2 (1984): 143-73.
53. Greenlee and Greenlee, *Genealogy of the Greenlee Families*, 235.
54. *Watts v Greenlee* (1827), 5.
55. For further information regarding the history of the Cherokee in North Carolina, see Robert L. Ganyard, "Threat from the West: North Carolina and the Cherokee, 1776-1778," *North Carolina Historical Review* 45, no. 1 (1968): 47-66; Joffre L. Coe, "The Indian in North Carolina," *North Carolina Historical Review* 56, no. 2 (1979): 158-61; Ruth Y. Wetmore, "The Role of the Indian in North Carolina History," *North Carolina Historical Review* 56, no. 2 (1979): 162-76; Ben Oshel Bridgers, "An Historical Analysis of the Legal Status of the North Carolina Chero-

kees," *North Carolina Law Review* 58, no. 6 (1980): 1075-131; John Ehle, *Trail of Tears: The Rise and Fall of the Cherokee Nation* (Doubleday, 1988).

56. Greenlee and Greenlee, *Genealogy of the Greenlee Families*, 237.
57. Purdue, "Race and Culture," 719.
58. *Smith v Hamilton*, 44 SCL 44 (1856).
59. Ibid., 48 (1856) (Justice Munro).
60. *McBrayer v Hill*, 26 NC 136 (1843); see also *McBrayer v Hill* (1843), original case file #3364, held by the North Carolina State Archives, Raleigh.
61. *McBrayer v Hill* (1843), 7.
62. Roscoe Pound, *The Formative Era of American Law* (Peter Smith, 1950), 4, 30 (note 2).
63. *State v Mann*, 13 NC (2 Dev.) 263 (1829).
64. Sally Greene and Eric L. Muller, "Introduction: State v. Mann and Thomas Ruffin in History and Memory," *North Carolina Law Review* 87, no. 3 (2009): 669-72. This issue of the *North Carolina Law Review*, titled "Thomas Ruffin and the Perils of Public Homage," was dedicated to unpacking Ruffin's complicated legacy. See also Sally Hadden, "Judging Slavery: Thomas Ruffin and State v. Mann," in *Local Matters: Race, Crime and Justice in the Nineteenth Century South*, eds. Christopher Waldrep and Donald G. Neiman (University of Georgia Press, 2011).
65. "Statue of Slave Owner, Former NC Supreme Court Chief Justice Thomas Ruffin Removed from Raleigh Court," *ABC11 News* (Raleigh, NC), 14 July 2020, https://abc11.com/thomas-ruffin-north-carolina-statue-removed-court/6315042/
66. "Supreme Court to Remove Portrait of Chief Justice Thomas Ruffin from Its Courtroom," Judicial Branch of North Carolina, Press Release, 22 December 2020, https://www.nccourts.gov/news/tag/press-release/supreme-court-to-remove-portrait-of-chief-justice-thomas-ruffin-from-its-courtroom
67. *McBrayer v Hill*, 26 NC 136, 139 (1843) (Chief Justice Ruffin).
68. Ibid., 140.
69. *Snow v Witcher*, 31 NC 346 (1849). *Snow v Wilches* [sic] (1849), original case file #4837, held at the North Carolina State Archives, Raleigh. In the published North Carolina Law Reports, the defendants' surname is spelled Witcher. But the case file folder held by NC State Archives is labeled "Snow v Wilches," and the original documents contained in the folder use the spelling Wilcher. See also William Witcher, US Census 1830, Surry County, North Carolina, p. 104, held by the US National Archives and Records Administration (NARA). I have used Witcher in my text and added "sic" to Wilcher and Wilches in case names. Re Huldah Snow, see US Census 1850, Surry County, North Carolina, House Number 1227, Line 24, held by the US National Archives and Records Administration (NARA).
70. *Snow v Wilcher* [sic] (1849), 6.
71. Ibid., 9-10.
72. *Snow v Witcher*, 31 NC 346, 348 (1849) (Justice Pearson).
73 *Watters* [sic] *v Smoot*, 33 NC 315 (1850). See also *John C. Waters and Wife v George W. Smoot* (1850), original case file #6605, held by the North Carolina State

Archives, Raleigh. In the published North Carolina Law Reports, the defendants' surname is spelled Watters. But the case file folder held by NC State Archives is labeled "Waters v Smoot." See also John Waters, US Census 1850, Wilkes County, North Carolina, p. 730, held by the US National Archives and Records Administration (NARA). I have used Waters in my text and added "sic" to Watters in case names.

74. *John C. Waters and Wife v George W. Smoot* (1850).

75. *Watters [sic] v Smoot*, 33 NC 315, 316 (1850) (Justice Pearson).

76. Re John Waters, see US Census 1850, Wilkes County, North Carolina, House Number 1828, Line 36, held by the US National Archives and Records Administration (NARA).

77. *State v John P Waters* (1809).

78. Linville M. Waters, application #22049, 13 June 13, 1907, Eastern Cherokee applications, Records of the US Court of Claims 1835-1984, National Archives identifier 56643034, National Archives, https://catalog.archives.gov/id/56643034

79. *State v William P. Watters [sic]* (1843). See also Charles Frank Robinson II, *Dangerous Liaisons: Sex and Love in the Segregated South* (University of Arkansas Press, 2003), 13.

80. *Lucas v Nichols*, 52 NC 32 (1859); see also *Candance Lucas v Gilbert R Nichols* (1859), original case file #7901, held by North Carolina State Archives, Raleigh.

81. *Candance Lucas v Gilbert R Nichols* (1859), 2.

82. Ibid.

83. *Lucas v Nichols*, 52 NC 32, 33-34 (1859).

84. Ibid., 35 (Justice Manly).

85. Bynum, *Unruly Women*, 41-44.

Chapter 4

1. *Lewis v Hudson*, 44 GA 568, 571 (1872) (Justice McCay).

2. Joseph Henry Lumpkin, "Law Reform in Georgia: Judge Lumpkin's Report," *Western Law Journal* 7 (1850): 384.

3. Noeleen McIlvenna, *Short Life of Free Georgia: Class and Slavery in the Colonial South* (University of North Carolina Press, 2015), 13.

4. Betty Wood, *Slavery in Colonial Georgia 1730-1775* (University of Georgia Press, 2007), 4.

5. Benjamin Martyn (board of trustee's secretary) quoted in Thomas A. Scott, ed., *Cornerstones of Georgia History: Documents That Formed the State* (University of Georgia Press, 1995), 30.

6. Watson W. Jennison, *Cultivating Race: The Expansion of Slavery in Georgia 1750-1860* (University Press of Kentucky, 2012), 189.

7. Ibid., 239.

8. Ibid., 4.

9. Jefferson James Davis, "The Georgia Code of 1863: America's First Comprehensive Code," *Journal of Southern Legal History* 4 (1995-1996): 1-44.

10. Erwin C. Surrency, "The First American Criminal Code: The Georgia Code of 1816," *Georgia Historical Quarterly* 63, no. 4 (1979): 420-34.

11. Lumpkin, "Law Reform in Georgia," 384.

12. Lucius Q. C. Lamar, *A Compilation of the Laws of the State of Georgia* (1821) (1811 act and 1812 amendment), https://digitalcommons.law.uGAedu/ga_code/22/

13. Ibid., ninth division, section 10, 594 (my emphasis).

14. Ibid, tenth division, section 6, 596.

15. See Andrew J. King, "Constructing Gender: Sexual Slander in Nineteenth-Century America," *Law and History Review* 13, no. 1 (Spring 1995): 84 (note 83). See also *Frisbee v Fowler and wife*, 2 CT 707 (1818); *Treat v Browning*, 4 CT 408 (1822); *Walton v Singleton*, 7 Serg. & Rawle 449 (PA 1821); *Klumph v Dunn*, 66 PA St. 141 (1870).

16. *Pledger v Hathcock*, 1 GA 550 (1846).

17. *Pledger v Hathcock* (1846), original case file #A-00042, held by the Georgia State Archives, Morrow, 3-4.

18. Ibid., 10.

19. Ibid., 6.

20. Ibid., 11.

21. *Pledger v Hathcock*, 1 GA 550, 550 (1846) (Justice Warner).

22. Ibid., 551.

23. Ibid.

24. An Act to Add an Additional Section to the Tenth Division of the Penal Code in This State (Act 161), 12 January 1852; See *Acts of the General Assembly of the State of Georgia, Passed in Milledgeville at a Biennial Session in November, December and January 1851-52* (Samuel J. Ray State Printer, 1852), 270.

25. Code of 1860, Title 2, chap. 1, § 50: "Persons have one eighth, or more, of negro or African blood in their veins, are not white persons in the meaning of this code." https://digitalcommons.law.uGAedu/ga_code/18/

26. *Castleberry v Kelly*, 26 GA 606 (1858).

27. US Census 1860 for Samuel S. Kelly and Martha Kelly, Warren County, Georgia, held by the US National Archives and Records Administration (NARA). Note: Samuel S. Kelly's entry has been incorrectly digitized as Samuel Skelly.

28. US Census 1860 for Ezra Castleberry and Sarah Castleberry, Warren County, Georgia, held by the US National Archives and Records Administration (NARA); US Census 1860 Slave Schedule for Ezra Castleberry, Warren County, Georgia, held by the US National Archives and Records Administration (NARA).

29. *Castleberry v Kelly*, 9-10.

30. Ibid., 9 (Judge Thomas).

31. Ibid., 10 (Judge Thomas).

32. *Castleberry v Kelly*, 26 GA 606, 608 (Justice McDonald).

33. Ibid.; the 1860 code of Georgia (written two years later) states, in its preliminary provisions: "'Person' includes a corporation, it does not include slaves or free persons of color, unless named." https://digitalcommons.law.uGAedu/ga_code/18/

34. *Castleberry v Kelly*, 606, 609 (Justice McDonald).

35. Ibid.

36. Robert Luckett, "Charles McDonald," *New Georgia Encyclopedia*, last modified 5 September 2014, https://www.georgiaencyclopedia.org/articles/government-politics/charles-mcdonald-1793-1860/

37. *Daily Chronicle & Sentinel* (Augusta, GA), 3 December 1858, p. 2; *The Daily Constitutionalist* (Augusta, GA), 3 December 1858, p. 3.

38. An Act to Declare Certain Words, Slanderous and Actionable Per Se, and for Other Purposes, No. 67 (17 December 1859) contained in *Acts of the General Assembly of the State of Georgia Passed in Milledgeville at an Annual Session in November and December 1859* (Boughton, Nisbet and Barnes State Printers, 1860).

39. Timothy Lockley, "Crossing the Race Divide: Interracial Sex in Antebellum Savannah," *Slavery and Abolition* 18, no. 3 (1997): 159-73.

40. *Beggarly v Craft* [sic], 31 GA 309 (1860). In the original court documents and the US Census, the plaintiff's name is clearly spelled Josaphine Croft, not Josephine Craft, as published in the official court reports. I believe the correct spelling is Josaphine Croft, which I use in my text.

41. US Census 1860 for Josaphine Croft, Atlanta, Fulton County, Georgia, held by the US National Archives and Records Administration (NARA); US Census 1860 Slave Schedule for G. W. Croft, Warren County, Georgia, held by the US National Archives and Records Administration (NARA).

42. *Beggarly v Craft* [sic] (1860) original case file #A-03337, held by the Georgia State Archives, Morrow, 6.

43. Ibid., 19.

44. Ibid., 2.

45. Ibid., 6-9.

46. Ibid., 10-11.

47. *Beggarly v Craft* [sic], 31 GA 309, 313 (1860) (Chief Justice Lumpkin).

48. Ibid., 314.

49. Ibid., 315.

50. Ibid.

51. Ibid., 316.

52. Legal historian Andrew King writes that Georgia codified its common law in 1852, and it was then that the legislature decided to include yet another category of slander *per se*. See King, "Constructing Gender," 63, 88. But the source he cites as authority—R. H. Clark, Thomas Cobb, and D. Irwin's second edition of the Code of the State of Georgia—was published in 1873, not 1852 (as King cites). The correct reference is R. H. Clark, et al., *The Code of the State of Georgia*, 2nd ed. (J. W. Burke & Co Publishers, 1873). This mistake as to the year of publication and thus codification is repeated within Lisa Pruitt's scholarship. See Lisa R Pruitt, "On the Chastity of Women All Property in the World Depends: Injury from Sexual Slander in the Nineteenth Century," *Indiana Law Journal* 78 (2003): 968 (note 8). In fact, Georgia did not codify its common law until the 1860s, and it was then that

slander *per se* was notably expanded. This explains why this new category—"debasing act"—which would have been critical in deciding the *Castleberry v King* decision of 1858, was never referred to or relied upon in that decision.

53. Charles Warren, *A History of the American Bar* (Little, Brown, 1913), 518.

54. Erwin C. Surrency, "The Georgia Code of 1863 and Its Place in the Codification Movement," *Journal of Southern Legal History* 11 (2003): 83.

55. Frederick Robinson, "A Letter to the Hon. Rufus Choate Containing a Brief Exposure of Law Craft and Some of the Encroachments of the Bar upon the Rights and Liberties of the People," (1832), quoted in Warren, *A History of the American Bar,* 511-512.

56. Oliver H. Prince, *Digest of the Laws of the State of Georgia* (Grantland & Orme, 1822), ix.

57. Lumpkin, "Law Reform in Georgia," 391.

58. Ibid. (my emphasis).

59. Ibid.

60. Ibid., 384 (emphasis in original).

61. Ibid.

62. "Judge Lumpkin's Report on Law Reform," *Milledgeville Southern Recorder,* 4 December 1849, p. 2; this report by Lumpkin was the same as the one published in the *Western Law Journal* in 1850 but in the latter version, Lumpkin's discussion of slavery towards the end of the report was omitted.

63. Joseph Henry Lumpkin to daughter Callie, 13 October 1853, quoted in Paul DeForest Hicks, *Joseph Henry Lumpkin: Georgia's First Chief Justice* (University of Georgia Press, 2002), 131-132.

64. Thomas Read Rootes Cobb, *An Inquiry into the Law of Negro Slavery in the United States of America: To Which Is Prefixed, An Historical Sketch of Slavery,* vol. 1 (T. & J. W. Johnson & Co (Philadelphia) and W. Thorne Williams (Savannah), 1858), 21-22.

65. Ibid., 49.

66. R. H. Clark, T. R. R. Cobb, and D. Irwin, *The Code of the State of Georgia* (John H. Seals, 1861), iii, viii.

67. For scholarship regarding the 1863 Code and its legacy, see Surrency, "The Georgia Code of 1863," 81; Davis, "The Georgia Code of 1863," 1; William B. McCash, "Thomas Cobb and the Codification of Georgia's Law," *Georgia Historical Quarterly* 62, no. 1 (1978): 9-23.

68. Roscoe Pound, "The Codification of American Law," in *Code Napoleon and the Common Law World,* ed. Bernard C. Schwartz (New York University Press, 1956), 273.

69. Lumpkin, "Law Reform in Georgia," 391.

70. *Central of Georgia Railway Co. v State of Georgia,* 104 GA 831, 855 (1898).

71. Ibid.

72. Ibid.

73. Clark, Cobb, and Irwin, *Code of the State of Georgia,* 544.

74. *Lewis v Hudson*, 44 GA 568 (1872); see also US Census 1870 for Evaline Lewis, Forsyth County, Georgia, held by the US National Archives and Records Administration (NARA); US Census 1870 for Ammon Hudson, Forsyth County, Georgia, held by the US National Archives and Records Administration (NARA).
75. *Lewis v Hudson*, 16-21.
76. Ibid., 23.
77. Ibid., 25-27.
78. *Lewis v Hudson*, 44 GA 568, 571 (1872).
79. Ibid.
80. Ibid.

Chapter 5

1. Edward Gibbon Wakefield, *Sketch for a Proposal for Colonizing Australasia* (J. Dove, 1830), Article VI, 4-5; see http://nla.gov.au/nla.obj-52759924; see also W. K. Hastings, "The Wakefield Colonisation Plan and Constitutional Development in South Australia, Canada and New Zealand," *Journal of Legal History* 11, no. 2 (1990): 279-299.
2. Eric Richards, ed., *The Flinders History of South Australia: Social History* (Wakefield Press, 1986), 1.
3. Paul Sendziuk and Robert Foster, *A History of South Australia* (Cambridge University Press, 2018), 41.
4. T. L. Stevenson, "Population Change Since 1836," in *The Flinders History of South Australia*, 172-173.
5. Catherine Spence, "Some Social Aspects of Early Colonial Life, by a Colonist of 1839," *South Australian Register* (Adelaide, SA), Saturday 26 October 1878, p. 5.
6. For further information regarding women and marriage in colonial South Australia, see Helen Jones, *In Her Own Name: A History of Women in South Australia from 1836* (Wakefield Press, 1994).
7. Mandy Paul and Robert Foster, "Married to the Land: Land Grants to Aboriginal Women in South Australia 1848-1911," *Australian Historical Studies* 34, no. 121 (2003): 48-68.
8. See also Amanda Nettelbeck, *Indigenous Rights and Colonial Subjecthood: Protection and Reform in the Nineteenth-Century British Empire* (Cambridge University Press, 2019).
9. Therese McCarthy and Paul Sendziuk, "Deserted Women and the Law in Colonial South Australia," *Journal of Australian Colonial History* 20 (2018): 63-82.
10. See Jones, *In Her Own Name*, 9.
11. Carol Bacchi, "The 'Woman Question' in South Australia," in *The Flinders History of South Australia History*, 413.
12. For details of Inskip's migration, see "Shipping Intelligence," *South Australian Register* (Adelaide, SA), 24 October 1849, p. 3.
13. *Inskip v Swailes* [1856] SASC, reported in *South Australian Register* (Adelaide, SA), 8 April 1856, p. 3.

NOTES TO CHAPTER 5

14. Patrick Parkinson, "An Ugly Rumour," *Adelaide Observer* (Adelaide, SA), 12 January 1856, p. 8.
15. *South Australian Register* (Adelaide, SA), 8 April 1856, p. 3.
16. Ibid.
17. Ibid.
18. Ibid.
19. Ibid.
20. *Adelaide Times* (Adelaide, SA) 8 April 1856, p. 3.
21. *South Australian Register* (Adelaide, SA), 8 April 1856, p. 3.
22. Ibid.
23. Ibid.
24. *Ward v Weeks* (1830) 7 Bing 211; Chief Justice Tindal: "Every man must be taken to be answerable for the necessary consequences of his own wrongful acts: but such a spontaneous and unauthorised communication cannot be considered as the necessary consequence of the original uttering of the words."
25. *South Australian Register* (Adelaide, SA), 15 April 1856, p. 3.
26. *South Australian Register* (Adelaide, SA), 25 June 1856, p. 3.
27. Ibid.
28. *South Australian Register* (Adelaide, SA), 6 November 1856, p. 2. In the marriage notice, John Hearn is spelled Hearne.
29. *Bell v Allen* [1862] SASC, reported in *South Australian Register* (Adelaide, SA), 9 September 1862, p. 3.
30. *South Australian Advertiser* (Adelaide, SA), 9 September 1862, p. 3.
31. *South Australian Weekly Chronicle* (Adelaide, SA), 13 September 1862, p. 5.
32. *South Australian Register* (Adelaide, SA), 9 September 1862, p. 3.
33. *South Australian Weekly Chronicle* (Adelaide, SA), 13 September 1862, p. 5.
34. *South Australian Register* (Adelaide, SA), 15 November 1862, p. 3.
35. *South Australian Register* (Adelaide, SA), 1 October 1862, p. 3.
36. *Wishart v Peryman* [1863] SASC, reported in *Adelaide Observer* (Adelaide, SA) 6 June 1863, p. 3.
37. *South Australian Advertiser* (Adelaide, SA), 5 June 1863, p. 3.
38. *South Australian Register* (Adelaide, SA), 5 June 1863, p. 3.
39. "Obituary. The Late Mr Justice Andrews," *South Australian Register* (Adelaide, SA), 3 July 1884, p. 3.
40. *South Australian Advertiser* (Adelaide, SA), 5 June 1863, p. 3.
41. Ibid.
42. Ibid.
43. *South Australian Weekly Chronicle* (Adelaide, SA), 6 June 1863, p. 7.
44. *Adelaide Observer* (Adelaide, SA), 6 June 1863, p. 3.
45. *South Australian Advertiser* (Adelaide, SA), 6 June 1863, p. 3.
46. "Legal Anomalies," *Adelaide Observer* (Adelaide, SA), 27 June 1863, p. 1.
47. Ibid.

48. *South Australian Register* (Adelaide, SA), 17 July 1863, p. 3; *South Australian Weekly Chronicle* (Adelaide, SA), 18 July 1863, p. 7.

49. See *South Australian Register* (Adelaide, SA), 1 October 1863, p. 3; *South Australian Advertiser* (Adelaide, SA), 1 October 1863, p. 3; *Adelaide Observer* (Adelaide, SA) 3 October 1863, p. 6; *South Australian Weekly Chronicle* (Adelaide, SA), 3 October 1863, p. 6.

50. *South Australian Advertiser* (Adelaide, SA), 1 October 1863, p. 3.

51. Ibid.

52. *South Australian Register* (Adelaide, SA), 28 September 1863, p. 2.

53. *South Australian Weekly Chronicle* (Adelaide, SA), 17 October 1863, p. 7.

54. "Waterhouse, Hon. George Marsden," from *An Encyclopedia of New Zealand*, ed. A. H. McLintock, orig. pub. 1966, http://www.TeAra.govt.nz/en/1966/waterhouse-hon-george-marsden

55. *Adelaide Observer* (Adelaide, SA), 21 May 1853, p. 5.

56. *South Australian Weekly Chronicle* (Adelaide, SA), 17 October 1863, p. 7.

57. Ibid.

58. An Act to Amend the Law Relating to Defamatory Words 1863 (South Australia).

59. *South Australian Weekly Chronicle* (Adelaide, SA), 25 June 1864, p. 5.

60. Ibid.

61. *Adelaide Observer* (Adelaide, SA), 12 November 1864, p. 6.

62. *Adelaide Observer* (Adelaide, SA), 19 November 1864, p. 3.

63. Ibid.

64. *Adelaide Observer* (Adelaide, SA), 18 March 1865, p. 2.

65. Ibid.

66. *Adelaide Express* (Adelaide, SA), 28 March 1865, p. 3.

67. *South Australian Register* (Adelaide, SA), 29 March 1865, p. 3.

68. Ibid.

69. *Adelaide Express* (Adelaide, SA), 12 May 1865, p. 3.

70. *South Australian Register* (Adelaide, SA), 13 May 1865, p. 3.

71. Ibid.

72. Ibid.

73. "Angas, George Fife (1789-1879)," from *Australian Dictionary of Biography*, National Centre of Biography, Australian National University, https://adb.anu.edu.au/biography/angas-george-fife-1707/text1855

74. *South Australian Advertiser* (Adelaide, SA), 28 June 1865, p. 2.

75. Ibid.

76. Ibid.

77. Ibid.

78. Ibid.

79. An Act to Amend the Law of Slander 1865 (South Australia).

Chapter 6

1. For example, New Jersey in 1790, North Carolina in 1808, Kentucky in 1811, Indiana in 1813, Illinois in 1823, South Carolina in 1824, Massachusetts in 1829, Ohio in 1833, Missouri in 1835, Arkansas in 1837, Maryland in 1838, Alabama in 1839, Iowa in 1844, Georgia in 1959.

2. See, e.g., *Raleigh Register* (Raleigh, NC), 29 April 1825, p. 3; "Ladies' Cabinet," *Vermont Gazette* (Bennington, VT), 31 May 1825, p. 1; Slander of Females," *Vermont Watchman and State Journal* (Montpelier, VT), 10 May 1825, p. 2; "Slander of Females," *Pittsfield Sun* (Pittsfield, MA), 12 May 1825, p. 1; "New York State Legislature," *Charleston Mercury and Morning Advertiser* (Charleston, SC), 5 April 1825, p. 2; *Poughkeepsie Journal* (Poughkeepsie, NY), 30 March 1825, p. 2; *Evening Post* (New York, NY), 25 March 1825, p. 2; *Phenix Gazette* (Alexandria, VA), 28 April 1925.

3. "Slander of Females," *Pittsfield Sun* (Pittsfield, MA), 12 May 1825, p. 1.

4. Barbara Welter, "The Cult of True Womanhood: 1820-1860," *American Quarterly* 18, no. 2 (1966): 151-74.

5. "Slander of Females," *Vermont Watchman and State Journal* (Montpelier, VT), 10 May 1825, p. 2.

6. See, e.g., Laurie Kaiser, "The Black Madonna: Notions of True Womanhood from Jacobs to Hurston," *South Atlantic Review* 60, no. 1 (1995): 97-109; Nancy Hewitt, "Taking the True Woman Hostage," *Journal of Women's History* 14, no. 1 (2002): 156-62; Donna J. Guy, "True Womanhood in Latin America," *Journal of Women's History* 14, no. 1 (2002): 170-73; Shirley Yee, *Black Women Abolitionists: A Study in Activism* (University of Tennessee Press, 1992).

7. *Buys v Gillespie*, 2 Johns. 115, 115 (1807).

8. Herbie J. DiFonzo and Ruth C. Stern, "Addicted to Fault: Why Divorce Reform Has Lagged in New York," *Pace Law Review* 27 (2006): 564.

9. *Buys v Gillespie*, 2 Johns. 115, 116 (1807).

10. Ibid.

11. Ibid., 115, 115 (1807).

12. Ibid., 115, 117 (1807).

13. The 1848 Seneca Falls Declaration of Sentiments and Resolutions described married women as "civilly dead." "Declaration of Sentiments and Resolutions," in *The American Sisterhood: Writings of the Feminist Movement from Colonial Times to Present*, ed. Wendy Martin (Harper and Row, 1972), 42-46; see also Isabel Marcus, "Locked in and Locked Out: Reflections on the History of Divorce Law Reform in New York State," *Buffalo Law Review* 37 (1988): 393.

14. See Marcus, "Locked in and Locked Out."

15. Michael Grossberg, "Who Gets the Child: Custody, Guardianship, and the Rise of a Judicial Patriarchy in Nineteenth-Century America," *Feminist Studies* 9, no. 2 (1983): 238: "Traditionally in Anglo-American Law fathers had an almost unlimited right to the custody of their minor, legitimate children." This didn't start to change in New York until the 1830s.

16. *Brooker v Coffin*, 5 Johns. 188, 188 (1809).

17. Ibid., 189 (1809).

18. *Brooker v Coffin*, 5 Johns. 188, 192 (1809).

19. Andrew J. King, "Constructing Gender: Sexual Slander in Nineteenth-Century America," *Law and History Review* 13, no. 1 (Spring 1995): 83.

20. "Blue Ey'd Mary," *Evening Post* (New York, NY), 29 August 1810.

21. See Ibram X. Kendi, *Stamped from the Beginning: The Definitive History of Racist Ideas in America* (Nation Books, 2016); Nell Irvin Painter, *The History of White People* (Norton, 2011).

22. Thomas Branagan, *The Excellency of the Female Character Vindicated: Being an Investigation Relative to the Cause and Effects of the Encroachments of Men Upon the Rights of Women, and the Too Frequent Degradation and Consequent Misfortunes of the Fair Sex* (Samuel Wood, 1807), 252.

23. Leslie M. Harris, *In the Shadow of Slavery: African Americans in New York City, 1626-1863* (University of Chicago Press, 2004), 59.

24. Shane White, *Stories of Freedom in Black New York* (Harvard University Press, 2007), 59.

25. Shane White, *Somewhat More Independent: The End of Slavery in New York City, 1770-1810* (University of Georgia Press, 1991), 3 (my emphasis).

26. L. E. L., "The Portrait," *Godey's Lady's Book* 1 (1830): 246.

27. See *Smith v Minor*, 1 NJL 16 (1790) and Chapter 1.

28. See *Sexton v Todd*, Ohio (Wright) 316 (1833); *Cox and wife v Bunker and wife*, 1 Morris 269 (1844).

29. *Poughkeepsie Journal* (Poughkeepsie, NY), 30 March 1825; *Charleston Mercury and Morning Advertiser* (Charleston, SC), 5 April 1825; *Evening Post* (New York, NY), 25 March 1825; *Raleigh Register* (Raleigh, NC), 29 April 1825; *Vermont Watchman and State Journal* (Montpelier, VT), 10 May 1825.

30. *Evening Post* (New York, NY), 25 March 1825.

31. *Poughkeepsie Journal* (Poughkeepsie, NY), 30 March 1825.

32. *Vermont Watchman and State Journal* (Montpelier, VT), 10 May 1825 (my emphasis).

33. Ibid.

34. See, e.g., Regina Graycar, "The Gender of Judgments: Some Reflections on Bias," *University of British Columbia Law Review* 32 (1998): 1-14; Margaret Thornton, ed., *Public and Private: Feminist Legal Debates* (Oxford University Press, 1995).

35. *Evening Post* (New York, NY), 25 March 1825.

36. *Vermont Watchman and State Journal* (Montpelier, VT), 10 May 1825.

37. Ibid.

38. *Evening Post* (New York, NY), 25 March 1825 (my emphasis).

39. For discussions of manliness and whiteness in the United States during the nineteenth century, see Gail Bederman, *Manliness and Civilization: A Cultural History of Gender and Race in the United States, 1880-1917* (University of Chicago Press, 1995); and Michael Kimmel, *Manhood in America: A Cultural History* (Free Press, 1996).

40. *Olmstead v Miller*, 1 Wend. 506, 506 (1828).
41. Ibid., 506, 510 (1828).
42. See also *Bradt v Towsley*, 13 Wend. 253 (1835).
43. *Beach v Ranney*, 2 Hill 309 (1842).
44. Ibid., 309, 310 (1842).
45. *Olmsted v Brown*, 12 Barb. 657 (1852).
46. Ibid., 657, 658 (1852).
47. Ibid., 657, 659 (1852).
48. Ibid., 657, 660 (1852).
49. *Terwilliger v Wands*, 17 NY 54 (1858), "Complaint," Record and Brief held by the New York State Archives, Albany.
50. *Terwilliger v Wands*, 17 NY 54 (1858), Testimony of John Neipier, Record & Brief, held by the New York State Archives, Albany, 10.
51. *Terwilliger v Wands*, 17 NY 54 (1858), Testimony of Nancy Harpbun, Record & Brief, held by the New York State Archives, Albany, 13.
52. *Terwilliger v Wands*, 17 NY 54 (1858), Testimony of George Terwilliger, Record & Brief, held by the New York State Archives, Albany, 14.
53. *Terwilliger v Wands*, 25 Barb. 313, 317 (1855) (Justice Allen).
54. *Terwilliger v Wands*, 17 NY 54, 60 (1858) (Justice Strong).
55. *Wilson v Goit*, 17 NY 442 (1858).
56. *Wilson v Goit*, "Complaint", Record & Brief, held by the New York State Library Special Collections, Albany, 4-5.
57. Ibid.
58. *Wilson v Goit*, Testimony of John Wilson, Record & Brief, held by the New York State Library Special Collections, Albany, 12-13.
59. *Wilson v Goit*, Testimony of Ann Wilson, Record & Brief, held by the New York State Library Special Collections, Albany, 14.
60. *Wilson v Goit*, "Points for Appellant," Record & Brief, held by the New York State Library Special Collections, Albany, 4.
61. *Wilson v Goit*, 17 NY 442 (1858).
62. *Wilson v Goit*, 17 NY 442 (1858) (my emphasis).
63. *Wilson v Goit*, 17 NY 442 (1858).
64. Vindex, "The Action of Slander as Expounded by the Court of Appeals," *Buffalo Morning Express and Illustrated Buffalo Express* (Buffalo, NY), 24 November 1859.
65. Re the rural nature of the New York slander cases, see King, "Constructing Gender," 77: "Most slander cases came from rural communities."
66. Vindex, "The Action of Slander as Expounded by the Court of Appeals"; Vindex, "The Action of Slander, Rejoinder to T's Reply," *Buffalo Morning Express and Illustrated Buffalo Express* (Buffalo, NY), 3 December 1859.
67. Vindex, "The Action of Slander, Rejoinder to T's Reply."
68. Ibid.
69. Vindex, "The Action of Slander as Expounded by the Court of Appeals."

70. Vindex, "The Action of Slander, Rebutter to T's Surrejoinder," *Buffalo Morning Express and Illustrated Buffalo Express* (Buffalo, NY), 10 December 1859.

71. See *New York Tribune* (New York, NY), 2 April 1869; *Buffalo Commercial* (Buffalo, NY), 10 April 1869; *New York Times*, 30 March 1869.

72. *Buffalo Commercial*, p. 2.

73. *New York Times*, p. 4.

74. "Slandered Chastity and Special Damages," *Albany Law Journal* 2 (December 24, 1870): 490.

75. See 1871 NY Laws, c. 219.

76. See New York Civil Rights, Ch. 6, Art. 7, § 77: "In an action of slander of a woman imputing unchastity to her, it is not necessary to allege or prove special damages."

Chapter 7

1. *North Melbourne Advertiser* (North Melbourne, VIC), 23 July 1874; *The Age* (Melbourne, VIC), 23 July 1874, p. 3; *The Leader* (Melbourne, VIC), 25 July 1874, p. 13; *The Argus* (Melbourne, VIC), 25 July 1874, p. 10.

2. Re Francis Quinlan, see obituary in *Advocate* (Melbourne, VIC), 9 April 1910, p. 41.

3. "Women Slanderers," *Australian Jurist* 2, no. 13 (28 August 1871): 2.

4. *The Argus* (Melbourne, VIC), 25 July 1874.

5. *The Age* (Melbourne, VIC), 23 July 1874; *The Leader* (Melbourne, VIC), 25 July 1874.

6. *North Melbourne Advertiser* (North Melbourne, VIC), 23 July 1874.

7. *The Age* (Melbourne, VIC), 23 July 1874.

8. "What Is Thought of Us in America," *Australian Jurist* 3, no. 5 (23 July 1872): 15.

9. "Death of Mr. J. L. Purves," *The Argus* (Melbourne, VIC), 25 November 1910, p. 6.

10. Hansard, *Victoria Parliamentary Debates, Session 1876, Legislative Council and Legislative Assembly*, vol. 25 (John Ferres Printer, 1877), 961.

11. See, e.g., Australian Law Reform, *Recognition of Aboriginal Customary Laws*, report no. 31 (June 1986); Leigh Boucher and Lynette Russell, *Settler Colonial Governance in Nineteenth-Century Victoria* (Australian National University Press, 2015); P. Grimshaw et al., *Equal Subjects, Unequal Rights: Indigenous Peoples in British Settler Colonies, 1830-1910* (Manchester University Press, 2003).

12. An Act to Provide for the Protection and Management of the Aboriginal Natives of Victoria 1869 (Victoria).

13. Leigh Boucher, "The 1869 Aborigines Protection Act: Vernacular Ethnography and the Governance of Aboriginal Subjects," in *Settler Colonial Governance*, 64.

14. See Diane Kirkby, *Barmaids: A History of Women's Work in Pubs* (Cambridge University Press, 1997); Diane Kirkby, "Writing the History of Women Working: Photographic Evidence and the Disreputable Occupation of Barmaid," *Labour His-*

tory, no. 61 (1991): 3-16; Clare Wright, *Beyond the Ladies Lounge: Australia's Female Publicans* (Text Publishing, 2014); Clare Wright, "Of Public Houses and Private Lives Female Hotelkeepers as Domestic Entrepreneurs," *Australian Historical Studies* 32, no. 116 (2001): 57-75.

15. Graeme Davison, *The Rise and Fall of Marvellous Melbourne*, 2nd ed. (Melbourne University Press, 2004), 7.

16. *White v Jordan* (1880) 6 VLR 11.

17. Davison, *Marvellous Melbourne*, 58.

18. *White v Jordan* (1880) "Cross Examination of John Jordan." Civil case files held by State Archives of Victoria, North Melbourne.

19. *Herald* (Melbourne, VIC), 18 March 1880.

20. *White v Jordan* (1880) "Affidavit of Maria White" sworn 26 January 1880. Civil case files held by State Archives of Victoria, North Melbourne.

21. See *White v Jordan* (1880) 6 VLR 11; *The Age* (Melbourne, VIC), 19 March 1880, p. 2.

22. *Bendigo Advertiser* (Bendigo, VIC), 17 March 1880.

23. *Weekly Times* (Melbourne, VIC), 20 March 1880.

24. *The Age* (Melbourne, VIC), 19 March 1880.

25. *The Age* (Melbourne, VIC), 29 March 1880.

26. *Albrecht v Patterson* (1886) 7 VLR 597.

27. *Albrecht v Patterson* (1885) "Statement of Claim." Civil case files held by Public Record Office Victoria, North Melbourne.

28. Ibid.; see also *The Age* (Melbourne, VIC), 20 April 1886; *Herald* (Melbourne, VIC), 21 April 1886; *Albrecht v Patterson* (1886) 7 VLR 597.

29. *Herald* (Melbourne, VIC), 21 April 1886.

30. *The Age* (Melbourne, VIC), 20 April 1886, p. 4.

31. Margot Beever, "Kerferd, George Briscoe (1831-1889)," *Australian Dictionary of Biography*, National Centre of Biography, Australian National University, https://adb.anu.edu.au/biography/kerferd-george-briscoe-3947/text6217 (published first in print in 1974).

32. *Herald* (Melbourne, VIC), 21 April 1886, p. 4.

33. *Albrecht v Patterson* (1886) 7 VLR 597, 599.

34. *Albrecht v Patterson* (1886) 7 VLR 597, 602.

35. *Albrecht v Patterson* (1886) 7 VLR 597, 603.

36. Ibid.

37. *Albrecht v Patterson* (1886) 7 VLR 821, 827 (Justices Williams and Webb).

38. *Albrecht v Patterson* (1886) 7 VLR 821, 828 (Justices Williams and Webb).

39. *Albrecht v Patterson* (1886) 7 VLR 821, 826 (Higinbotham CJ dissented, stating they were of no obligation to extend the current law's injurious effects, holding: "The inevitable hardship of the existing rule will be mitigated by holding that as soon as that condition is satisfied, and special damage has been proved, the jury will be at liberty to award general damages.")

40. "Slandering a Woman," *Table Talk* (Melbourne, VIC), 10 September 1886, p. 9.

41. Hansard, Victorian Parliamentary Debates, Legislative Council and Legislative Assembly, 14 December 1887, p. 1398.

42. *The Age* (Melbourne, VIC), 23 February 1887, p. 5; *The Age* (Melbourne, VIC), 24 February 1887, p. 4; *The Age* (Melbourne, VIC), 25 February 1887, p. 5.

43. *The Age* (Melbourne, VIC), 25 February 1887, p. 5; slightly different version given by *The Argus* (Melbourne, VIC), 28 February 1887, p. 6.

44. *The Argus* (Melbourne, VIC), 28 February 1887, p. 6

45. *The Age* (Melbourne, VIC), 1 March 1887, p. 7.

46. "An Unmarried Woman's Difficulty," *Geelong Advertiser* (Geelong, VIC), 7 March 1887, p. 4.

47. "A Woman's Reputation," *Table Talk* (Melbourne, VIC), 4 March 1887, p. 8.

48. Hansard, Victorian Parliamentary Debates, 13th Parliament, Legislative Council and Legislative Assembly, vol. 56, 16 November 1887, 2138.

49. Ibid., 2139.

50. Hansard, Victoria Parliamentary Debates, 13th Parliament, Legislative Council and Legislative Assembly, vol. 56, 14 December 1887, 2639.

51. Hansard, Victorian Parliamentary Debates, 13th Parliament, Legislative Council and Legislative Assembly, vol. 56, 16 November 1887, 2640.

52. Ibid.

53. "Slander," *Table Talk* (Melbourne, VIC), 25 November 1887, p. 8.

54. See Diane Kirkby, ed., *Sex, Power and Justice: Historical Perspectives on Law in Australia* (Oxford University Press, 1995); Marilyn Lake, *Getting Equal: The History of Australian Feminism* (Allen & Unwin, 1999), 23-24; Judy Mackinolty and Heather Radi, eds., *In Pursuit of Justice: Australian Women and the Law 1788-1979* (Hale & Iremonger, 1979).

55. Audrey Oldfield, *Woman Suffrage in Australia* (Cambridge University Press, 1992), 134.

56. See Geoffrey Serle, "Shiels, William (1847-1904)," *Australian Dictionary of Biography*, vol. 11 (Melbourne University Press, 1988).

57. See Janette Bomford, *That Dangerous and Persuasive Woman: Vida Goldstein* (Melbourne University Press, 1993).

58. See Oldfield, *Woman Suffrage in Australia*.

Chapter 8

1. "Ecclesiastical Report," *Law Magazine* 7, no. 2 (1832): 263-98.

2. Ibid., 291.

3. Ibid., 292.

4. Hansard, UK Parliament, House of Commons, vol. 66, 13 February 1843, column 395, https://api.parliament.uk/historic-hansard/lords/1843/feb/13/the-law-of-libel

5. House of Lords Select Committee, *Report from the Select Committee of the House of Lords Appointed to Consider the Law of Defamation and Libel and to Report Thereon to the House; With Minutes of Evidence Taken Before the Committee, and an Index* (London, 1843), iii.

6. The attorney general: "But to the first clause of this Bill, which gave a right of action for verbal slander, he felt great objection.... There he would make his stand; and, instead of passing a law to raise the law of slander to the law of libel, he would rather cut down the law of libel to the level of the law of slander." Hansard, UK Parliament, House of Commons, vol. 71, 16 August 1843, column 875, https://api.parliament.uk/historic-hansard/commons/1843/aug/16/defamation-and-libel-bill

7. *The Law Times* quoted in Anthony Hugh Manchester, "Reform of the Ecclesiastical Courts," *American Journal of Legal History* 10, no. 1 (1966): 75.

8. Ibid.

9. Hansard, UK Parliament, House of Lords, vol. 130, 16 February 1854, column 371, https://hansard.parliament.uk/Lords/1854-02-16/debates/fec61113-2dea-440b-9b79-fb84b8bcd4b5/TestamentaryJurisdictionBill

10. Stephen Waddams, *Sexual Slander in Nineteenth Century England* (University of Toronto Press, 2016).

11. "Law Intelligence," *Derby Mercury* (Derby, England), 2 May 1860, p. 6; *Morning Chronicle* (London), 26 April 1860, p. 8.

12. *Allsop v Allsop* (1860) 5 H & N 534, 538.

13. Ibid., 539.

14. *Lynch v Knight*, original case file held at Parliamentary Archives UK, Westminster (House of Lords Appeal Cases and Writs of Error, series 3-1861, H-M).

15. Ibid.

16. Ibid.

17. Ibid.

18. *Lynch v Knight* (1861) 9 HLC 576, 588.

19. Ibid., 593.

20. Ibid., 596.

21. Ibid., 593.

22. Ibid., 594.

23. Ibid., 598.

24. Ibid.

25. *Roberts v Roberts* (1864) 5 B & S 384.

26. Ibid., 389.

27. Ibid., 390.

28. Ibid.

29. *Davies v Solomon* (1871) 7 LR QB 112.

30. Ibid., 114.

31. Ibid.

32. "Victoria, Australia," *The Times* (London), 2 February 1888, p. 13.

33. 19th Century House of Commons Hansard Sessional Papers, third series, vol. 328, 1888, 15-154, 75.

34. Ibid.

35. "Slander," *The Guardian* (London), 3 July 1888, p. 6; Slander Law Amendment Bill, Hansard, UK Parliament, House of Commons, vol. 328, 2 July 1888, p. 154.

36. "Slander of Women," *The Times* (London), 5 July 1888, p. 9; "Slander of Women," *Pall Mall Gazette* (London), 5 July 1888, p. 10.

37. "From Our London Correspondent," *Manchester Courier and Lancashire General Advertiser* (Manchester, England), 4 July 1888, p. 5.

38. "Our London Correspondence," *Liverpool Mercury* (Liverpool, England), 5 July 1888, p. 5.

39. C. H. M. Wharton, "Absurdities of English Law—Slander," *Stockport Advertiser* (Manchester, England), 10 January 1890, p. 4.

40. See "Lewis, Elizabeth Ann," in Ernest Hurst Cherrington, ed., *Standard Encyclopedia of the Alcohol Problem*, vol. 4, Kansas-Newton (American Issue Publishing Co., 1928), 1536-1537; see Ros Black, *Scandal, Salvation and Suffrage: The Amazing Women of the Temperance Movement* (Matador, 2015), 23-30.

41. John Anson, "The 'Drunkard's Friend' Who Hoped to Turn Blackburn Teetotal," *Lancashire Telegraph* (Lancashire, England), 11 June 2023, https://www.lancashiretelegraph.co.uk/news/23579134.drunkards-friend-hoped-turn-blackburn-teetotal/

42. Black, *Scandal, Salvation and Suffrage*, 30.

43. "Extraordinary Slander Case," *Manchester Evening News* (Manchester, England), 1 April 1890, p. 3.

44. "The Lewis-Shaw Case," *Weekly Standard and Express* (Blackburn, England), 5 April 1890, p. 6.

45. "Blackburn Slander Case," *Liverpool Echo* (Liverpool, England), 1 April 1890, p. 4.

46. Ibid.

47. "The Lewis-Shaw Case."

48. Ibid.

49. "Presentation to a Temperance Advocate," *Manchester Weekly Times and Examiner* (Manchester, England), 28 November 1890, p. 7.

50. *Liverpool Mercury* (Liverpool, England), 3 April 1890, p. 5.

51. Slander Law Amendment Bill, Hansard, UK Parliament, House of Commons, vol. 344, 15 May 1890, column 1060, https://api.parliament.uk/historic-hansard/commons/1890/may/15/slander-law-amendment-bill

52. *Weekly Standard and Express* (Blackburn, England), 24 May 1890, p. 5.

53. Slander Law Amendment Bill (No. 278), Hansard, UK Parliament, House of Commons, vol. 346, 9 July 1890, column 1227, https://api.parliament.uk/historic-hansard/commons/1890/jul/09/slander-law-amendment-bill-no-278; see also "Slander Law Amendment Bill," *The Times* (London), 10 July 1890, p. 8.

54. Slander of Women Bill, Hansard, UK Parliament, House of Commons, vol. 349, 4 December 1890, column 629, https://api.parliament.uk/historic-hansard/commons/1890/dec/04/slander-of-women-bill

55. Slander of Women Bill (no. 150), Hansard, UK Parliament, House of Commons, vol. 351, 23 March 1891, column 1755, https://api.parliament.uk/historic-hansard/commons/1891/mar/23/slander-of-women-bill-no-150

56. *Speight v Gosnay* [1891] 60 LJQB 231.

57. *Liverpool Mercury* (Liverpool, England), 3 February 1891, p. 5; see also *Lichfield Mercury* (Lichfield, England), 6 February 1891, p. 6.

58. Sandra Stanley Holton, "'To Educate Women into Rebellion': Elizabeth Cady Stanton and the Creation of a Transatlantic Network of Radical Suffragists," *American Historical Review* 99, no. 4 (October 1994): 1130; see also Ellen Carol Dubois, *Harriot Stanton Blatch and the Winning of Women's Suffrage* (Yale University Press, 1997), 1112–1136.

59. *Birmingham Daily Post* (Birmingham, England), 21 May 1889, p. 4.

60. Susan Kent, *Sex and Suffrage in Britain, 1860–1914* (Routledge, 2005), 141–142.

61. *Liverpool Mercury* (Liverpool, England), 9 May 1891, p. 5.

62. "Notes from the Law Courts," *The Observer* (London), 10 May 1891, p. 6.

63. *Weekly Standard and Express* (Blackburn, England), 16 May 1891, p. 2.

64. Slander of Women Bill (no. 1111), Hansard, UK Parliament, House of Lords, vol. 354, 29 June 1891, columns 1704–1711, https://api.parliament.uk/historic-hansard/lords/1891/jun/29/second-reading-5

65. Slander of Women Bill (no. 233), Hansard, UK Parliament, House of Lords, vol. 356, 30 July 1891, column 705, https://api.parliament.uk/historic-hansard/lords/1891/jul/30/slander-of-women-bill-no-233

Conclusion

1. *Ward v Klein*, 809 NYS 2d 828 (2005).

2. *US Restatement of Torts, Second* § 574 (1977) (June 2024 update).

3. See Daniel L. Stephens, "The Evolution and Confusion of the Sexual Misconduct Category of Slander Per Se," *Regent University Law Review* 31 (2018–2019): 277.

4. *Gallo v Alitalia*, 585 F Supp 2d 520 (SDNY 2008).

5. *Butler v Town of Argo*, 871 So 2d 1 (AL 2003).

6. *Wardlaw v Peck*, 318 SE 2d 270, 275 (SC Ct App. 1984).

7. *Walia v Vivek Purmasir & Associates Inc*, 160 F Supp 2d 380 (2000).

8. *Rangel v American Medical Response West*, Unreported, US District Court, ED California, No 1:09-cv-01467-AWI-BAM (2013).

9. *Doe v Simone*, Unreported, US District Court D, New Jersey, Civil Action No 12-5825 (2013).

10. *Mallory v Simon & Schuster Publishers*, 168 F Supp 3d 760 (2016).

11. Russell Spivak, "'Deepfakes': The Newest Way to Commit One of the Oldest Crimes," *Georgetown Law Technology Review* 3, no. 2 (2019): 339–401.

12. In 1822, the Court of Appeals of Kentucky interpreted their gender-specific slander of women act of 1811 as capable of applying to men. See *Morris v Blakely*, 1 Litt. 64 (1822). Whereas in Ohio the court refused to extend their judicial innovations making the sexual slander of women actionable *per se* to men. See *Davis v Brown*, 27 Ohio St. 326 (1875).

13. See Andrew J. King, "Constructing Gender: Sexual Slander in Nineteenth Century America," *Law and History Review* 13 (1995): 63-110; Lisa R. Pruitt, "On the Chastity of Women All Property in the World Depends: Injury from Sexual Slander in the Nineteenth Century," *Indiana Law Journal* 78 (2003): 965-1018; Lisa R. Pruitt, "Her Own Good Name: Two Centuries of Talk About Chastity," *Maryland Law Review* 63, no. 3 (2003): 401-539.

14. For example, see Defamation Act 2005 (Victoria), Sch 4, s 3 repealed Wrongs Act 1958 (Victoria) s 7 re slander of women.

15. *Lachaux v Independent Print Ltd and another* [2019] UKSC 27; [2020] AC 612.

16. Act of 1811, 4, W. Littell, The Statute Law of Kentucky 38.

17. 1813 Indiana Acts 110.

18. 1823 Illinois Laws 82.

19. 1824 South Carolina Acts, c4, s3.

20. *Miller v Parish* 25 Mass (8 Pick) 384 (1829).

21. *Sexton v Todd* 316, 317 (Ohio 1833).

22. 1845 Mo. Rev. Code 100.

23. 1837 Arkansas Acts 729 (Act of 13 December 1837).

24. 1838 Maryland Laws c 114.

25. 1839 Alabama Acts 96.

26. *Cox v Bunker*, 1 Morris 269 (IA 1844).

27. 1 Civil Code of the State of California 24 (1874).

28. See R. Knox-Mawer, "Some Indian Precedents and the Common Law," *International and Comparative Law Quarterly* 5, no. 2 (1956): 282-285.

29. See John King, *The Law of Defamation in Canada* (Law Publishers, 1907).

30. An Act to Declare and Amend the Law Relating to Defamation 1895 (TAS); An Act to Amend the Law Relating to the Slander of Women 1900 (WA).

31. See Alice Krzanich, "Virtue and Vindication: An Historical Analysis of Sexual Slander and a Woman's Good Name," *Auckland University Law Review* 17 (2011): 33-59.

32. "Slander Actions Are Made Easier," *Straits Times*, 9 May 1957, p. 11; see also "Defaming of Women," *Singapore Free Press*, 13 May 1957, p. 5.

33. See Kathleen A. Feeley and Jennifer Frost, eds., *When Private Talk Goes Public: Gossip in American History* (Palgrave MacMillan, 2014).

34. Ibid., 5.

35. See Diane L. Borden, "Reputational Assault: A Critical and Historical Analysis of Gender and the Law of Defamation," *Journalism and Mass Communication* 75, no. 1 (1998): 98-111.

36. *Gates v New York Recorder* (1898) 49 NE 769.

37. *McFadden v Morning Journal Ass'n*, 28 AD 508 (1898).

38. See Henry Ajder et al., "The State of Deepfakes: Landscape, Threats, and Impact," *Deeptrace*, September 2019, https://regmedia.co.uk/2019/10/08/deepfake_report.pdf

INDEX

Aboriginal Australians, 39, 42, 51-52, 102, 142
Adelaide Observer, 105, 108, 113, 181
Adultery: allegations against men, 117-18; criminalization, 79, 84-86, 88; double standard, 170; grounds for divorce, 103, 123-24; imputations, 44, 64, 133, 146, 165, 176; special damage, 5, 15, 55, 158-59, 161, 163; spiritual matter, 4, 27, 52, 102, 123; whiteness, 122-23
African Americans: Georgia, 80-82, 86; New Jersey, 20; North Carolina, 60, 62, 77. *See also* Black women; Black men; Race; Slavery
Agency, 17, 26, 77
Age, The, 139, 141
Albany Law Journal, 136, 140
Albrecht, Elizabeth, 9, 15, 145-50, 178, 180
Albrecht v Patterson, 145-50
Allen, Joseph, 2, 108-10
Allsop, Hannah, 155-57, 159-60
Allsop v Allsop, 155-57, 159-60, 164
American Revolution, 6, 19-20, 22, 26-27, 33, 39, 177

An Appeal to the Tribunal of Public Justice (Hopkins), 32
Andrews, Richard Bullock, 112
Angas, George Fife, 119-20
Antebellum period, 13, 60-62, 78
Apologies, 4, 115, 144
Argus, The, 149
Australian colonies, 5-6, 27, 38, 88, 104, 120, 139-40, 143, 153-54, 172, 183. *See also* New South Wales; South Australia; Victoria
Australian Natives' Association, 141
Aurora General Advertiser, 59
Australian Jurist, The, 138, 140-41
Autonomy, 15, 103

Bakewell, William, 114-20
Bastard: criminalization, 19, 26; imputations of being pregnant with, 2, 28, 73, 164
Beach v Ranney, 130-31
Beggarly, Clark, 90-92
Bell, Elizabeth, 2, 108-13
Bell v Allen, 108-113
Bentham, Jeremy, 92-93, 100
Bigamy, 103

Bitch (as insult), 176
Blackburn (England), 164-65, 167
Black men, 35, 51, 63, 79, 86-89. *See also* African Americans; Race; Slavery
Black women, 10, 14, 23, 34, 36, 51, 60, 86, 122, 179. *See also* African Americans; Race; Slavery
Block, Ruth, 59-60
Boothby, Benjamin, 107-10, 117-19
Botany Bay (New South Wales), 37, 39, 183
Boucaut, James, 110-11, 119
Boudinot, Annis, 28
Branagan, Thomas, 15, 126
Breach of promise to marry, 106
Bright, Ursula, 169-170
British Empire: backwardness, 150; development of defamation law, 3-5; English slander reforms, 164; New South Wales, 40-41, 45, 47
British India, 12, 183
British Temperance League, 165
British Women's Temperance Association, 165
Brooker, Nancy, 2, 124-26
Brooker v Coffin, 85, 124-26
Brothels, 56, 88. *See also* Disorderly houses; Prostitution
Buffalo Commercial, 136
Burke county (North Carolina), 62, 66, 68-70
Burke, Tarana, 11
Burlington county (New Jersey), 25, 28
Butler, Josephine, 170
Buys v Gillespie, 123-25
Bynum, Victoria, 61, 76

Cady Stanton, Elizabeth, 170
Campbell, Margaret, 48-50, 53
Campbell, John, 54-55, 115, 119, 153-55, 158-61, 178
Canada, 3, 12, 183
Castleberry, Ezra, 14, 86-89

Castleberry, Sarah, 14, 86-89
Castleberry v Kelly, 14, 86-89
Centinel of Freedom, 24
Chastity: at common law, 55-56, 153, 159, 161-63, 169; femininity, 2, 10, 103; imputations of unchastity, 29, 67, 70, 105, 109, 131, 155; male chastity, 120, 132, 141, 170; men's duty to protect, 107, 119, 141; paid work, 146-148; poverty, 74; spiritual matter, 5, 27, 52, 108; whiteness, 10, 15, 61, 89-90, 126-30, 137, 179-80
Citron, Danielle Keats, 3
Civility, 38
Civilization: Aboriginal peoples, 39, 51-52, 180; anxieties about, 38-40; femininity, 44, 51, 56, 122; ideas of savagery, 38-40, 51; law reform, 136, 149, 168, 172; manners and conduct, 41; masculinity, 46; modern societies, 66; speech and language, 46; violence, 38-39, 135, 140; whiteness, 10, 51, 134, 180. *See also* Civility; Civil Law
Civil law, 3, 5, 45, 51, 77-78, 142
Citizenship: African Americans, 20, 34, 36; disenfranchisement, 36; immigrants, 20, 36; men, 36, 60, 94, 135; property, 23, 36; women, 10, 13, 20-24, 28, 31, 34-36. *See also* Suffrage
Civil War, 33, 61, 80, 96-97
Class: ambiguity and fluidity, 49; citizenship, 23, 28, 36; conduct and behaviour, 53. *See also* Status
development of defamation law: 3, 52; elites, 98; equality, 55; illiteracy, 45; lower classes, 44-45, 76, 98, 127, 152, 163; middle class, 98, 104; race, 61-63, 76, 80, 90, 127; respectability, 38, 44
Clayton, George, 138-39
Cobb, Thomas, 94-97

INDEX

Codification, 14, 79-98
Cohabitation, 64, 73, 75, 84, 88
Common law: adoption by Australian colonies, 40, 47, 102; American adoption, 6, 57, 87, 122; barbarous, 66, 92-93, 136, 148-149, 151, 153, 159, 162, 164, 168; cruel, 113, 119, 154, 161; defective, 54, 114, 116, 134, 139, 153; grotesque, 168; hostility towards, 26-27; masculine in orientation, 4-5, 52, 129; monstrous, 113, 149-150; subjecthood, 22; transnational, 3, 5, 8-9; uncertainty of, 125; unjust, 147-48. *See also* Transnational
Continental Congress, 25
Convicts, 39-41, 44-45, 55-56
Cooper, Joseph, 25
Costs (of legal actions), 108, 110, 113-14, 166-67
Coverture, 23, 102, 123-24, 160-61
Criminal intercourse, 13, 38, 50, 74
Criminalization: extramarital sex, 79, 84-86; giving birth to a bastard, 26; interracial sex, 81, 86-89; nonconsensual pornography, 3; punishment, 140; of speech, 63-64, 152-53
Croft, Josaphine, 90-92
Croft v Beggarly, 90-92
Cult of domesticity, 122. *See also* True Womanhood; Domesticity
Cursing, 45
Custody, 124, 151, 170, 178

Davies, Isabella, 161-62
Davies v Solomon, 161-62
Debasing acts, 14, 79, 96-98
Declaration of Independence, 28
Deepfake pornography, 2, 3, 177, 185
Defamation law: English origins, 3-6; existing scholarship, 10-11; current issues, 11-12, 181

Defences. *See* Truth; Qualified Privilege
Democracy, 53, 80, 82, 93-94
Denigration, 2-3, 70, 78, 178-79, 185
Depp, Johnny, 11
Dignity, 6, 35, 184
Disorderly houses, 146. *See also* Brothels; Prostitution
Divorce, 103, 123-124, 169-70
Doe v Simone, 176
Domesticity, 24, 59-60, 104, 122, 134-35, 179
Dunk, James, 40

Early modern period, 4, 10
Ecclesiastical courts: abolition of, 16, 55, 152-55; British colonies 5, 46-47, 102; English law 3, 4; New Jersey, 26; Royal Commission into, 152-53; "women's court", 4. *See also* Spiritual offenses
Economic loss, 4, 31, 127-35
Egalitarianism, 22-23, 48-49, 56
Elkins, Lois, 20
Elite, 77, 90, 98
Emotional distress, 131-34
Enfranchisement, 20-25, 28, 33, 36
England: abolition of ecclesiastical courts, 152-55; influenced by Victoria, 162; marriage roles and expectations, 159; parliamentary debates about slander, 162-63, 167-69, 171; slander reforms, 172; women's suffrage, 169-71. *See also* British Empire
Equal protection clause (US Constitution), 174
Equality, 16, 25, 80, 101, 150-51, 168-69
Equal rights, 6, 55, 147, 150-51, 154, 169-70
Evening Post, 128
Excellency of the Female Character Vindicated, The (Branagan), 15, 126

INDEX

Facebook, 11
Face that Launched a Thousand Lawsuits, The (Lake), 2
Family, 6, 92, 101-104
Farley, Lin, 3
Federalist, 33
Federalist party, 23, 31, 36
Femininity: civilization, 39, 44, 46, 51, 56, 122, 179; modesty, 46, 169; repressive standards, 2, 8, 9, 185; respectability, 38; whiteness, 10, 122, 179. *See also* Chastity; Purity; True Womanhood; Domesticity
Fisher, James Hurtle, 106-107
First Fleet, 39
Floodgates, 153, 163, 171, 179
Fornication: criminalization, 79, 84-86, 88; by men, 86, 170; spiritual offense, 4, 18, 26-27
Franks, Mary Anne, 3
Freedom of expression, 3, 29. *See also* Free speech
Free speech, 154. *See also* Freedom of expression

Gates, Ida, 184
Gates v New York Recorder, 184
Gaunson, David, 141-42, 177
Geelong Advertiser, The, 150
Gender: abuse, 1, 11; citizenship, 13, 20, 23, 36; civilization, 39-41; defamation scholarship, 11-12; English slander law, 3-5; gender-neutral reforms, 16, 27, 59, 116, 119, 169, 174, 177, 182; gender-specific reforms, 27, 120, 154, 174, 177; hate speech, 2, 185; race, 10, 62, 102; reform movement, 7-9. *See also* Femininity; Masculinity
Gertzog, Irwin, 23
Genius of Liberty, 24
Georgia: agriculture, 80-82; early governance and legal system, 80-83;
population demographics, 82, 87; slander reforms, 89-90, 96; slavery, 79-82, 86-90, 94-95, 98; speech suppression, 79, 97. *See also* Codification; Whiteness; White Supremacy
Giles, George Hartley, 110
Godey's Lady Book, 127
Goit, James, 2, 133
Gossip, 10, 183
Governess, 48-49, 52-53, 114, 159
Gowing, Laura, 4
Green, Ashbel, 34
Greene, Sally, 72
Greenlee, John Mitchell, 14, 66-71, 78
Griffith, William, 23
Gully, William, 16, 165-68, 171, 179

Hackensack county, 35
Hanson, Richard, 105-106
Harris, Kamala, 2
Hate speech, 2-3, 185
Hathcock, Middleton, 84-85
Hearn, John, 106-108
Henderson, Leonard, 67-68
Higinbotham, George, 147-49, 151
Hillsborough Recorder, 65
Hodes, Martha, 62
Holt, Elizabeth, 63-64
Honor, 21, 52, 54, 121, 129, 135, 139
Hopkins, Thomas, 28-33
Horton, Dolly, 64-65
Horton v Reavis, 64-65
Hotels, 108-109, 143, 145-46, 149. *See also* Publican
House of Commons, 16, 55, 115, 162-63, 165, 167-68, 170-171
House of Lords, 54, 153, 157, 158, 168, 171, 182
Housework, 131-134, 159. *See also* Domesticity; True Womanhood
Hudson, Ammon, 96-97
Hulbert, John Whitefield, 15, 121-23, 128-30, 137, 178

INDEX

Humiliation, 2-3, 8, 17, 134-35, 176, 183, 185

Illiteracy, 13, 45, 183-84
Illness, 131-34, 159-60
Images, 2, 185
Incest: accusations, 105, 107-108, 117-19; criminalization, 84; divorce, 103
Incontinence (sexual): accusations, 66-67, 71-76, 130, 132, 152; criminalization, 85; North Carolina slander act, 59
Indentured servitude, 28-32, 34
Indictable offenses, 19, 57, 84-85, 88, 120, 125
Indigenous women, 10, 51-52, 180. See also Aboriginal Australians; Native Americans
Infidelity, 124, 131
Innuendo, 67
Inskip, Lucy, 105-108, 111, 114, 119
Inskip v Swailes, 105-108, 110-111, 114, 119
Internet, 2, 185
Interracial: marriage, 75, 102, 127; sex, 10, 14, 35, 61-64, 65, 81, 87-90, 96-98, 130, 179; social relations, 92, 97. See also Race; Slavery

Jeffery, Robert, 38, 47-53
Johnson, Richard, 43-44
Jones, William W, 13, 58-59, 77
Jordan, John, 143-144
Justification (defence of), See Truth

Kelly, Martha, 9, 14, 86-89
Kendi, Ibram, 126
Kept woman, 44, 64, 72-73, 145-46
Kerber, Linda, 20, 24, 59
Khan, Irene, 11-12
Kinsey, James, 13, 25-27, 31, 127, 177, 182
Kinsey, John, 25

Kirkby, Diane, 143
Klinghoffer, Judith, 20
Knight, Jane, 156-160

Ladies' National Association for the Repeal of the Contagious Diseases Acts, 170
Language: abusive, 35, 46; gross, 44, 46; coarse, 139; masculinity, 45-46. See also Cursing; Hate speech; Oral Culture; Tongue
Law Magazine, 152
Lehrmann, Bruce, 11
Lewdness, 73-74, 84, 131, 177
Lewin, John, 13, 41-42
Lewin, Maria, 13, 41-47
Lewin v Thompson, 13, 41-47, 52
Lewis, Elizabeth Ann, 2, 9, 16
Lewis, Evaline J, 96
Lewis v Hudson, 96-97
Lewis, Jan, 21, 36, 59
Libel: Australian Uniform Defamation Acts, 181; cases, 184; common law, 4; England, 153, 163; Georgia laws, 83-84; New South Wales, 45, 54-56; Victoria, 148
Liberty's Daughters (Norton), 20
Literacy. See Illiteracy
Liverpool Mercury, The, 163, 167-68, 171
Lucas, Candance, 76-77
Lumpkin, Joseph Henry, 80, 83, 85, 91-95
Lynch, James, 156-60
Lynch v Knight, 156-62, 164

Mackinnon, Catherine, 3
Madison, James, 92-93
Malice, 19, 117, 134
Mallory v Simon & Schuster Publishers, 176
Manchester Society for Women's Suffrage, 170
Manly, Matthias, 76

Manners: civilization, 41; masculinity, 45–47; status, 53–54
Mansfield, James, 4–5
Marriage: cancellation of upcoming, 5, 15, 57, 107–108, 138, 181; desertion or abandonment, 102–3; England, 159; Georgia, 79, 86; interracial, 75, 102, 127; loss of consortium, 157–61; New Jersey, 22, 24; New York, 123–124; respectability, 110–11; South Australia, 15, 100–104; Victoria, 138–39, 144, 146–47. *See also* Divorce; Adultery
Married Women's Property Acts, 7, 104, 136, 151, 170
Maryland, 5, 57, 182
Masculinity: Brutish, 1; called into question, 177; savage, 13, 38, 45–46
Matra, James Mario 39
McFadden, Nellie, 184–85
McFadden v Morning Journal, 184–85
Melbourne, 2, 138–39, 143, 151, 162
Men: as plaintiffs, 116–18, 131–33; gallantry, 9, 121, 128–29, 135, 139, 142, 150; imputations of criminality, 4; manliness, 129, 131–33, 135; recent defamation claims, 11; sexual imputations as trivial, 5, 132–33; trades and professions, 4–5, 52, 54. *See also* Masculinity
Methodology, 8, 12
Me Too movement, 11–12
McBrayer, Frances, 2, 71–73
McBrayer v Hill, 71–74
McDonald, Charles James, 88–89
McIlquham, Harriet, 170
McLachlan, Craig, 11
Milano, Alyssa, 11
Miller, Mary, 130
Miller v Olmsted, 130
Milvain, Thomas, 163, 167
Migration, 15, 48, 53, 100–101
Modesty, 46, 110, 159, 169, 183

Moore v Meagher, 161
Moore, William, 52–53
Morality: double standard, 16, 154, 169–71; civic, 59–60, 92; offenses, 84–85; men, 58; paid work, 52, 112, 146, 180–81; sexual, 2, 5, 17, 27, 41, 96, 111; shifting community standards, 174; whiteness, 10, 13, 59–60, 77, 122, 126–27, 179; women's enfranchisement, 104
Muecke, Carle, 116–17
Muecke v Roundfeldt, 116–17
Muller, Eric L, 72

Native Americans: Cherokee nation, 68–69, 75, 79; Creek Nation, 79, 81; Trail of Tears, 69; women plaintiffs, 10, 14, 60–61, 66–71, 77, 179. *See also* Indigenous women; Race
Neese, Sampson, 63–64
New Hanover county (North Carolina), 58–59
New Jersey: change in slander law, 26–27; colonial slander cases 19; enfranchisement, 20–23; party politics, 22–23, 25, 36; population demographics, 20, 33; Princeton University, 28–29; Quakers, 22–23, 25–26; slavery, 20, 29, 33–34; women's political activity, 21, 22, 24. *See also* Citizenship, Suffrage
New South Wales: Aboriginal peoples, 39–40, 51–52; early governance and legal system, 40, 45, 47; egalitarian market society, 48, 52–54; libel actions, 54; population demographics, 39–40, 45, 53; slander reforms, 55–56. *See also* Civilization, Manners, Class
New world, 6, 8–9, 26, 48, 56, 115, 121, 136
New York: divorce laws, 123–24; emancipation, 127; men's cases, 131–33; slander reforms, 134–35. *See also*

True Womanhood, Domesticity, Coverture
New York Times, 136
New Zealand, 3, 12, 183
Nichols, Gilbert, 76
Niemcewicz, Julian Ursyn, 24
Nonconsensual pornography, 2, 3, 185
North Carolina: colonial legal history, 5, 57, 61; population demographics, 62, 69; slander reforms, 59, 77; slavery, 60-63, 72; Native Americans, 66-71, 75. *See also* Race; Class; Purity; Interracial
Norton, Mary Beth, 20

Odersook, Nicolas, 28-32
Oglethorpe, James, 80
Olmsted, Joseph, 130
Olmsted v Brown, 131
Olmsted v Miller, 130, 147
Online culture, 2-3, 11, 177, 185
Oral culture, 10, 45, 183

Paid work, 9-10, 52, 104, 134-35, 143, 146-47, 180-81. *See also* Professions and Trades; Status; Victoria
Painter, Nell, 126
Pankhurst, Emmeline, 169-70
Pankhurst, Richard, 169-70
Paternalism, 7, 27, 101-104, 106, 108, 111, 147
Patterson, Annie, 145-50
Peace of society, 27, 117, 177
Pearson, Richard Mumford, 74, 77
Peryman, Catherine, 111-14
Philadelphia Aurora, 31
Philip, Arthur, 39
Pickersgill, Edward, 162-63
Pledger, Matilda, 84-85, 87
Pledger v Hathcock, 84-85, 87-88, 125
Poetry (about slander), 47, 99, 126-27
Pollock, Frederick, 55, 153-54
Pornography, 2-3, 177, 185

Pound, Roscoe, 6, 26, 72, 95-96
Poverty, 60-61, 77, 100. *See also* Class
Privacy laws, 2-3, 173, 176, 185
Private sphere, 7, 135
Professions and trades: men, 5, 54-55; women, 7, 15, 104, 112-16, 146, 148, 180. *See also* Paid work; Status
Progress, 9-10, 15, 55, 83, 102-104, 115, 120, 140, 180
Prostitution, 44, 55, 73, 91-92, 124-26, 128, 136. *See also* Brothels; Disorderly houses
Publican, 2, 4, 16, 138, 143, 145-46, 165, 181, 187
Public house. *See* Hotels; Publican
Public record, 14, 31, 78
Purdue, Theda, 68, 70
Purity: double standard, 169; true womanhood, 122; unsullied, 59-63, 74, 77; whiteness, 14, 121, 123, 126-27, 129, 179. *See also* Modesty; Morality; Chastity; Femininity
Purves, James, 141, 142, 144-47, 150, 179

Quakers, 13, 22-23, 25, 26
Qualified privilege (as defence), 117, 148
Quick, John, 148
Quinlan, Francis, 138-39

Race: chastity, 10; children, 63, 88; citizenship, 20, 23, 36; civilization, 51; defamation scholarship on, 11; language of staining, 122-23, 126, 127, 129, 142, 179; mixed race, 70, 75; paternalism, 102; racial misidentification slander, 11; racial status of plaintiff, 68, 71; slavery, 33, 89, 94-95. *See also* Aboriginal Australians; Black Men; Black Women; Indigenous women; Interracial; Native Americans; Whiteness; White supremacy; Slavery

Raleigh Minerva, 58
Rangel v American Medical Response West, 176
Rape, 1, 2, 60, 62. *See also* Sexual assault
Reavis, William Whitfield, 64-65
Redman, Rebecca, 138-39, 143, 146
Redman v Clayton, 138-39
Republican party, 23-24, 36
Reputation: change in meaning/function, 38, 39, 46, 54; civilization, 51-52, 180; elite women, 77; importance for women, 7, 58, 61, 150; marriage, 104, 111, 114, 124; men, 116-18, 129, 132, 135-36, 146; protection by defamation law, 3; reputational rights, 137, 147, 169-70; subjecthood, 19, 22, 35; white women, 89, 97-98, 128, 130, 179; written attacks, 84
Respectability, 38, 45-46, 51, 53-54, 108, 110-11, 142
Richter, Rosalyn, 173-74
Roberts, Margaret, 160-161
Roberts v Roberts, 160-161, 164
Rogers, John Warrington, 138-39
Ruffin, Thomas, 72-74, 76-77
Rumors, 10, 44-45, 105-109
Rush, Geoffrey, 11
Russell, Penny, 39-40, 45

Scandalum magnatum, 55
Servants, 29, 32, 38, 44-45, 49-50, 53, 56, 77, 110
Sexual assault, 11, 109
Sexual harassment, 3, 10, 11, 109, 175-76
Sexual impropriety, 43, 47-48, 145
Shame, 8, 17, 126, 178, 183, 185
Sharp, James Anthony, 4
Shaw, John, 16, 165-167
Shiels, William, 150-151
Silencing, 6, 9, 11, 32, 56, 137, 150, 178, 185

Simmons, Gene, 173-174
Singapore, 3, 12, 183
Slander of Women Act 1808 (North Carolina), 59
Slander of Women movement, 7-10, 27
Slavery: Georgia, 79-82, 86-90, 94-95, 98; New Jersey, 20, 23, 26, 29, 33-36; New South Wales, 39; New York, 127; North Carolina, 59-63, 69, 72, 76. *See also* African Americans, Black men, Black women, Interracial, Race
Slut, 2, 8, 16, 72, 175-77, 184
Slut shaming, 2. *See also* Shame
Special damage: causation, 106-108; legal definition, 4-5; remoteness, 156-59. *See also* Defamation law
Spence, Catherine, 101-111
Spencer, Harriet, 2, 9, 13, 38, 47-54, 56
Spencer v Jeffrey, 38, 47-54
Spindel, Donna, 57, 61
Spiritual offenses, 3-4, 18, 26-27, 52, 54, 112, 123, 155. *See also* Ecclesiastical courts
Spiritual courts. *See* Ecclesiastical courts
Society of Friends, 25-26, 33
South Australia: Aboriginal Australians, 102; early governance, 100; equal migration of the sexes, 101; men's cases, 116-18; parliamentary debate about slander, 114-16, 119-20; regulation of marriage and family, 102-104. *See also* Marriage
South Australian Advertiser, 113
South Australian Register, 101, 108, 115, 117
South Carolina, 62, 65-66, 71, 81, 124, 174-75
Smith, Mary, 2, 6, 9, 12-13, 18-22, 25-27, 31, 35, 37, 177-78
Smith, Nathan Button, 136
Smith v Minor, 2, 12, 18-27, 33, 127

Snow, Huldah, 73-74
Snow v Witcher, 73-74, 77
Streetcar Named Desire, A (Williams), 1
Staining (language of), 10, 15, 121-22, 126-30, 135, 179
Stanton-Blatch, Harriet, 169
Starkie, Thomas, 4-5, 85, 146, 178
State building, 99
State v Neese, 63-64
Status: class, 49, 53, 76, 127; economic, 9, 54, 70; immigration 32, 33; marriage, 110, 111, 130; political, 21-22, 31, 178; professional, 54; public, 181; racial, 10, 61, 68, 71, 82, 88, 126; social, 7, 9, 32, 39, 44-45, 68, 70, 101, 114
Stephen, John, 38, 51-52, 180
Stephens v Verner, 117-19
Stigma, 2, 10, 126, 178
Stillwell, Sally, 34-35
Stillwell v Syme, 34-35
Stockport Advertiser, 164
Stockton, Betsey, 34
Stockton, Mary Field, 28-33
Stockton, Richard Sr., 28-33
Stockton v Hopkins, 28-33
Stow, Randolph, 109, 112, 116, 117
Suffrage: African Americans, 13, 20, 23, 36; disenfranchisement, 36; England, 165, 169-71, 182; immigrants, 13, 20, 36; New Jersey, 13, 20-23, 25-26, 36; property requirements, 23, 36; South Australia, 105, 119; Victoria, 16, 147, 151; voter fraud, 36; women, 10, 20-23, 25-26, 36, 147, 151, 165, 169-71, 182. *See also* Citizenship; Women's Franchise League
Swearing, 45
Sydney (Australia), 13, 39, 45, 48, 52
Sydney Morning Herald, 56
Syme, James, 34-35

Table Talk, 148, 150-51
Temperance, 16, 164-67
Temporal damage, 144, 147, 159-61
Temporal offenses, 3. *See also* Spiritual offenses
Terwilliger, John, 131-33, 177
Terwilliger v Wands, 131-33
Thompson, George, 43-46
Times, The, 162
Todd, Nathaniel, 34
Tongues, 45-46, 58, 79, 91, 122, 136, 183
Transnational common law, 3, 8-9, 12, 182. *See also* Common law; Methodology
Trenton (New Jersey), 18, 19, 23, 29-30
True American, 23
True womanhood, 122, 127, 137. *See also* Domesticity; Housework; Femininity
Truth (as defence), 16-17, 43, 73-74, 90-92, 106, 166
Turner, Raymond, 21

Unchastity. *See* Chastity
Uncivilized. *See* Civilization; Civility; Manners
United States Gazette, 31, 59
Under their Vine and Fig Tree (Niemcewicz), 24
US Constitution, 69, 174-75
US Restatement of Torts, Second, 174-75

Vexatious litigants, 16, 115, 119, 153-154, 156, 163, 168, 171, 179
Victoria: Aboriginal Australians, 142; connection with New York, 140-41; influence on English parliament, 162; parliamentary debates about slander, 141-42, 150-51; population demographics, 138, 143; women in paid work, 146-47; slander reforms, 151. *See also* Equal rights; Paid work; Suffrage

Victorian Women's Suffrage Society, 151
Vindication, 98, 108, 154, 166-67, 171
Virtue: class, 44, 53; commodified, 7, 178; civic, 60, 179; civilization, 39, 51, 56, 180; whiteness, 96, 122, 179. *See also* Chastity; Modesty; Femininity; Purity

Waddams, Stephen, 4, 155
Wakefield, Edward Gibbon, 100-101
Walia v Purmasir, 175-76
Ward, Georgeann Walsh, 173-74
Wardlaw v Peck, 174-75, 177
Ward v Klein, 173-74
Warner, Hiram, 85
Washington, George, 20
Waterhouse, George Marsden, 115, 121, 182
Waters, John, 74-75
Waters, Nancy, 75
Waters v Smoot, 74-75
Watts, Catherine, 9, 14, 66-71, 78, 179
Watts, Mary, 9, 14, 66-71, 78, 179
Watts, John, 68-69
Watts v Greenlee, 66-71
Webster, Richard, 16, 162, 168
Weekly Standard and Express, 171
Weinstein, Harvey, 11
Welter, Barbara, 122, 127
When KISS Rules the World, 173
White, Maria, 143-44

White v Jordan, 143-44, 147
Whitehead, John, 25
Wigley, William, 109
Williamstown (Victoria), 143-44
Wilson, Lucy, 2, 9, 133-35
Wilson v Goit, 133-35, 147
Windeyer, Richard, 55-56, 177
Wishart, Suzanna, 9, 14, 111-116, 147, 178, 180
Wishart v Peryman, 111-16
White, Deborah Gray, 60
White, Shane, 127
Whiteness: civilization, 51; degrees of, 90; plaintiff's status, 71, 98; sexual purity, 122-23, 126-28, 179. *See also* Staining (language of); Race; White Supremacy
White supremacy, 82, 98, 179
Williams, Hartley, 15, 149, 180
Williams, Tennessee, 1
Wood, Betty, 80
Woman Christian Temperance Movement, 151
Woman Movement, 16, 151
Women of the Republic (Kerber), 20
Women's Franchise League, 169-71
Wright, Clare, 143

X (formerly Twitter), 2, 11

Young Tassel, 68-69

THE CULTURAL LIVES OF LAW
Austin Sarat, Editor

The Cultural Lives of Law series brings insights and approaches from cultural studies to law and tries to secure for law a place in cultural analysis. Books in the series focus on the production, interpretation, consumption, and circulation of legal meanings. They take up the challenges posed as boundaries collapse between as well as within cultures, and as the circulation of legal meanings becomes more fluid. They also attend to the ways law's power in cultural production is renewed and resisted.

Marie-Eve Loiselle, *Building Walls, Constructing Identities: Legal Discourse and the Creation of National Borders*
2025

Joseph Mello, *Pot for Profit: Cannabis Legalization, Racial Capitalism, and the Expansion of the Carceral State*
2024

Chloé Deambrogio, *Judging Insanity, Punishing Difference: A History of Mental Illness in the Criminal Court*
2024

Daniel LaChance and Paul Kaplan, *Crimesploitation: Crime, Punishment, and Pleasure on Reality Television*
2022

Nesam McMillan, *Imagining the International: Crime, Justice, and the Promise of Community*
2020

Jeffrey R. Dudas, *Raised Right: Fatherhood in Modern American Conservatism*
2017

Renée Ann Cramer, *Pregnant with the Stars: Watching and Wanting the Celebrity Baby Bump*
2015

Sora Y. Han, *Letters of the Law: Race and the Fantasy of Colorblindness*
2015

Marianne Constable, *Our Word Is Our Bond: How Legal Speech Acts*
2014

Joshua C. Wilson, *The Street Politics of Abortion: Speech, Violence, and America's Culture Wars*
2013

Irus Braverman, *Zooland: The Institution of Captivity*
2012

Nora Gilbert, *Better Left Unsaid: Victorian Novels, Hays Code Films, and the Benefits of Censorship*
2012

Edited by Winnifred Fallers Sullivan, *Robert A. Yelle, and Mateo Taussig-Rubbo, After Secular Law*
2011

Keith J. Bybee, *All Judges Are Political—Except When They Are Not: Acceptable Hypocrisies and the Rule of Law*
2010

Susan Sage Heinzelman, *Riding the Black Ram: Law, Literature, and Gender*
2010

David M. Engel and Jaruwan S. Engel, *Tort, Custom, and Karma: Globalization and Legal Consciousness in Thailand*
2010

Ruth A. Miller, *Law in Crisis: The Ecstatic Subject of Natural Disaster*
2009

Ravit Reichman, *The Affective Life of Law: Legal Modernism and the Literary Imagination*
2009

Edited by David M. Engel and Michael McCann, *Fault Lines: Tort Law as Cultural Practice*
2008

William P. MacNeil, *Lex Populi: The Jurisprudence of Popular Culture*
2007

Edited by Austin Sarat and Christian Boulanger, *The Cultural Lives of Capital Punishment: Comparative Perspectives*
2005